THE POLITICS OF BLACKNESS

This book uses an intersectional approach to analyze the impact of the experience of race on Afro-Brazilian political behavior in the cities of Salvador, São Paulo, and Rio de Janeiro. Using a theoretical framework that takes into account racial group attachment and the experience of racial discrimination, it seeks to explain Afro-Brazilian political behavior with a focus on affirmative action policy and Law 10.639/03 (which requires that African and Afro-Brazilian history be taught in schools). It fills an important gap in studies of Afro-Brazilian underrepresentation by using an intersectional framework to examine the perspectives of everyday citizens. It will be an important reference for scholars and students interested in the issue of racial politics in Latin America and beyond.

Dr. Gladys L. Mitchell-Walthour is a political scientist in the Department of Africology at the University of Wisconsin–Milwaukee. She was the 2013–2014 Lemann Visiting Scholar at the David Rockefeller Center for Latin American Studies at Harvard University. In 2016, she was elected Vice President of the Brazil Studies Association. She has coedited both *Race and the Politics of Knowledge Production: Diaspora and Black Transnational Scholarship in the United States and Brazil* (2016) and *Brazil's New Racial Politics* (2010).

CAMBRIDGE STUDIES IN STRATIFICATION ECONOMICS: ECONOMICS AND SOCIAL IDENTITY

Series Editor: William A. Darity Jr., *Duke University*

The *Cambridge Studies in Stratification Economics: Economics and Social Identity* series encourages book proposals that emphasize structural sources of group-based inequality, rather than cultural or genetic factors. Studies in this series will utilize the underlying economic principles of self-interested behavior and substantive rationality in conjunction with sociology's emphasis on group behavior and identity formation. The series is interdisciplinary, drawing authors from various fields including economics, sociology, social psychology, history, and anthropology, with all projects focused on topics dealing with group-based inequality, identity, and economic well-being.

Books in the Series

The Hidden Rules of Race: Barriers to an Inclusive Economy Andrea Flynn, Dorian T. Warren, Felicia J. Wong, Susan R. Holmberg

The Politics of Blackness

Racial Identity and Political Behavior in Contemporary Brazil

GLADYS L. MITCHELL-WALTHOUR

CAMBRIDGE
UNIVERSITY PRESS

CAMBRIDGE
UNIVERSITY PRESS

University Printing House, Cambridge CB2 8BS, United Kingdom

One Liberty Plaza, 20th Floor, New York, NY 10006, USA

477 Williamstown Road, Port Melbourne, VIC 3207, Australia

314–321, 3rd Floor, Plot 3, Splendor Forum, Jasola District Centre,
New Delhi – 110025, India

79 Anson Road, #06–04/06, Singapore 079906

Cambridge University Press is part of the University of Cambridge.

It furthers the University's mission by disseminating knowledge in the pursuit of
education, learning, and research at the highest international levels of excellence.

www.cambridge.org
Information on this title: www.cambridge.org/9781107186101
DOI: 10.1017/9781316888742

© Gladys L. Mitchell-Walthour 2018

First published 2018

Printed in the United States of America by Sheridan Books, Inc.

A catalogue record for this publication is available from the British Library.

ISBN 978-1-107-18610-1 Hardback
ISBN 978-1-316-63704-3 Paperback

Cambridge University Press has no responsibility for the persistence or accuracy of
URLs for external or third-party internet websites referred to in this publication
and does not guarantee that any content on such websites is, or will remain,
accurate or appropriate.

For my husband, Anthony Walthour, who has always believed in me even when I felt discouraged and whose spirit and smile exudes positivity. I love you!

Contents

Figures

Tables

Maps

Acknowledgments

This book is an eleven-year-old project that developed as I traveled and lived in five states in Brazil and nine states in the United States. Despite the moving, my faith, family, and friends have remained a constant. I first thank God for the many blessings and people in my life to have this project come to fruition. I give respect and honor to my African ancestors who came before me, as well as to African descendants throughout the diaspora who resist and work tirelessly to live in dignity despite the injustice and everyday forms of violence we experience.

During the writing of this book I gave birth to my daughter, Truth, a beautiful, intelligent, and strong-willed girl. Thank you for being a great baby when I worked on this book as a Lemann Visiting Scholar at Harvard University. Even when you grew into a toddler when we moved to Wisconsin, you still allowed me to work, and I am forever grateful for our learning time at coffee shops, our walks on the Oak Leaf Trail, and all the time we spent and continue to spend laughing together. You already display Sojourner Truth's courageous and intellectual spirit. I'm a very proud mom! I thank my husband, Anthony Walthour, who always has an encouraging word and who has always supported me in my scholarly pursuits. I thank my late father, David Mitchell Jr., who first taught me about the important contributions of African descendants and the value of blackness. While he was passionate about his academic training in engineering and shared his passion of mathematics with my sisters and me, he was equally passionate and committed to the self-study of black and social justice issues. I am immensely thankful for his intelligence and unconditional love.

I thank my sisters, Cornelia Smith, Julia Elam, and Davia Lee, who have always provided love, support, and inspiration. They are truly brilliant and beautiful. I am forever inspired by these three in all they do. I thank my mother, Violet Mitchell, whose humor has provided great relief when I visited "home" in North Carolina. I thank my grandmother Gladys H. Mitchell, whose intellect and love have always provided immeasurable support. I draw great energy and hope from all of my nieces and nephews: Chay Smith, Julianne Elam, Anthony Lee, Robbie Elam, Andrew Lee, and Josephine Elam. They are all black excellence and I hope they will shed hope, peace, and love in the world. I am grateful for my late Uncle James, who always slipped me money when I was "home" in NC, and for Shirley Ann Walthour, who attended my dissertation defense. Both Uncle James and Mrs. Walthour transitioned during the duration of this project but are both fondly remembered. To family members such as "Godmother" Elnora Barrier and Aunt Julia Morris who brightened my day with a holiday card or simple phone call, I am grateful. I also am thankful for Rev. Dr. Jeremiah Wright Jr., whom I have never had the good fortune to meet face to face but who served as a spiritual guide through his commitment to Africans and African descendants. It was truly rewarding to hear Dr. Wright speak about the situation of Afro-Brazilians during one of his many sermons on social justice. I am grateful he is an example of someone who is Unapologetically Black and committed to black empowerment.

This project would not have been possible without the graciousness of Brazilian scholars, students, and friends. Cloves Oliveira, Paula Barreto, and Gislene Santos were all helpful in choosing neighborhoods to conduct my surveys. I extend my gratitude to Hugo Barbosa de Gusmão for creating maps despite the time constraints. I thank the following for their excellent work serving as assistants or transcribers during this work: Ana Luiza Alves, Ivanilda Amado, Edson Arruda, Leandro Freire, Magda Lorena, Leon Padial, Rosana Paiva, Ardjana Robalo, Jacqueline Romio, Jaqueline Santos, Kledir Salgado, Thabatha Silva, Darlene Sousa, Ricardo Summers, Keise Valverde, Gloria Ventapane, and Gabriela Watson.

I am thankful to all my friends who encouraged me as I worked on this project: Reighan Gillam, Jaira Harrington, Elizabeth Hordge-Freeman, Keisha Lindsay, Tehama Lopez Bunyasi, Bernd Reiter, Tanya Saunders, and Paxton Williams.

I give an *abração* to Michel Chagas and his wife, Ecyla Borges, for their hospitality letting me stay with them in Salvador, Jacqueline Santos for her hospitality in São Paulo, and Tanya Saunders for opening up her home to me in Rio de Janeiro.

I would like to thank some of my former students who made teaching rewarding. They are equally as brilliant as they are kind and thoughtful: Abdi Ali, Leyla Falhan, and Alfonso Henderson.

I would also like to recognize two native Milwaukeeans involved in social justice work for Afro-descendants in Latin America. Somer Nowak and Bryan Rogers, you both inspire me and I am proud of the work you are doing and your dedication.

Special thanks to John French, because I took his class on Afro-Brazilian History and Culture as a second-year undergraduate student at Duke University in 1997 and it opened my eyes to understanding the culture and lives of African descendants outside of the United States and the continent of Africa. After taking this class I knew I would continue studying Brazil, and here we are!

I am thankful to the following people for babysitting my daughter even for a couple hours, which allowed me to work on this project or make presentations about this project: Abdi Ali, Fleming Daugaard-Hansen, Crystal Ellis, Reighan Gillam, Basha Harris, Eliza Hawkins, Changoumei Liu, Mara Ostfeld, Charmane Perry, Ermitte St. Jacques, and John Walthour.

Finally, I would like to thank William "Sandy" Darity Jr. for his mentorship. Sandy is not only a committed scholar to issues relevant to African descendants but is an excellent mentor who is truly committed to developing scholars of African descent.

I received financial support at various stages of this project from the following: the Overseas Dissertation Fellowship at the University of Chicago, Denison University, the Samuel Dubois Cook Fellowship at Duke University (special thanks to Paula McClain and Kerry Haynie), the Erskine Peters Fellowship University of Notre Dame (special thanks to Dianne Pinderhughes and Richard Pierce), the Lemann Visiting Scholar Fellowship at Harvard University's David Rockefeller Center for Latin American Studies, the Center for Africana Studies Postdoctoral Fellowship at Johns Hopkins University (special thanks to Michael Hanchard and Floyd Hayes III), the Africology Department at the University of Wisconsin Milwaukee (special thanks to former chair Erin Winkler and current chair Anika Wilson), and the Center for Latin American and Caribbean Studies at the University of Wisconsin–Milwaukee.

I thank the Latin American Public Opinion Project (LAPOP) and its major supporters (the United States Agency for International Development, the Inter-American Development Bank, and Vanderbilt University) for making its data available.

Finally, for all those involved in the struggle for freedom of thought, dignity, movement, and citizenship of African descendants in Brazil and elsewhere, I hope this book is a small contribution. *Axé*!

Introduction

[*Negros* are underrepresented in politics because of] white supremacy. Salvador is a city with a [large] *negro* population in relation to the number of [*negros* in other] cities in Brazil . . . but there is still a sense of supremacy from the white race. They watch and control us. They do not give opportunities to *negro* people to arrive, to get what they have so they try to do the most they can to impede *negro* people from getting more . . .

      30-year-old dark-skinned black man in Salvador with a college degree

This book uses an intersectional approach to analyze the impact the experience of race has on Afro-Brazilian political behavior and black and brown Brazilians' race-based vision of the political world in the cities of Salvador, São Paulo, and Rio de Janeiro. It addresses the importance of focusing on how race-related experiences affect individual and group political behavior among Brazilians. In a country where over half of the population identifies as black (*preto*) or brown (*pardo*), it is crucial to examine Brazilian experiences of race in order to capture and predict Afro-Brazilian political behavior. I use the term Afro-Brazilian in the same way the mainstream Brazilian media uses the racial category *negro*, which includes the census categories "browns" (*pardos*) and "blacks" (*pretos*). The respondent quoted above, explains Afro-Brazilian underrepresentation through a lens of white domination despite living in a majority Afro-Brazilian city. The perspectives of everyday citizens as an explanation of Afro-Brazilian underrepresentation are understudied in scholarship on Brazilian politics. Much contemporary literature on electoral politics ignores the reality that Brazilians do indeed have a racial identification and that individual life experiences are largely influenced, if not determined by, racial identification and/or racial classification. This book relies on a theoretical framework that takes into account the *experience* of race by considering racial-group attachment, or what

1

Michael Dawson (1994) calls "black-linked fate," and the experience of racial discrimination. The book seeks to explain Afro-Brazilian political behavior by focusing on support of affirmative action policy, Law 10.639/03 (requiring that African and Afro-Brazilian history be taught in schools), support of the idea that the president should nominate Afro-Brazilians to political positions, and political opinions about black political underrepresentation. Although Brazil is the focus of this book, specifically because of the proliferation of the political and social mobilization of African descendants throughout Latin America in the 1990s, it is an important area of study for scholars, students, and the general public who are interested in the issue of racial politics in Latin America and elsewhere. The mixed-method approach to studying political behavior bridges studies on race and ethnicity across fields. Scholars of identity politics in the fields of sociology, political science, anthropology, and history – and specifically those studying black politics, Latino politics, and Asian politics in the United States – should consider studies on Afro-Brazilians. Brazilian racial politics demonstrate a complex picture of how experiences are shaped based on skin color and physical aesthetics. Some North American political scientists have considered skin color and found that it has an impact on the likeability of political candidates (Hochschild and Weaver 2007; Valentino, Hutchings, and White 2002). This study's intersectional approach contributes to growing literature on skin color, politics, and racial group identity.

Brazil is a country stratified by race, class, and gender, among other social categories.[1] One of the goals of the book is to examine how Afro-Brazilians explain political inequality. Although Afro-Brazilians comprise 53 percent of the population (Bianchi and Vilela 2014), they hold less than 10 percent of the seats in the national congress. A study incorporating the experience of race rather than solely considering individual variables of racial or color identification is important because experiences based on race, class, and gender lead people to make certain political choices. It may be argued, however, that choices such as racial identification are rooted in self-interested behavioral decisions. Conversely one may support certain policies that support the group even if one does not individually benefit from such policies.

---

[1] The 2013 Ethno-Racial Characteristics of the Population Research (*Pesquisa de Características Étnico-Raciais da População*) carried out by the Brazilian Institute for Geography and Statistics finds that 64 percent of Brazilians believe that race or color influences their lives. This study was carried out in São Paulo, Paraiba, Amazonas, Distrito Federal, Rio Grande do Sul, and Mato Grosso. There are differences according to racial identification and location. Nonetheless, this speaks to the significance of race or color in Brazilian society.

A second goal of the book is to consider whether intersectional identities lead to variance in identifying as *negro* and in explaining political inequality. Social categories are not isolated; they intersect. These intersecting identities result in different experiences. Kimberlé Crenshaw's (1991) notion of "structural intersectionality" is particularly useful when considering the interplay of race, class, and gender in Brazil. Structural intersectionality is concerned with "the ways in which the location of women of color at the intersection of race and gender" make their experiences qualitatively different from those of white women (Crenshaw 1991: 1245). In my analysis I am concerned with how an Afro-Brazilian woman's location at the intersection of race, class, and gender may or may not result in different interpretations of her life experiences and outlook on the political world compared to an Afro-Brazilian man.

Of course, an individual's experience is shaped by the environment in which he or she lives, as well as the structures, institutions, and various discourses of race in any given society. The Brazilian case is unique in that it has experienced authoritarian and democratic political regimes and changing racial discourse. Afro-Brazilians' understanding of their everyday lives and experiences may be interpreted differently because of changes in racial discourse, and those interpretations may be reinterpreted with new changes in discourse.[2] For example an older Afro-Brazilian who lived through a repressive military dictatorship may be more likely to deny racism than a younger Afro-Brazilian born during the 1990s, when black movement discourse of race and racism had more of an influence on public discourse during a democratic era. Scott (1991) believes historians should not simply focus on experience but should historicize experiences and acknowledge that individual experiences exist in relation to others. I believe that throughout Latin America, some Afro-descendants are

---

[2] Joan Scott's (1991) article, "The Evidence of Experience," is important because she discusses how historians rely too heavily on personal experiences, especially as they relate to difference and may only reify norms if they do not question experience within a historical context. She states, "Making visible the experience of a different group exposes the existence of repressive mechanisms, but not their inner workings or logics; we know that difference exists, but we don't understand it as relationally constituted. For that we need to attend to the historical processes that, through discourse, position subjects and produce their experiences. It is not individuals who have experience, but subjects who are constituted through experience. Experience in this definition then becomes not the origin of our explanation, not the authoritative (because seen or felt) evidence that grounds what is known, but rather that which we seek to explain, that about which knowledge is produced. To think about experience in this way is to historicize it as well as to historicize the identities it produces" (779–780).

*re*interpreting life experiences as racialized subjects who, as marginalized people, are seeking rights based on these identities.

This book is unique because I argue that central to the understanding of Afro-Brazilian political behavior is the consideration of group-based and individual behaviors, along with racial inequality. For example, I can examine if Afro-Brazilians overwhelmingly support certain policies because they believe they are necessary for Afro-Brazilians as a group or if they have individual preferences that will benefit them personally. Another example of individual behavior is one's choice of racial identification. Despite the assumed ambiguity of race, many respondents do not feel like they have options in their choice. To be sure, there is inconsistency in classification depending on classification in a census category, binary format such as white or black, and skin color and physical characteristics (Bailey, Loveman, and Muniz 2013). However, in terms of self-identification there is less ambiguity. In fact, Lamont et al. (2016) find in their study, in answer to the question "What is your race?" that 60 percent of respondents said *negro/negra*. In my research many respondents base their choice on physical features. Afro-Brazilians who have experienced discrimination, those with darker skin and with higher incomes, are more likely to claim a *negro* identification. Afro-Brazilians who identify as *preto* or *negro* demonstrate group-based political behavior (Aguilar et al. 2015; Janusz 2017; and Mitchell 2010). Afro-Brazilians who have experienced discrimination and those who are younger are more likely to demonstrate a sense of *negro* linked fate. Interview and survey questions employed the Portuguese term *negro*, which includes census category *pretos* (blacks) and *pardos* (browns). Analysis reveals that those demonstrating *negro* linked fate are more likely to support racial policies for *negros*. Group attachment is different from self-identification. Lamont et al. (2016: 138) concludes that self-identification as *negro* does not always lead to racial political consciousness. However, this conclusion is based on self-identification and not *negro* linked fate.

The academic relevance of such a book is clear, given the significant increase in scholarship dealing with race in Brazil in recent years (Lamont et al. 2016; Paschel 2016; Smith 2016; Hordge-Freeman 2015; Joseph 2016; Lima 2015; Perry 2013; Williams 2013; Costa 2014; Santos 2014). Since Brazil hosted the 2014 World Cup and the 2016 Olympics, its racial past and politics have been a hot topic in the media, including the *New York Times*, the *Guardian*, National Public Radio, and the *Economist*. In preparation for both of these events, the Brazilian state repressed and inflicted violence on Afro-Brazilian communities as neighborhoods were supposedly "pacified" and "cleaned" of drug activity and crime. Cases of innocent people dying in these efforts are being discussed in black social networks and media in Brazil and the United States. As such, this book gives voice to Afro-Brazilians who have a voice in the digital world but often are silenced in the social and political worlds, and whose issues are likewise silenced in the academic world. Too often, the issues of race and racism are considered secondary to the issue of class.

THEORETICAL FRAMEWORK

The theoretical framework for this book is an intersectional analysis based on black feminism broadly and as articulated from Brazilian intellectuals. Although many aspects of intersectionality and black feminism are similar in the United States and Brazil, it is important to highlight how Afro-Brazilian women theorists articulate intersectionality. In the Brazilian context, black feminism acknowledges the role that race, class, aesthetics, and gender play in society and how Afro-Brazilian women are particularly marginalized due to racism, classism, and sexism (González 1988; Nascimento 2009; Bairros 1991; Carneiro 2003). Sueli Carneiro challenges feminism that ignores the experiences of black women. She believes that feminism should challenge both racial and gender domination. She proposes a number of initiatives black women should promote, including recognizing that poverty has a racial dimension and that race should be included in analyses of the feminization of poverty. She also advocates for a recognition of the "symbolic violence and oppression that whiteness as the hegemonic and privileged aesthetic standard has over non-white women" (Carneiro 2003: 130). I point out the aesthetic dimension because one's appearance is particularly valued in Latin America and especially Brazil. Very curly hair has been stigmatized in Brazilian society, and black women's hair is commonly described as "hard hair" and "bad hair." An intersectional framework in the Brazilian case has to take into account aesthetics and physical characteristics such as one's hair texture or hairstyle. My qualitative interviews include information on skin color and hairstyle.

It is important in approaching black feminism to understand that one's experiences inform identity. Just as Crenshaw argues that intersecting identities shape experience, it is important to note that experiences shape identity. Daniela Ikawa (2014), who writes from an intersectional and critical race perspective, argues that, in Brazil, many public policies have ignored the experiences of Afro-descendant women. She believes policies should be designed for differently situated women such as black women or poor black women. Their experiences lead to different policy needs as well as how they might articulate these needs. In Cecilia McCallum's (2007) work on black women and white women activists in Brazil, she discusses "the formation of distinct subjectivities" as articulated by Creusa Maria de Oliveira, an Afro-Brazilian woman activist who heads the National Federation of Labor Union for Domestic workers (*Federação Nacional das Empregadas Domésticas*) (2007: 66). Creusa believes there is a difference between the life experiences of poor black women and white women. McCallum emphasizes that these differences are not essentialized identities but are products of specific life histories (2007: 66). Even among Afro-Brazilian women, there are differences based on skin color, self-identification, hair texture, age, and class that lead to *differently situated* women and experiences. I am most interested in whether responses to the question about *negro* underrepresentation is linked to these different subjectivities. All social categories are experienced by individuals, and I contend that these experiences have an impact on political opinion and behavior

I situate my work within studies of race in Brazil and the US. Because of multicultural movements in the US, there has been an expansion of the study of racial politics that go beyond the black/white paradigm to include Latino politics (Zepeda-Millán 2016; Lopez Bunyasi 2015; Affigne 2014; Carey, Branton, and Martinez-Ebers 2014; Garcia and Sanchez 2008; Fraga et al. 2006; Barreto 2007; Leal 1999), Asian politics (Wong, Ramakrishnan, Lee, and Junn 2011), studies on biracial Americans (Davenport 2016), and black immigrants (Rogers 2006; C.W. Smith 2014). Today some scholars believe race in Brazil is becoming more dichotomous while race in the US is becoming more Latin American. While I agree that racial discourse and race relations are changing in both countries, I challenge the Latin Americanization thesis, as I believe it assumes that race relations or racial politics are linear. I discuss this later in this chapter.

Before my discussion of my methodology and the outline of the book, I give background about race in Brazil. I first discuss how race was conceptualized historically. I follow with a discussion of Brazilian black movement activism as it shaped changing notions of race. Lastly, I challenge convergence theses that Brazil is becoming like the United States and vice versa. Challenging these theses is important because Brazilian racial politics are not static and are changing in a way particular to Brazil. Mixed-methods studies such as this one are essential to providing a fuller understanding of how Brazilians themselves explain these dynamics.

Race/Color In Brazil

Historically, many scholars have found that race in Brazil is different than race in the US because race is based on ancestry in the US rather than phenotype, physical features, and class status such as in Brazil (Nogueira 2007; Degler 1986; Telles 2004). Race in the US has been understood as binary (white and black), and the one-drop rule of having any African ancestry determined if a person was black, regardless of phenotype. This concept stands in opposition to Brazil, where race or color is viewed as ambiguous. The word *cor* (color) is more commonly used in Brazil than the word *raça* (race), although black activists increasingly use the term race. Skin color and race are distinct as race is based on parentage and is viewed as something one cannot change. Color is based on skin color and other traits such as social status. However, it is important to acknowledge that both are racialized or certain racial or color categories take on certain meanings. Scholars discuss the fact that color is racialized in Brazil (Caldwell 2007; Nascimento 2009). Color is racialized in the same way as race, in that lighter colors are generally more valued than darker ones and African traits are viewed as less attractive than European traits (Sheriff 2001; Hordge-Freeman 2015). Racialization is an important concept because it implies that race is socially constructed. Furthermore, Christen Smith's (2016) claim that scholars should pay attention to the performative aspects of identity is extremely useful when considering race and color as identities. Bodies perform "race," and agents of the state construct race in their varied treatment of certain bodies. In other words, phenotype, whether light or dark in color, coupled with physical features may determine the interplay of violence against those with curly hair and African features regardless of skin color. In this instance, race is performed and experienced. Many people cite Marvin Harris's (1970) finding that there are over 100 color categories in Brazil. However, Telles (2004) finds that 94 percent of responses about race or color fall into one of six categories. In this way, self-identification is not as ambiguous as it may seem.

There are three important aspects to emphasize in a discussion of color in Brazil. These aspects are social status, physical characteristics such as skin tone or hair type, and gender. All of these aspects play a role in how strangers and friends determine a person's color identification. The historical context of whitening and the belief in racial democracy is also important to this discussion. In Brazil, one can have African ancestry but not be considered black (Telles 2004; Nogueira 2007).

Color and social status in Brazil intersect in profound ways that can also determine how one identifies or is classified.[3] Blackness is associated with negative stereotypes such as unattractiveness, poverty, and less intelligence. Calling a stranger *preto* is still considered offensive, and saying the aphorism *coisa de preta* or "that's a black thing" when someone makes a mistake demonstrates the pejorative and engrained nature of the word *preto*. The most common identification in everyday language is *moreno* (Baran 2007; Caldwell 2006, Telles 2004). This is especially the case for women. A stranger might believe it impolite to call a woman *preta* or *negra*, and so may use the term *morena*. *Morena* is an ambiguous term that includes a range that spans from very light-skinned people with brunette or dark hair to very dark-skinned people. The same holds for self-identification. If someone is uncomfortable calling themselves *preto* or *negro*, they may refer to themselves as *moreno*. Yet Telles (2004) finds that Brazilians with more income identify as *preto*.

A dark-skinned person can be described as brown if he or she is highly educated or holds a prestigious job. Even when status is not a marker of whether Brazilians will classify others in non-black categories, this act may take place in an effort to show good manners. Robin Sheriff (2001) notes, in her anthropological study of a slum community in Rio de Janeiro, that residents referred to acquaintances as having lighter colors in an effort to be polite. In contrast to how darker-skinned people's color may be manipulated by acquaintances to "lighten" them, some Afro-Brazilians identify as *preto* or *negro*, and while this is generally associated with having dark skin, it is also associated with higher income or higher education (Mitchell-Walthour and Darity 2014). Younger Afro-Brazilians and higher income Afro-Brazilians are more likely to claim a *negro* racial identification (Telles 2004; Bailey and Telles 2006; Mitchell 2010).

As I explained earlier in the case of Afro-Brazilians, color is racialized but is different from race. This racialization is exemplified in the fact that there are a number of skin color designations for Afro-Brazilians. Curiously, there are not numerous terms for the color white nor for the white census category, but there are multiple societal terms for Afro-Brazilians. The census includes the terms *pardo*,[4] which is designated for

---

[3] Alberto Carlos Almeida (2007) challenges this idea, as he found in an experimental setting that varying clothing did not have an impact on how one was racially classified.

[4] The census category *pardo* includes African descendants and other racially mixed people including people of indigenous and European ancestry. Theoretically any Brazilian could choose this category, including those of Middle Eastern descent. However, researchers commonly understand the census category *pardo* to denote racially mixed people of African descent.

racially mixed people and *preto* for blacks. As noted earlier, there are numerous terms to denote skin colors for Afro-Brazilians. Yet, social scientists, the media, and black activists often combine the census categories *preto* and *pardo* to describe *negros*, a racial category.

Race is based on parentage, such that someone with one white parent and one black parent may identify as *pardo*, and despite the fact that Brazil is often understood as a country with ambiguous racial categories, many Brazilians view themselves in a binary fashion. Sheriff (2001) finds that respondents view the world, in racial terms, as either black or white. Thus, in determining one's race, people of various colors or shades of brown identify as *negro* or racially black.

Physical attributes such as hair texture and skin tone can also have an impact on how others identify people. Those with coarse hair or more African features may be identified in categories that imply a darker color or that are actually meant to describe someone with light skin but who has African features. An example is the term *sarará* which in Salvador, Bahia describes a light-skinned person with African features. Determining a person's color comes with certain rules and as Hordge-Freeman (2016) explains, there is a certain racial etiquette to determine one's color. She shows how very young children do not know this etiquette but later learn the rules or etiquette to determine one's color. Social status can play a role in how an individual is classified yet for young children who have not learned the rules of classification they may not consider social status but simply a person's skin color.

Gender has an impact on classification as gender can intersect with social status. Gender, alone can also play a role in how one is classified. Kia Caldwell (2007) discusses the idea of the *mulata* which is often a hyper-sexualized idea of Afro-descendant women. A woman's social status can also determine how she is classified by others. Telles (2004) finds that Brazilians are less likely to classify high-status self-identified *preta* women as *preta*.

In summary, both race and color are racialized. Brazilians often racially identify according to parentage, while they consider skin color and other physical traits to determine their color. When Brazilians are identified by others they may consider perceived parentage to determine another person's race or may rely on a binary notion of black and white. In contrast, when identifying another person's color, social status, demonstrating good manners by showing respect by identifying an acquaintance in a lighter color, and one's gender may all be considered as determinants of a person's color. Oftentimes, this calculus is made according to the rules of racial etiquette Hordge-Freeman identifies (2016). In order to understand why race and color exist as such, I turn to a historical discussion.

The Historical Making of Race

In this section I discuss the history of race-making, both biologically and through census categories. The Brazilian system of racial stratification has roots in white supremacy which is manifested in the belief that African origins denote inferiority while European origins denote superiority. Although racial mixture is celebrated and characterized as the product of romantic relationships between Portuguese settlers and Indigenous women and African women in the sixteenth century, Anthony Marx (1998) claims this is a remaking of history. According to Marx (1998), history was remade and retold in this way to better align with Brazil's identity as a multiracial non-racist nation. In fact, African and Indigenous women were often raped by Portuguese settlers who left their wives and families in Portugal. As a result, the racial groups acknowledged as contributing to Brazil's racial mixture consist of Africans, the Indigenous, and the Portuguese.

Between four and five million Africans were brought to Brazil as part of the transatlantic slave trade. Brazil had one of the harshest systems of slavery: in some regions of the country, children as young as age seven died enslaved (Marx 1998). With Brazil's proximity to Africa, it was easy for the Portuguese to continue transporting Africans to Brazil when enslaved people ran away or died. Brazil abolished slavery in 1888, making it the last country in the western hemisphere to do so. Not all Africans and African descendants were enslaved. Some were free and others were able to buy their freedom by earning money for their skilled services. The constant influx of enslaved Africans led to large numbers of African descendants in the country. To address the "problem," the political elite actively sought to whiten the population.

The state promoted race-making through racial mixture with the goal of ridding its society of black people and black culture during the early twentieth century (Nascimento 1989; Marx 1998). It later embraced racial miscegenation and racial ambiguity as part of its national identity.

The ideology of whitening Brazil's population has to be understood in the context of racial ideologies. Thomas Skidmore (1974) identifies three main schools of racial ideology that influenced Brazilian thought. By 1860, racial theory was supported by scientific theory in Europe and the United States. These theories subsequently affected racial theories in Brazil.

One theory held that physical differences indicated different species or races. This allowed scientific support for the concept of white superiority. This ideology was first formulated in the US in the 1840s and 1850s (Skidmore 1974: 49). Darwinian theory eventually replaced a strictly biological ideology of race. Many studies were conducted using skull measurements and other markers to define races and compare their development to the "superior" white race. Darwinian theory emanated from the "ethnological-biological" school and aided in supporting racist ideas about black inferiority (Skidmore 1974: 50).

The second racial ideology prominent at this time was the historical approach. It examined the history of the Anglo-Saxon or Aryan race to make the claim that it dominated the world and would continue to do so because of its inherent superiority (Skidmore 1974: 51). The third school of racial ideology was social Darwinism, which proclaimed that as time progressed, the higher race would continue, while the weak or lower ones would disappear. These various schools of thought influenced how Brazilians thought about race and Skidmore claims that social Darwinism was most accepted in Brazil. Brazil accepted the third approach with the belief that blacks would eventually disappear from the population.

The role of mixed-race people was that they served as an intermediary group that did not face economic and racial inequality. Brazil has always been viewed as a unique case because of the existence of a multiracial group of people who do not neatly fit into the categories of black or white, and there has been debate about measuring inequality in Brazil by separating this group or by combining mixed-race people with blacks. Degler's "*mulato* escape hatch" indicates that *mulatos* are closer to whites and thus have a better chance of social ascendance. Additionally, the idea of whitening indicates that if one intermarries or has a high social status, one will not be viewed as black.

Immigration and Whitening

Political elites began to socially and biologically construct race through the ideology and practice of whitening the population with European immigration. The Constitution of 1891 banned African and Asian immigration (Andrews 1991: 52). To encourage European immigration, the federal government established a program to subsidize European travel to Brazil. This program ended in 1927. By then, over two million European immigrants had already traveled to São Paulo, more than half of them having travel subsidized by the São Paulo state government (Andrews 1991: 58). Although subsidies may not have played the most significant role in immigration, it is important to note that they were given to Europeans rather than Africans or Asians. Europeans worked in factories and on coffee plantations. For this reason, the immigration program can also be understood in economic terms since planters' main concern was to produce coffee at production levels set during slavery.

The fact remains, however, that European and white Brazilian workers were favored over Brazilians of African descent. In addition, most factory jobs gave preferential treatment to white Brazilians and Europeans, while Brazilians of African descent worked as domestics or on large plantations (Andrews 1991: 68).[5] During this time, the pervasive ideology among scholars and political elites was that white immigrants could mix with non-whites to better the Brazilian population by ridding it of its degenerate African and Indigenous blood. Oliveira Vianna was a lawyer and historian who was a popular advocate of whitening. He referred to whitening as *Aryanization* because of his belief in European superiority (Skidmore 1974: 200–201). He wanted to support the idea that Brazil was becoming whiter. He compared racial percentages in the 1872 and 1890 censuses, claiming there was a white increase of 6 percent, a 5 percent decrease in blacks, and that the mixed-race population decreased by 6 percent (Skidmore 1974: 201). Despite their desires, there was still a significant Afro-Brazilian population.

Embracing Racial Mixture

It is important to note the national shift in views of race from rejecting African descendants to accepting race mixture. Gilberto Freyre (1956) add was not the first to introduce the idea of racial democracy in the 1930s but is most known. He referred to racial democracy as a "brotherhood or fluid social relations rather than to a type of political institution" (Telles 2004: 33). He believed that miscegenation had allowed a diffusion of racial difference that would alleviate racism in society. His work promoted national unity and a unified Brazilian culture (Telles 2004: 35). The idea was that racial mixture implied more tolerance. Racially mixed people served as an intermediary group between blacks and whites. Some scholars supported the idea that racially mixed people served as a buffer between whites and blacks. Carl Degler (1986) maintained that racially mixed people were not subject to racism because they were not a distinct group. Anthony Marx (1998) argues that political elites saw embracing racial mixture as essential

---

[5] George Reid Andrews in *Blacks and Whites in São Paulo 1888–1988* (1991), notes that most European immigrants were low skilled and that factory jobs required on the job training. Therefore, it was not true that European immigrants were more skilled than Brazilians of African descent (1991: 75).

to the national project. By creating a national identity, they also encouraged national unity. Those who did not subscribe to this ideology were seen as anti-Brazilian.

In Brazil, terms such as the census category *pardo* indicate a multiracial background, while in common parlance, *moreno* is the term used most often to denote an ambiguous identification (Telles 2004). Terms such as *mulato* and *mestiço* are also used in everyday language but less often than *moreno*. These terms are also used more in certain regions and also in certain contexts. For example, during Carnival, Afro-Brazilian women's bodies are upheld as a societal representation of the sexualized and racialized "*mulata*" (Caldwell 2007).

Racial democracy as an ideology is still supported by some Brazilian elites and citizens. However, this idea has been greatly challenged by black movement activists and academics. Many scholars refer to it as a myth because of research documenting economic and educational inequality between Afro-Brazilians and white Brazilians. Critiquing racial democracy, Elisa Nascimento (2009) believes racial democracy still has an impact on society when people deny the existence of racism. She also critiques people who deny that inequality in society is solely due to past racism. In Nascimento's critique, the "sorcery of color" or inequality is explained in a race-neutral way and the continuation of racial stratification and inequality is viewed as a leftover effect of the structure of the system of slavery and that, as if by magic, blacks continue to remain on the bottom rungs of the societal ladder. Denying persistent racism reinforces the idea of racial democracy. With the continued activity of black movement and grassroots activism, racial democracy is not as prevalent as it was in the past but still remains a part of Brazilian society. While black activism challenged racism and the idea that Brazil was free of race-based discrimination, black organizing predates the proliferation of the idea of racial democracy.

BLACK ACTIVISM

I date black activism to the slavery era when Africans and African descendants escaped and formed communities known as *quilombos*. These *quilombos* were multiracial and not limited to Africans or African descendants. Running away and revolts were forms of resistance. There were a number of revolts led by enslaved people. One of the most famous, the Malê revolt, was led by enslaved Muslims (Reis 1995). Post-abolition, Afro-Brazilians organized to support each other. They created autonomous social and cultural institutions. During the late nineteenth century, Afro-Brazilians founded religious brotherhoods in Salvador. One such brotherhood was the *Rosário às Portas do Carmo*, which lasted from 1888 to 1938 (Butler 1998: 147). As early as 1832, the mutual aid society *Sociedade Protectora dos Desvalidos* was created, and membership was restricted to *pretos* (Butler 1998: 158–159). There were also religiously affiliated groups led by Afro-Brazilian women, such as the *Irmãndade de Boa Morte* in Cachoeira, in Bahia.

Upwardly mobile Afro-Brazilians were excluded from exclusive white social clubs, so they started their own. One such group was the Black Gloves (*Luvas Pretas*), which was started in 1904. The Palmares Civic Center was created in 1927. Originally a library, it later served as a meeting place for Afro-Brazilians. Black movements were both cultural and political, and some were involved in challenging the government. An example is the 1928 campaign against the decree that Afro-Brazilians could not enlist in the São Paulo Civil Guard militia (Andrews 1991: 147). These historical moments show that Afro-Brazilians challenged racial exclusion.

The imposition of Getúlio Vargas's New State (*Estado Novo*), from 1937 to 1945, made political mobilization difficult. The Black Brazilian Front (*Frente Negra Brasileira*) is recognized as Brazil's first black political party. It was created to combat racism. It lasted from 1931 until 1937 when it was shut down, as were all political parties during this period (Hanchard 1994: 105). Although this period was repressive, Vargas did approve the Law of Naturalization of Labor in 1931, requiring that labor forces be composed of at least two-thirds Brazilian-born people (Andrews 1991: 147). This greatly affected Afro-Brazilians because European immigrants were favored over them. For this reason, Vargas gained support among Afro-Brazilian activists during this time.

Before the 1940s, Afro-Brazilians developed their own newspapers, social clubs, and dance groups. A small black elite led the intellectual thought that circulated in São Paulo's Black Press. As Hanchard notes, "The intensity of market and racial competition in São Paulo appears to have greatly influenced the formation of racial consciousness and race-specific institutions at an earlier period than in Rio de Janeiro" (1994: 30).

Yet since the 1930s, Rio de Janeiro has been a principal site of Afro-Brazilian social mobilization and is where many national organizations were created (Hanchard 1994: 9). Abdias do Nascimento's theater ensemble, the Black Experimental Theatre, was created in Rio de Janeiro in 1944. Although it ascribed to folkloric notions of African culture, the group embraced blackness and, through their work, challenged racism.

Challenging racism in Rio de Janeiro was not limited to cultural groups. The cultural tendency toward activism became more political as embracing blackness was a part of the emergence of Black Soul in Rio de Janeiro, which popularized black-power symbols such as Afro hairstyles from the US. Black activism was challenged as embracing a black racial identity was viewed as anti-Brazilian. Yet activism continued and the conflict between black activists' attempt to create a black culture with black cultural markers and commemorations ran in contrast with political elites' notion of a singular Brazilian culture where the focus should be on the people they believed should be celebrated during certain commemorations. An example of this tension is the centennial commemoration of abolition.

The Centennial Commemoration of Abolition

One of the most important events giving visibility to Brazil's black movements was the 1988 centennial celebration. May 13, 1888, was the day Princess Isabel signed the Golden Law to abolish slavery. Although this date has long been celebrated in Brazil, it was especially important to Brazil's black movement, as it marked 100 years of abolition from slavery. In some circles, the celebration was questioned because of the enormous amount of economic, social, and political inequality Afro-Brazilians continued to face. A debate entitled "Abolition: Myth or Reality?," sponsored by the Ministry of Culture, was canceled in Rio de Janeiro (Andrews 1991). In many cases, Black movement activists, in protest, did not celebrate on May 13. They preferred to not give credit to Princess Isabel's "freeing of enslaved people" but sought to recognize resistance movements of African descendants such as Zumbi dos Palmares, the leader of a runaway community of enslaved people. In 1988, in Salvador and Rio de Janeiro, black movement organizations did not hold events on May 13, and in Salvador, local and state governments were persuaded not to have events on the date. On May 12, in Salvador, a public demonstration was held, entitled "*Cem anos Sem abolição*." The phrase translates as "100 Years Without Abolition." Andrews notes this is a play on the Portuguese words *cem* and *sem*.

In Rio de Janeiro, a march took place on May 11, 1988. The police met the marchers with hostility. About 5,000 marchers were met by 750 troops to prevent them from marching past the Pantheon, where the Duke of Caxias, a commander in the Brazilian military during the Paraguayan War (1864–1870), is buried (Andrews 1991). He, along with Princess Isabel, were no longer recognized as heroes by Afro-Brazilian activists. As Andrews notes, the activists, in a 1987 pamphlet issued by the Rio de Janeiro Commission of Black Religious Seminarians and Priests, claimed they were "false heroes who contributed to the massacres of blacks in Brazil." In Brasília, the nation's capital, tensions were also high, and members of the Black United Movement protested Congress against the lack of employment opportunities for blacks (Andrews 1991).

Both Andrews (1991) and Hanchard (1994) note differences in how Brazilians focused on the commemoration of abolition. Some viewed slavery as a past historical event, choosing to focus on its legacy as a contributor to present-day inequality. Black movement activists wanted to focus on current-day inequalities, while those who held on to the belief of racial democracy wanted to emphasize inequalities arising during slavery. This last group saw inequalities as a past, rather than a current-day problem. Referring to the *Catalogo: Centenario da Abolição*, Hanchard found that of 1,702 events in capital cities, 500 were under the category of black culture. Of these, 224 were supported by federal, state, and municipal governments, while the black movement supported only 64. Race relations were the lowest category with only 38 events. What is most important, Hanchard points out, is that events discussing contemporary issues related to inequalities comprised the smallest number of events. Hanchard also notes that government entities and black movement organizations overwhelmingly focused on categories of black culture and abolition related to conditions during slavery, as opposed to present-day conditions. This logic is precisely what Nascimento (2009) criticizes, as it denies persistent domination of African descendants.

As Andrews (1991) shows, even before the events commemorating the 100-year anniversary of abolition, there was tension between the black movement and the state. The former sought recognition of resistance efforts while the latter promoted a history of Brazil that was more appropriate for its reputation as a racial democracy. Celebrations of abolition had been celebrated ever since the actual event in 1888, even if they were not always recognized as such. Black activists upheld November 20, Zumbi Day, as the holiday that Afro-Brazilians should celebrate. This day continues to be celebrated as a national holiday, although it is now named the Day of Black Consciousness. Black movement activists' effort to promote a holiday held in honor of a black hero was an effort to uphold black culture and to have the Brazilian nation embrace Afro-Brazilians contributions to the nation. In terms of racial identity, acknowledging African descendants' contributions to the nation was important because this recognition would encourage Afro-descendants to be proud of being black and the contributions of blacks to the nation.

Black movement activists wanted to raise racial consciousness but also put pressure on political elites. Former President Fernando Henrique Cardoso played a significant role in responding to black movement demands. An important event that forced the government to recognize the growing importance and concerns of the black movement was the commemoration of Zumbi dos Palmares, on November 20, 1995. Thousands of marchers met in Brasília and voiced their concerns. Black movement activists and labor leaders met with President Cardoso to ask for concrete measures to be taken to combat racism. President Cardoso created the Interministerial Working Group for the Development of Public Policies to Valorize the Black Population (Telles 2004: 56). The group eventually published a document on ways to integrate blacks into society. It was not effective, however, because the government provided no support to achieve these goals. Although Cardoso was supportive of affirmative action, his administration was hesitant to implement such policies.

Rejecting Racial Democracy

Political elites challenged the existence of racial democracy by acknowledging racial inequality and discrimination in society. Former President Luiz Inácio "Lula" da Silva denounced racism in Brazilian society. He can also be credited with intentionally increasing Afro-Brazilian political representation at the national level.[6] He created the Special Secretariat of Policies for the Promotion of Racial Equality (*Secretaria de Políticas de Promoção da Igualdade Racial*) and appointed Matilde Ribeiro, an Afro-Brazilian woman, to lead it. He appointed Joaquim Benedito Barbosa Gomes to the Brazilian Supreme Court, making him the first Afro-Brazilian person to ever serve on the court. Barbosa later became the president of the Brazilian Supreme Court but left there in 2014. Gilberto Gil, a well-known Afro-Brazilian singer, was chosen to head the Ministry of Culture. Benedita da Silva, an Afro-Brazilian woman, well known for speaking out on issues affecting poor Afro-Brazilians and women and who had served as a senator and governor of Rio de Janeiro, was appointed as the Minister for the Promotion of Social Assistance. Benedita da Silva now serves as a federal deputy. Marina Silva was

---

[6] My discussion of representation should be put in context. Between 2003 and 2010, Lula appointed about 90 Ministers. While less than 10 percent of these appointees were Afro-Brazilian, he still appointed more Afro-Brazilians than his predecessors.

appointed to direct the Ministry of the Environment (Telles 2004: 73). Silva unsuccessfully ran for president in the 2014 election. In October of 2015, then President Dilma Rousseff combined the Ministries of Women, Racial Equality and Human Rights and Nilma Lino Gomes, an Afro-Brazilian was nominated to lead the newly formed ministry. In May of 2016, when former Vice President Michel Temer took over as president he initially made his cabinet all white and all male, dismantling years of representation of Afro-Brazilians and women. In June of 2016, however, he appointed Luislinda Dias de Valois Santos (from the state of Bahia) as president of SEPPIR, making her his first Afro-Brazilian appointee. Although he assured the public that he believes the issues SEPPIR addresses are important, the composition, in racial and gender terms, of his initial cabinet members made it difficult to accept the sincerity of his commitment to diversity. Black movement and social movement activists continue to protest and demand rights under Temer's conservative government. Black movement activism is practiced in formal and informal ways, and it shapes and influences individual racial identity – and perhaps whether some Afro-Brazilians think in group terms.

Black Movement Activism and Recent Successes

Activists have played a critical role in changing the discourse on race and challenging negative stereotypes of blackness. Black activism now includes formal non-governmental and non-profit organizations where the focus is on Afro-Brazilians. Hip-hop music and the organizations of some of these artists also serve as forums of black activism: artists provide workshops where issues of racial discrimination are addressed (Pardue 2004). Activism also includes free pre-*vestibular* courses, such as in the case of the non-governmental organization Educafro. These courses prepare students for the college entrance exam. Educafro requires a citizenship course in which students discuss racism and issues of race, serving as an avenue for developing racial consciousness (Santos 2010). Some Afro-Brazilian politicians discuss racism and racial issues while campaigning and the use of political campaigns serve as a means of racial mobilization and teaching racial consciousness (Mitchell 2009a). More importantly, grassroots organizations are sites where black women organize, asserting their racial and gender identities (Caldwell 2007; Perry 2013). Christen Smith (2016) shows the important work that artistic groups and political groups, such as "*Reaja ou Será Morto!*" in Salvador, do to highlight racism and police brutality. Lastly, social networking sites such as Facebook, YouTube, and Twitter serve as more recent mediums of black activism.

This new racial climate may bring about new ways of viewing social experiences, for example viewing discrimination as racial in nature rather than only a class issue, a legacy Nascimento (2009) posits is Brazil's "sorcery of color." Perceptions of discrimination differ according to the intersection of race, class, and gender. Layton and Smith (2017) find that considering all Brazilians, those with darker skin tones are more likely to perceive class, gender, and race discrimination. When considering racial discrimination, age is negatively associated with perceived discrimination and education is positively associated with perceiving discrimination. Lower levels of income are positively associated with perceived class discrimination. Similarly, darker skin tones are positively associated with perceived class discrimination. For women, those with darker skin tones are more likely to report gender discrimination. These women also face race discrimination. Variance in discrimination may be the result of exposure to black movement activists discourse. Younger people and people with more education may be more perceptive of racial discrimination. These various forms of activism may play an important role on racial identity. Afro-Brazilians who embrace blackness due to exposure to black movement activists discourse may me more likely to support racial policies for Afro-Brazilians as a racial group. Racial policies directed at Afro-Brazilians may also influence racial identity.

Three such policies are Law 10.639/03, which was passed in 2003 and requires schools teach African and Afro-Brazilian history; federal legislation enacted in 2012 requires all federal public universities to reserve sub-quotas for Afro-Brazilian and Indigenous students that reflect their population percentage in the state; and Law 12.990, which was enacted in 2014, sets a 20 percent quota for Afro-Brazilians in civil service jobs in the Foreign Ministry. These are all policies that have potential to influence whether Afro-Brazilians claim an Afro-Brazilian identity as black or brown. The law regarding teaching African and Afro-Brazilian history has the potential to de-stigmatize African descended people. Black movement activists are not only concerned with increasing the visibility of blacks in civil society and the media but also with lifting Afro-Brazilians' self-esteem. For black activists, one way of doing this is through education, so they advocated for Law 10.639 (Nascimento 2009; Santos 2014).

Black movement activists supported and pushed for affirmative action policies, while simultaneously encouraging Afro-Brazilians to embrace the *negro* racial identity. Some universities that have implemented affirmative action policies for Afro-Brazilian students have formed campus organizations. There are also research groups that focus on racial discrimination and issues relevant to blacks in Brazil (Penha-Lopes 2013). The experience Afro-Brazilians undergo in these new learning spaces, in which they may confront racial discrimination or learn about blackness in a different way from what they have experienced in home or public life where blackness may not be valued, is relevant to this book. Those who embrace these new ways of thinking about blackness may have a propensity toward blackness not felt by previous generations.

Black movement activism has resulted in policies that have the potential to democratize universities and in some areas of employment. Through education, young Brazilians can learn about the contributions of Africans and African descendants to the Brazilian nation. The successes of black movement activism is that their discourse of embracing blackness and policies aimed at Afro-Brazilians may lead to more Afro-Brazilians embracing blackness. Furthermore, black movement activism that involves multiple issues and views issues such as women's rights, LGBTQ rights, and Afro-Brazilian rights through an intersectional lens will allow people to see how various oppressions are linked. Awareness of these various forms of domination can lead to support of certain policies based on attachment to a group.

Racism and Inequality in Brazilian Society

As the previous section on activism highlights, inequality persist in Brazilian society and black activists have struggled to create a more equitable society. In this section I discuss racism and inequality in Brazilian society. Brazilians often say American racism is explicit, whereas Brazilian racism and discrimination are *mascarada*, or masked. For this reason, social relations in Brazil appear to be fairly integrated and racially harmonious among racial groups. Edward Telles (2004) proposes the notion of vertical and horizontal social relations to explain Brazilian inequality. Telles claims that from the 1930s until 1972, scholars such as Gilberto Freyre (1956), Marvin Harris (1970), Charles Wagley (1971), Donald Pierson (1942), and Carl Degler (1986) promoted the idea of racial democracy and that these scholars focused on horizontal social relations and equality in these relations. In this view, there is less racism in the private spheres of home and social life. Telles finds that, when compared to the United States, there is less residential segregation and more interracial marriage in Brazil. Scholars such as Carlos Hasenbalg and Nelson do Valle Silva (1988) focused on racism and racial inequality in vertical social relations, sometimes comparing Brazilian racism to American racism. Florestan Fernandes (1965), UNESCO-sponsored research, also demonstrated racial inequality. Examples of vertical relations are inequality in employment and educational attainment. There is evidence of inequality between whites and Afro-Brazilians in employment and education. Despite evidence of more equality in horizontal relations compared to vertical relations, some scholars have found evidence of racial inequality in vertical relations or the private sphere.

Racism in the Private Sphere

A number of scholars have documented discrimination in the private sphere. France Winddance Twine's (1998) anthropological research in a rural town outside of Rio de Janeiro revealed racism in homes and schools where school-age Afro-Brazilian girls served as *criadas*, or maids who were adopted and raised to work in households without receiving pay. Racial discrimination was also present in schools, where teachers negatively viewed Afro-Brazilian students. Robin Sherriff's (2001) and Donna Goldstein's (1999) research projects reveal racism in the private sphere and negative views of blackness, even among Afro-Brazilians. Men view Afro-Brazilian women with African features and/or dark skin as less suitable marriage partners (Goldstein 1999; Caldwell 2007). Chinyere Osuji (2013) finds that, despite Brazil's reputation as a racial paradise with many interracial couples, it was challenging to find interracial couples in her research in Rio de Janeiro. Furthermore, when she did study these couples, many revealed that their families hold prejudice against Afro-Brazilian partners. Both Marcos Rangel (2015) and Elizabeth Hordge-Freeman (2015) find that within families, children are treated differently according to their skin color. Rangel finds that parents invest more in lighter-skinned children than their darker-skinned siblings. Hordge-Freeman finds that parents praise lighter-skinned children's physical features, and some show less affection to their darker-skinned children. Yet she did find evidence of resistance where parents embraced blackness. All of these examples demonstrate that even in the private sphere, racial prejudice has a negative impact on Afro-Brazilians.

Racism in the Public Sphere

Researchers continue to document inequality in the public sphere. Some examples of racism in the public sphere are in the domains of education, health, employment, and even public social spaces. Paixão, Rossetto, Montovanele, and Carvano (2011) have shown that even though there was a general increase in the number of Afro-Brazilians moving out of poverty during former President Lula's time in office, there was still significant income inequality between Afro-Brazilians and non-Afro-Brazilians in Brazilian society. Statistical comparisons of infant mortality show that in 2005, infant mortality was slightly higher for blacks and browns than whites; 24.4 percent for *pretas* and *pardas*, and 23.7 percent for *brancas* (Paixão and Carvano 2008: 38). The number of whites attending university was over four times the number of blacks and browns attending university in 2006 (Paixão and Carvano 2008: 81). Mitchell and Wood (1998) find that darker-skinned men report higher incidences of police brutality.

As wages increase, the difference in wage earnings between whites and Afro-Brazilians increases (Telles and Lim 1998; Arias et al. 2004; Bailey et al. 2013). It appears there is an "elite profile of discrimination" against Afro-Brazilians (Silva and Reis 2011). Those with higher incomes and more prestigious jobs face barriers despite having equivalent or superior credentials to their non-Afro-Brazilian peers. Professionals such as engineers, lawyers, and doctors in Rio de Janeiro work in white-dominated environments where they are a minority. Respondents typically pointed to the workplace and the public sphere as the most common sites of discrimination. Silva and Reis find that respondents noted prejudice against them in interactions with strangers, such as being mistaken for a nurse when one is a doctor. Angela Figureido (2010) finds that professionals in Salvador face a similar form of discrimination. A study conducted by Arias et al. (2004) reveals that the largest discriminatory wage penalties for Afro-Brazilians exist in the highest paid occupations. Paixão and Carvano (2008) show that *pretos* and *pardos* who have finished college are 1.2 times more likely to be unemployed compared to whites with the same schooling. Paixão (2015) also finds that Afro-Brazilian entrepreneurs report experiencing racism.

In terms of income inequality, studies focusing on inequalities between whites and Afro-Brazilians have employed a number of methods to grasp the cause of inequality. The degree of inequality depends on whether a researcher uses self-identification, how the respondent identifies herself or the interviewer's classification, and how the interviewer classifies the respondent. Using the interviewer classification gives a closer approximation to how one is identified by others in society. Arcand and D'Hombres (2004) find employment gaps between whites and browns and whites and blacks, but they point out that the gap between whites and blacks is due to endowment effects and discrimination, while for browns, it is mainly due to endowment effects or inherited social inequalities. Bailey et al. (2013) demonstrate that the composition of the Brazilian population changes depending on varying classification systems based on descent, photography, a binary classification, or restrictive census categories used by the respondent or the interviewer.

When considering ascribed identities or those the interviewer ascribes to a respondent, income inequality between blacks and whites is higher at some deciles than it is between whites and browns. Such differences are lost when only a binary schema is used. Considering multiple classification schemes is important because inequality differs according to these schemes.

Wage inequality between Afro-Brazilians and whites is higher for Afro-Brazilians with higher wages than those with lower wages. Bailey et al.'s (2013) work confirms that there is a penalty for blackness, so those with darker skin are paid less than those with lighter skin. Arias et al. (2004) rely on self-identification and only include men in the labor market. They use quantile regressions that allow them to examine wage differences between whites and Afro-Brazilians (*pardo*s and *pretos*) at various income levels, taking into account returns on education in the labor market. They find that differences in parental education and quality of education account for some of these income differences; however, they also believe discrimination is a factor since these disparities do not entirely explain differences in returns on education. Quality of education is measured by teacher-pupil ratio. In the Northeast, which tends to have a higher percentage of Afro-Brazilians, there are more students for every one teacher than in the South, which tends to have higher percentages of white Brazilians. Although mixed-race people have closer returns on educational investments at higher income levels, mixed-race people are paid closer to blacks at the lower end of the pay scale.

Using more recent data from the Brazilian Institute of Geography and Statistics (IBGE), Paixão et al. (2010) find that in the six metropolitan regions on which they focus, monthly salaries among *pretos, pardos,* and whites are more equal for lower status jobs such as domestic workers than for positions with more prestige. The greatest inequality they find among these groups is in public sector employment. They believe occupational discrimination may account for some of the differences in this sector, considering that *concursos* (exams) are sometimes required as a basis for determining promotions.

It is clear that income disparities exist between Afro-Brazilians and whites. Some of these differences can be explained in terms of human capital such as parents' education and an individual's capital. However, even considering these factors, there are still differences that may be better explained by racial discrimination. Lovell (2006) finds that Afro-Brazilians and women make less than white men. In 2014, while there was a decrease in the wage gap, *negra* women still earned 40 percent less than white men.[7] Inequality in the public sphere is based on intersectional identities including race and gender.

Today's economic downturn has been particularly harmful to Afro-Brazilians; the Brazilian real is at a low point while the price of goods has risen. Although average salaries of Afro-Brazilians rose 51.4 percent between 2003 and 2013 compared to 27.8 percent for whites, Afro-Brazilians incomes still amounts to only 57.4 percent of whites' incomes (Lisboa 2014). In 2015, *preto* and *pardo* workers in Salvador received only 48 percent of what whites earned; in Rio de Janeiro, *pretos* and *pardos* received 55.5 percent of white earnings; and in São Paulo, they received 59.4 percent of what whites earned (Carta Capital 2016).

Considering persistent inequalities in the public sphere is important. However, it is also important to consider discrimination in the private sphere. Black movement activists challenge discrimination in both spheres by advocating for policies and by embracing blackness and African features. Both are necessary to change the mindsets of people that people with dark skin and African features are intellectually inferior and not as attractive as those with European features and light skin. It is at this critical time period that this book, *The Politics of Blackness*, analyzes how Afro-Brazilians think they are viewed in society, how they interpret experiences of racial discrimination, whether they feel linked to blacks, and if there is a positive relationship between *negro* linked fate and support for racial policies. To address the critique that examining racial group attachment, racial identity, racism, and political behavior is an American framework, I examine the current line of thought that Brazilian race relations are becoming more American and that race relations in the Unites States are becoming more Latin American.

CHALLENGING CONVERGENCE THEORIES

There is a belief that North American scholars impose their understandings of race on Brazil without recognizing that Brazilian racial politics and North American racial politics are different. The first studies of race in Brazil often compared race in contrast to the United States. In the United States, many scholars define race in terms of the one-drop rule so that anyone with any African ancestry is considered black. This binary system

---

[7] 2016. Mulher negra ganha menos de 40% da renda de homem branco, diz Ipea. Veja.com http://veja.abril.com.br/economia/mulher-negra-ganha-menos-de-40-da-renda-de-homem-branco-diz-ipea/ (accessed on July 29, 2017).

of race in the US characterized American race relations up until the late twentieth century. In contrast, scholars view Brazil's racial system as a triracial system made of blacks, whites, and mixed-race people. Degler's (1986) "*mulato* escape hatch" indicates that *mulatos* can more easily ascend social and economic ladders. The *mulato* escape hatch is challenged because in reality, mixed-race people are still penalized in the labor market but to a lesser degree than *pretos*. Nonetheless, *pretos* report suffering more discrimination than *pardos* (Telles 2014).

Relying on Brazil's mixed-race population to characterize race relations in contrast to race-relations in the US does not acknowledge that most African Americans also have a mixed-race background. Furthermore, it does not allow a more complex analysis of variance in social, economic, or political behavior of mixed-race people and blacks in the United States. The debate about differences among mixed-race people and blacks in the US is not new. There was scholarly debate about the role of mixed-race people or the "mulatto's" place in the United States in the 1930s. An example is Park's comparative country analysis of mixed-race people. In Park's analysis, mixed-race people in the United States and South America, and he later discusses Brazil in the article, occupy a superior intellectual position to blacks. In his 1931 article he states the following:

... There is, nevertheless, no question at all in regard to the actual superiority of the mulatto in comparison to the Negro, provided superiority is measured by present achievements and by the relative status of each in the existing social order. Everywhere the mixed blood has, with certain outstanding exceptions, outclassed the *Negro* ... Not only in the learned professions and in politics, but particularly in literature and the expressive arts, the mulatto has outdistanced the Negro. This is perhaps less true in South Africa and the West Indies than it is in South America and the United States (Park 1931: 542).

In Park's analysis, mixed-race people in the United States and South America, and he later discusses Brazil in the article, occupy a superior intellectual position to blacks. This is an example that shows there was also a debate about the role of mixed-race people in the United States' position in society despite that many scholars only focus on segregation in the United States and do not acknowledge that mixed-race people may have had different life experiences than those not viewed as mixed race. Convergence theses suggest that race relations characteristic of Latin America and race relations characteristic of the United States are converging. Many do not acknowledge historical arguments about the role of mixed-race people in the United States.

While convergence theses about racial dynamics have recently emerged in sociological literature, there is a history of comparing Brazil and the US, most often in contrast to each other. However, Park, like Degler, believed mixed-race people were better off than blacks. In this way he believed the two countries were similar. I propose that scholars consider changes in racial dynamics in both countries and that North American scholars use what we learn about Brazil and Latin America generally to understand racial dynamics in the United States. Racial dynamics in the United States cannot simply be understood in a black/white paradigm. Multicultural movements in the US challenge binary notions of race (Hernandez 1998; Nobles 2001). Recent scholarship has shown that black-white biracial people often claim a biracial or multiracial identity (Rockquemore and Arend 2002; Davenport 2016). In addition, Latinos in the US challenge traditional notions of race, as some opt to identify as white (Darity et al. 2005) and some do not opt for a white or black label (Frank et al. 2010). These recent understandings of race stand in contrast to historic and current day analyses of race relations in the United States being defined by the one-drop rule where ancestry solely determines a person's race.

African-Americans' life experiences are shaped by intersectional identities of skin color, parentage, education, gender, and sexuality. These intersectional identities can lead to different experiences and political beliefs and behaviors. Teasing out intragroup differences may explain divergences in political opinion among Afro-descendants in the US. Afro-descendants in the United States include African immigrants, descendants of enslaved people from the United States, biracial Americans, and black-identified Latinos. Similar to Brazil, where Afro-descendants have varying phenotypes, these groups vary in phenotype and may interpret racialized experiences differently. Age may also explain varying racial attitudes. In Cathy Cohen's (2010) book, *Democracy Remixed: Black Youth and the Future of American Politics*, she finds that many black youth attribute their shortcomings to individual lack of effort rather than systemic racial discrimination. This is one example of an unexpected trend of young people in large cities.

Research that examines the political opinion of biracial Americans compared to monoracial Americans is also important and can benefit from studies on Afro-Brazilians. Lauren Davenport (2016a) has produced such work and draws upon some scholarship on Brazilian racial dynamics. Davenport finds that biracials who identify as white and black or those that identify as black support the same affirmative action policies as monoracial blacks. In addition, 90.6 percent of biracials who identify as white and black, 89.1 percent of biracials who identify as black and 88.8 percent of monoracial blacks believe racism is a problem. Biracials that identify as white are more similar to monoracial whites in these aspects. In contrast, in terms of non-racial issues such as abortion rights, biracials are more liberal than monoracial blacks and whites. In terms of identification, Davenport (2016b) finds that biracials in more affluent neighborhoods are more likely to identify as white or as white and black, and those living in black communities more likely to identify as black. Yet, considering the sample of biracials, most (55 percent) identify as both white and black. Davenport's study is an excellent example of going beyond convergence theses that do not consider present-day racial dynamics and differences in political behavior of biracial Americans compared to monoracial blacks.

Scholars such as Eduardo Bonilla-Silva propose the Latin Americanization thesis to describe a system of race in the US in which some minorities have gained status as honorary whites and that the US has moved beyond a binary framework of race (Bonilla-Silva 2004). Other scholars have criticized this thesis because it does not acknowledge the changing nature of race in Latin America, which in some cases has become more binary (Sue 2009).

I challenge the Latin Americanization thesis and other convergence theses because I do not think race relations in both countries will converge as reflections of each other at any given time. This is different than convergence theories and the theory of Latin Americanization of race in the US (Daniel 2006; and Bonilla-Silva and Glover 2006). A convergence assumes the two will meet at a point where they have similar racial structures of classification and race relations. Like Osuiji (2014), I offer a perspective that complicates the status of race relations in both countries. Racial progress exists alongside repression of Afro-descendants in both countries. While they are similar in terms of multiracial societies and the existence of racism, they are not exactly the same. While some mainstream media believed the US was heading toward a post-racial society because of the election of Barack Obama, America's first African American president, the current climate demonstrates how the country is regressing. There is open expression of racial hostility and hatred toward African Americans, Muslims, gays, transgender people, and immigrants. Consider laws such as the state of North Carolina's 2016 regulations barring transgender people from using public restrooms that do not correspond to their "biological" gender. At the national level, a travel ban was proposed for people coming from six predominantly Muslim countries. Despite racial, religious, and sexuality diversity in the United States, intolerance remains. Many Latin Americans national identities are rooted in the idea that diversity or racial mixture indicates fluid social relations and that these nations are racially tolerant because of diversity. Yet, we can see that that diversity does not lead to more tolerance.

In order to highlight diversity and a multiracial population today the US census has more flexible census categories (Hernandez 1998), which have led to over 100 possible racial combinations. This means the one-drop rule as an analytical category for studying race in the US and comparing it in direct contrast to other countries is less appropriate. Yet claiming that the US is now more Latin American because of a multiracial population does not acknowledge the complexity of race relations and the way multiple identities intersect. While the US is becoming more diverse, some say that Brazilian race relations are becoming less diverse or less of a tri-racial system in favor of a biracial system. This assessment does not acknowledge the work that black movement activists continue to do to convince mixed-race people to claim a *negro* identity and to view issues such as economic marginalization in racial group terms.

Rather than rely on the idea that race relations in the US and Brazil will converge, a focus on the complex ways these societies are changing and how race relations are progressing and retrenching as political climates become more conservative will allow for more insightful analyses on race relations and political behavior. This book is situated in Brazil's current climate in which understandings of race are fundamentally different than what they were in the past. During the duration of this project, from 2005 when the Workers' Party dominated national politics, to 2017 where austerity measures have been taken after Workers' Party president Dilma Rousseff was impeached, racial politics have changed. More liberal political climates are more amendable to racially progressive policies. Yet, policies that threaten the well-being of citizens especially those most marginalized such as low-income black and brown people give rise to black and social activism. Black activism can influence race relations by challenging Afro-Brazilians ways of thinking about economic marginalization and the needs of Afro-Brazilians as a racial group.

TERMS

Throughout the book I use the term Afro-Brazilian, Afro-descendant, and *negro* when referring to the census categories *pardos* (browns) and *pretos* (blacks). *Negro* is also employed when referencing how a respondent self-identified. I analyze my quantitative and qualitative data by separating these groups (*negros, pretos, pardos, morenos, mulatos,* etc.) and relying on the categories in which respondents self-identify in an open-ended question. By relying on their self-identification, I am restricted to Brazilian color and race classifications rather than "imposed categorizations." These respondents use terms such as *pardo, negro,* and *preto, mulato, moreno,* and rarely *mestiço.* When the survey questions use the term *negro,* they are understood as the combination of the census categories *preto* and *pardo.* When respondents identified as *negro, preto, moreno, mulato,* or any other identification, I report these identifications without combining them. For this reason, I am using a Brazilian framework, not a US framework.

In Brazil, the term *negro* is employed to refer to Afro-Brazilians, including *pardos* and *pretos.* I do not combine the groups when using the term *negro.* Rather, I use *negro* when respondents use the term, or I specify the use of *negro* when used by other scholars. Self-reported terms, such as *mulatto,* meaning racially mixed, or *moreno,* which can have an ambiguous meaning, are explained in the text. The term racial identification is employed throughout the text when referring to self-categorization and emphasizes that choosing identity is a process not an innate identity.

CITY SELECTION

This book focuses on Rio de Janeiro, Salvador, and São Paulo for comparative analyses. They are three of the largest cities in Brazil. Map I.1 shows where these cities are located and the composition of Afro-Brazilians (*pretos* and *pardos*) in the states where these cities are located.[8] These cities differ in racial composition, geographic location, income inequality, and racial politics. All of these factors make for interesting comparisons of how Afro-Brazilians experience race, interpret blackness and racialized experiences, and form political opinions on racial policies. Map I.2–I.4 show where *pretos* and *pardos* live at the subdistrict level based on the 2010 Brazilian Census. Map I.5–I.7 show these subdistricts by income. Historically these cities are important sites of black movement activism, and a number of well-known Afro-Brazilian politicians come from these cities (Hanchard 1994; Butler 1998; Covin 2006; Mitchell 2009a; Johnson 2006). Early studies on race relations and racial politics included Salvador (Azevedo 1996 [1953]), São Paulo (Bastide and Fernandes 1959; Nogueira 1985[1954]; and Valente 1986), and Rio de Janeiro (Souza 1971). My study builds upon both past and current research that tends to focus on one city.

---

[8] It is important to note that the map combines *pretos* and *pardos,* and despite high percentages in some of these regions, *pardos* are the vast majority and not *pretos.*

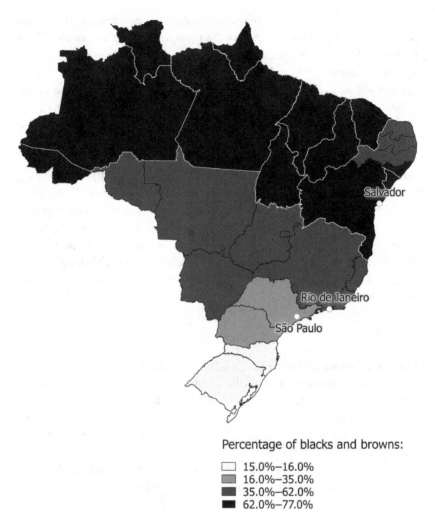

Percentage of blacks and browns:

☐ 15.0%–16.0%
⬜ 16.0%–35.0%
⬛ 35.0%–62.0%
■ 62.0%–77.0%

Map I.1 Afro-Brazilian Population by State

These cities differ in demographic composition of Afro-Brazilians and economic inequality. Salvador has the highest level of economic inequality between Afro-Brazilians and whites among the three cities. Studying these three major cities sheds light on regional difference in contemporary Brazil.

São Paulo has the largest number (4.2 million) of *pretos* and *pardos* in Brazil, followed by Rio de Janeiro (3 million) and Salvador (2.7 million) ("Negros e Pardos..." Terra 2011). When considering only those that are

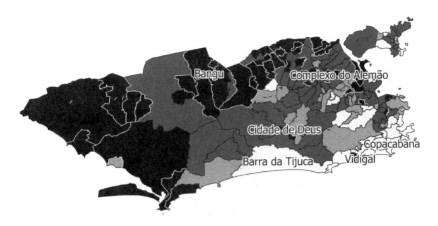

Percentage of blacks and browns:

☐ 8%–27%
▨ 27%–43%
■ 43%–56%
■ 56%–83%

Map I.2 Afro-Brazilian Population by District in Rio de Janeiro

preto, Salvador has the most (743,700), followed by São Paulo (736,000), and Rio de Janeiro (724,000) ("Negros e Pardos..." Terra 2011). The Northeast, the region where Salvador is located, is 96.1 percent Afro-Brazilian, and the Southeast where both Rio de Janeiro and São Paulo are located is 37.1 percent Afro-Brazilian. The percentage of *pretos* and *pardos* have increased in São Paulo and Rio de Janeiro, while it has remained relatively the same since the 2000 census in Salvador. Rio de Janeiro is 53 percent *preto* and *pardo*, Salvador is 80 percent and São Paulo 37 percent. In the article "Negros e Pardos são Maioria em 56,8% das Cidades, diz estudo" on Terra.com, Marcelo Paixão notes that changing demographics "were influenced by the process of valorization of the Afro-descendant presence in Brazilian society and by the adoption of affirmative policies" and further states "these data demonstrate not only the demographic change but also the political, social, and cultural change in expressing a new form of visibility of the black Brazilian population to encourage people to accept their skin color in a more open manner" (Terra 2011). In terms of economic differences, including all racial groups, São Paulo has the highest average monthly family salary (US$1,277.09) followed by Rio de Janeiro (US$1,275.88). On the lower end, Salvador's monthly family average is US

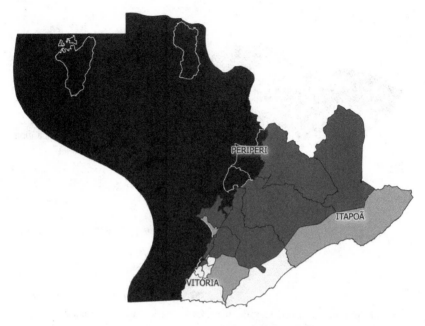

Percentage of blacks and browns:

- ☐ 64.0%–69.0%
- ▦ 69.0%–77.0%
- ▨ 77.0%–85.0%
- ■ 85.0%–89.0%

Map I.3 Afro-Brazilian Population by District in Salvador

$909.51[9] (Lisboa 2014). Differences in economic conditions of these cities also offer insight into the context in which Afro-Brazilians live. In Chapter 1, I discuss more details of the economic, political, and racial character-istics of each city.

METHODOLOGY

This book employs a mixed-method approach using original survey data collected in 2005–2006 and original survey data collected in 2008. I also

---

[9] Monthly salaries are converted to US dollars using the purchasing power parity of 1.606 provided by the Organization for Economic Cooperation and Development. Salaries in the Brazilian *real* are as follows: R$2,051.01 (US$1,277.09); R$2,049.07 (US$1,275.88); R$1,460.68 (US$909.51).

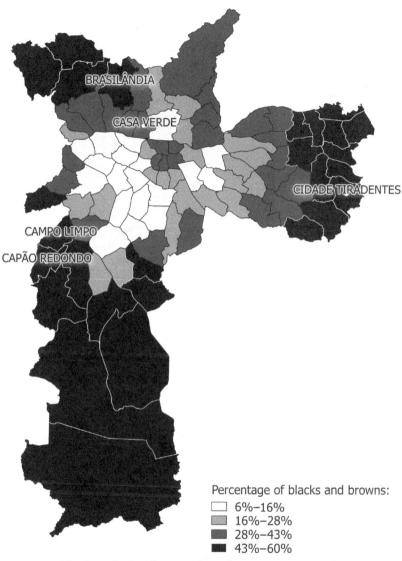

Map I.4 Afro-Brazilian Population by District in São Paulo

rely on survey data from the Latin American Political Opinion Project (LAPOP) from the years 2010 and 2012. The 2010 LAPOP national survey data includes 1,500 respondents. The 2012 LAPOP survey also has 1,500 respondents. In-depth interviews were conducted in 2012 and include the

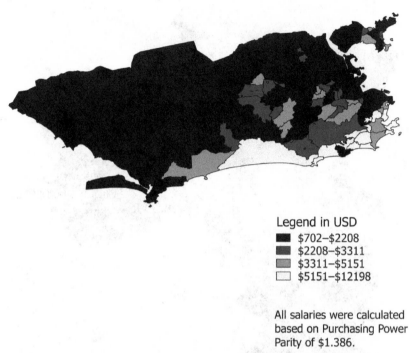

Legend in USD
- ■ $702–$2208
- ■ $2208–$3311
- ▨ $3311–$5151
- ☐ $5151–$12198

All salaries were calculated based on Purchasing Power Parity of $1.386.

Map I.5 Average Monthly Household Income by District in Rio de Janeiro

cities Salvador, São Paulo, and Rio de Janeiro. The original survey data collected from 2005 to 2006 and 2008 only include Salvador and São Paulo due to financial constraints. The 2005–2006 research and the 2008 research are separate surveys that are not different waves of the same survey. The 2005–2006 survey is entitled "Survey of Political Opinion, Racial Attitudes and Candidate Preference." The 2008 survey was a survey about political candidate preference. It was administered with an experimental design but had no effects. In 2012, 76 in-depth interviews were conducted in Salvador, São Paulo, and Rio de Janeiro. Funding limitations prevented me from including Rio de Janeiro in the 2005–2006 survey and the 2008 survey. Original survey data of 674 survey interviews were collected in the 2005–2006 survey, and 200 survey interviews were conducted in 2008. When analyzing data from the LAPOP survey, I rely on respondents' self-identification as census categories *preto* and *pardo*, and when analyzing the 2006 and 2008 data, I rely on their self-identification in an open-ended question. Similarly, when analyzing interviews, I rely on open-ended self-identification.

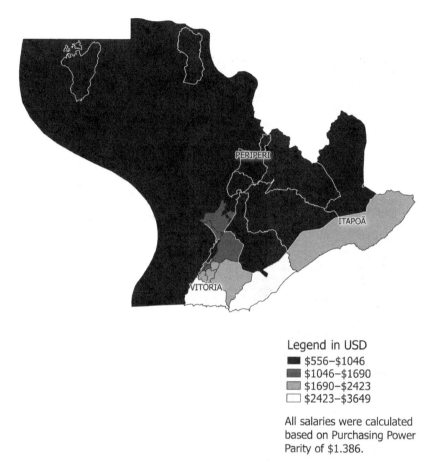

Legend in USD
◼ $556–$1046
◼ $1046–$1690
▨ $1690–$2423
☐ $2423–$3649

All salaries were calculated
based on Purchasing Power
Parity of $1.386.

Map I.6 Average Monthly Household Income by District in Salvador

2005–2006 Survey Data Collection

I hired and trained a team of Brazilian students in Salvador and São Paulo
in interviewing methods. The resulting interview samples were limited to
neighborhoods selected by professors from the Federal University of Bahia
(UFBA) and the University of São Paulo (USP) based on their knowledge
of neighborhoods where I could easily find high concentrations of Afro-
Brazilians with class heterogeneity. I obtained maps of the neighborhoods
from the Brazilian Institute of Geography and Statistics (IBGE). Students
were assigned to at least two neighborhoods. Randomization was introduced by arbitrarily selecting streets in these neighborhoods and

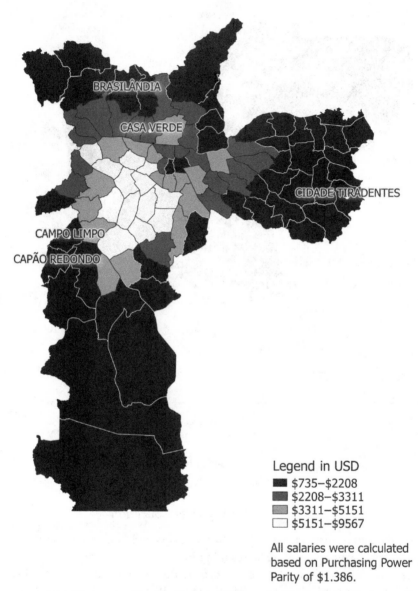

Map I.7 Average Monthly Household Income by District in São Paulo

employing a skip-number method to choose households. This step was
needed to make inferences from the samples taken in each city. On most
streets, interviewers conducted interviews at every fifth house on the

designated blocks. If the street did not contain many houses, interviewers went to every third house. This sample is not entirely random because of the pre-selected neighborhoods. Because of financial constraints, neighborhoods were pre-selected. I do not use these data to make generalizations about the entire country of Brazil. Results are limited to the cities of Salvador and São Paulo. Despite the limitations of data collection, there are currently no available survey data that measures the notion of *negro* linked fate in Brazil making this quantitative survey novel and important to analyze these data.

A total of 346 interviews were conducted across three neighborhoods in Salvador: Federação, Itapoãn, and Periperi. Federação is a socioeconomically heterogeneous neighborhood including both middle-class and very low-income households. Part of the Federal University of Bahia (UFBA) campus, a prestigious public university, is located in Federação. Itapoãn is also socioeconomically diverse, but it has a larger proportion of low-income households. Periperi, a low-income neighborhood, is located in the periphery of Salvador. It could almost be considered a suburb because it is located well away from the center of the city.

In São Paulo, neighborhoods included were Cidade Tiradentes, Casa Verde, Brasilândia, Campo Limpo, and Capão Redondo. A total of 328 interviews were conducted in São Paulo. Because of attacks on public buses by a gang called PCC (Primeiro Comando da Capital or the First Capital Command) and law enforcement's search for those associated with the gang, interviewing was discontinued. We continued after attacks from the gang and after attacks on communities from law enforcement calmed. The result is a lower number of respondents in São Paulo than in Salvador. Cidade Tiradentes is a low-income neighborhood located on the far-eastern side of São Paulo. Several non-governmental organizations operate there, including hip-hop organizations that support youth in the community. Casa Verde, located in northeastern São Paulo, is mostly middle class. Campo Limpo is located in the southwest and is known for its large social divisions. *Favelas* (shantytowns) are located beside condominiums of middle-income and upper-class households. Capâo Redondo, a low-income neighborhood, is in the southern periphery of the city.

Relying on obtained maps of these neighborhoods from the IBGE in São Paulo, I randomly selected streets for students to conduct face-to-face interviews. Interviewers were assigned to at least two neighborhoods. They used a skip-number method, choosing every fifth house. On streets with a small number of houses, interviewers went to every third house. Interviewers told potential respondents they were conducting research and that their personal information was not needed; no identifying information would be recorded. Similar to the interviews in Salvador, interviewers asked if anyone of African descent lived in the household. If the respondent identified herself as a person of African descent, the interview was conducted. This ensures that race identification was determined by the respondent. In our analysis, we only consider respondents' self-identification to avoid triggering bias towards a racialized identity; we did not specifically name racial groups or colors when asking for participation in the study. In the Brazilian context, the term "Afro-descendant" or asking if someone is of African ancestry is a matter of ancestry rather than an identity (Telles 2004). Unlike the US, in Brazil Africanness or African heritage is part of the Brazilian national identity and citizens openly accept that most Brazilians have African, indigenous, and Portuguese ancestry. In this way, the term "Afro-descendant" was a more appropriate term to describe potential respondents than a list of racial identifications. Respondents selected were of voting age.

2008 Survey Data Collection

The 2008 survey sample consists of 200 respondents in Salvador and São Paulo. Afro-Brazilian university students from UFBA conducted interviews in Salvador, and university graduates trained in interviewing methods conducted interviews in São Paulo. The survey was originally intended as an experiment to measure the effect of political advertisements on the racial identification of politicians. However, no effects were found. Unlike the larger 2006 survey, where specific neighborhoods were identified, in 2008, interviewers chose neighborhoods and, in some cases, conducted surveys outside of households in public places with people from various neighborhoods. Randomization was not introduced in this survey in the same manner as the 2006 survey, making claims about complete randomization limited. However, the value of the survey is that it includes survey questions on *negro* linked fate.

2012 In-Depth Interviews

Seventy-six in-depth interviews were conducted in Rio de Janeiro, São Paulo, and Salvador. I conducted interviews in company with one research assistant in each city. Research assistants conducted interviews with respondents who agreed to participate in a study of Afro-descendants. They chose respondents of varying ages, class and educational backgrounds. Respondents were interviewed in neighborhoods, city centers, universities, public spaces such as parks and, in São Paulo, the research assistant interviewed some people at bus stops. The spread of interviews is as follows: Salvador, 27; Rio de Janeiro, 26; São Paulo, 23. The research assistant in São Paulo interviewed individuals in low-income neighborhoods; I interviewed university students. As a result, responses in this sample differ from the other city samples. Low-income individuals in the São Paulo sample were less willing to expand their answers, mainly responding either "yes" or "no," making it difficult to analyze responses in the same way as respondents in other cities who gave more detailed answers.

In addition to survey questions, interviewers recorded the color or racial identification stated by respondents when asked "What is your color or race?" Interviewers also recorded hairstyle and skin tone, based on a memorized color palette with which they were provided. Skin tone is measured on a scale from one (lightest) to six (darkest). When quoting responses, I list the skin tone, education, self-identification, age, and hairstyle to give a fuller description of respondents.

In the racialized context of Brazil, hairstyles are politicized. Examples of hairstyles that mark one's blackness are braided hair (including cornrows and braided hair extensions) and Afros (called "black power," which Brazilians say in English). Such aesthetics are especially detrimental to black Brazilian women, who are aware that naturally curly hair is not looked upon positively in mainstream media (Caldwell 2007). However, as in the 1970s, the youth and some older Afro-Brazilians are sporting hairstyles that embrace blackness.

ORGANIZATION

Chapter 1: Afro-Brazilian Political Underrepresentation

This chapter examines how Afro-Brazilians in Salvador, Rio de Janeiro, and São Paulo explain *negro* underrepresentation in politics. I develop a theory of racial spatiality, which is the notion that spaces in society are naturalized as white spaces that exclude Afro-Brazilians – even when they are middle class and educated. Using an intersectional approach, I analyze how skin color, class, gender, and aesthetics intersect to produce varying accounts of underrepresentation. Interviews reveal that Afro-Brazilians believe racism, social exclusion, slavery, faulting *negros*, and political parties explain *negro* underrepresentation. Overwhelmingly they cite racism, social exclusion, and slavery, which are all related to spatial exclusion. However, these responses differ in regard to respondents' race, class, gender, skin color, and aesthetics.

Chapter 2: Blackness and Racial Identification in Contemporary Brazil

In this chapter, I examine confounding factors to choosing a *negro* identification. I also examine the endogeneity of racial identification, relying on quantitative and qualitative analyses. Much work in the social sciences considers racial identification a contributing factor to one's political behavior. Rather than continuing this trend without critique, I make the claim that racial identification in Brazil is endogenous to other variables, such as racial group identity and racial discrimination. This means, for example, that one may claim *negro* identification because of the experience of discrimination. On the other hand, people who identify as *negro* may be more likely to say they have experienced discrimination. My point is that I am critical of viewing race as a static category as opposed to understanding race as an experience. In Brazil, one becomes *negro* (Caldwell 2007). Understanding the concept of choosing blackness is important because it emphasizes the non-static notion of race, which is important when considering Afro-Brazilian political opinion and behavior.

To support this contention, I use variables that capture the experience of being Afro-Brazilian in my statistical analyses whenever possible. Rather than simply examining racial identification, I consider the racial discrimination variable. I made this choice based on in-depth interviews during which many Afro-Brazilian respondents placed the experience of discrimination as a common experience in daily life. Relying on seventy-six in-depth interviews conducted in Salvador, São Paulo, and Rio de Janeiro, I examine whether people choose black identifications and why they do so. I used the LAPOP survey to examine the endogeneity of race, based on statistical analysis. The statistical results support my claim that racial identification is endogenous. This finding serves as a basis for later chapters and challenges how social scientists conduct research where race is simply considered a demographic variable explaining behavior.

Chapter 3: *Negro* Group Attachment in Brazil

Relying on quantitative and qualitative data, I examine the notion of *negro* group attachment or *negro* linked fate in Brazil. Findings demonstrate that Afro-Brazilians in Salvador, Rio de Janeiro, and São Paulo feel linked to *negros* because of issues commonly faced by *negros* such as racial discrimination and challenges faced by economically marginalized people. This finding is in direct opposition to scholars who claim that Brazil is unique and that racial groups do not demonstrate collective political behavior.

Chapter 4: *Negro* Linked Fate and Racial Policies

I examine the role of *negro* linked fate in policymaking, including affirmative action, the requirement that African and Afro-Brazilian history be taught in schools, and whether the president should nominate blacks to important positions. Results show that a sense of *negro* linked fate has a positive impact in the support of racial policies. Not only does *negro* group identity exist in Brazil but there is also a positive relationship between *negro* linked fate and support for racial policies. This is similar to Michael Dawson's work on African Americans and political behavior. In this respect, Brazil is more similar than different from the United States. This is an important finding scholars should consider. Findings are based on quantitative and qualitative methods.

Chapter 5: Afro-Descendant Perceptions of Discrimination and Support for Affirmative Action

Black movement activism has taken place in a number of Latin American countries. However, because of differing histories and national myths not all black social movements have been effective. In this chapter, I focus on countries that have implemented policies for Afro-descendants. Relying on the 2012 LAPOP survey, I examine *negro* and mixed-race people's support of affirmative action policy. Not all surveys included the question on discrimination. I focus on countries with *negro* and mixed-race populations and surveys that included questions on affirmative action and discrimination. These countries include Bolivia, Brazil, Colombia, Honduras, and Nicaragua. I run three different multinomial regression analyses to examine if respondents who have experienced discrimination are more likely to support affirmative action. The results are not as expected when testing three different forms of discrimination which include discrimination in employment, in public places, and in government. I believe this is due to the fact that such an analysis is premature. However, considering this is useful for scholars that may examine such trends in the future.

Conclusion: The Racialization of Political Events

I focus on two events where race was salient in discussions of both events. One is President Dilma Rousseff's 2014 campaign and her subsequent removal from office in 2016, and the other is mobilization around police brutality. Rousseff's removal from office involved discussions around the *Bolsa Família* program, which if faced with budget cuts would have a negative effect on low-income Afro-Brazilian families. Mobilization around police brutality has taken place at the national level and has been discussed as a racialized issue relevant to Afro-Brazilians, not simply a class issue. Cuts to social programs and high rates of police killing and torturing of Afro-Brazilians have reinforced economic, social, and political exclusion. I close the chapter focusing on the suggestions that scholars of race and ethnicity need to discuss these forms of exclusion as violence. A mixed-method approach is most appropriate for such analysis.

Afro-Brazilian Political Underrepresentation

On July 4, 2014, some friends and I, who were mostly black, went to the Diplomat Bakery in downtown Belo Horizonte to buy drinks, when we decided to sit there to eat and converse. The bakery was full by it being the Brazilian soccer national team's game day, and besides employees, we were the only blacks there. Even with everyone having their bills in hand, a supposed manager of the bakery didn't stop exclusively questioning us blacks, if we had paid for the food. I emphasize that during the questioning, we were still eating. Our conversation was interrupted several times to know if we had intended to leave without paying. A friend politely told the manager that the situation was getting extremely uncomfortable when she was surprised with screams. The guy said he was only keeping an eye on his bakery, was just doing his job and didn't need us there. He then ordered us to leave.

Mirela Oliveira, "O Nosso Lugar É Na Periferia: O Racismo Sutil Deixando De Ser
    Sutil" Blog Post on *Blogueiras Negras*, author's translation

According to the blog post, when Oliveira and her friends refused to leave, the manager turned to the black woman and said, "This bakery is not for you. Your place is in a periphery bakery." They performed an act of resistance by filing a report. The author and her friends filed a report of discrimination at a military police station; however, they were met with racist insults. The *de jure* segregation that existed in the United States never existed in Brazil, yet Afro-Brazilians recall experiences reminiscent of segregation. Today Afro-Brazilians are still not welcome in certain social spaces and whites wish they would stay in the periphery neighborhoods. These everyday experiences show how nice places are informally reserved for whites while low-income places are marked as the domain of blacks. In interviews with Afro-Brazilians about political underrepresentation, some of them liken political inequality to their everyday experiences of racial and social exclusion.

The focus of this chapter is to show how Afro-Brazilians in Salvador, Rio de Janeiro, and São Paulo explain Afro-Brazilian political underrepresentation.

I situate my work within the larger body of literature on political representation and inclusion, race and politics, and race and identity in Latin America. The literature on race and politics or identity and blackness in Latin America generally focuses on individual countries such as Brazil (Hanchard 1994; Bailey 2009a; Costa 2014; Telles 2004; Guimarães 2002; Oliveira 2007, 1997; Souza 1971; Santos 2000; Mitchell 2009a; Mitchell 2009b; Johnson 2006, 1998; Pinho 2010; Soares and do Valle Silva 1987), Colombia (Escobar 2008), Cuba (Cleland 2017; Saunders 2015; Sawyer 2005; Fuente 2001), Honduras (Anderson 2009), Mexico (Sue 2013), Peru (Golash-Boza 2011), Venezuela (Fernandes 2014), or Ecuador (Johnson 2014). However there is a growing body of multi-country literature focusing on the role of race and ethnicity in politics in Latin America (Yashar 2015; Htun 2016; Hernandez 2013b; Johnson 2012; Madrid 2012; Sidanius et al. 2001).

Generally, there are similar racial narratives throughout Latin America. These nations view themselves as racially mixed and share similar histories of denying racism due to the existence of a racially mixed population. Tanya Hernandez (2016) questions scholars who believe the idea of racial democracy has actually led to more tolerant white Latin Americans. Further, she questions the outdated and inaccurate idea that the existence of segregation meant there was no race mixture in the US. Hernandez's concerns about scholarship predicated on the view that white Latin Americans are more tolerant than whites in other countries such as the US, is important because the assumption of a tolerant white political elite would indicate a high degree of Afro-descendant integration in all realms of life, including political life. Yet scholars have found that Afro-descendants remain excluded and politically underrepresented in Latin America.

Regarding political representation in electoral politics in Latin America, most literature focuses on indigenous representation (Madrid 2012) or quotas for women. Htun's (2016) work focuses on the inclusion of women, indigenous people, and Afro-descendants throughout Latin America. She argues that quotas have led to an increase in the number of women and members of ethnic and racial groups, but representatives do not always act in the best interests of these groups. Similarly, relying on plenary speeches, Crissien (2015) finds that Indigenous and Afro-descendant political candidates make identity relevant. However, when examining elections in minority-majority districts, Indigenous candidates were more successful at empowering their constituency, while Afro-descendants were not. Similar to Htun's point about representation versus inclusion, inclusion does not mean that the interests of Afro-descendants will be represented in political institutions. In the case of Colombia, the only Latin American country that has reserved seats for Afro-descendants, there was no electoral creation of Afro-descendant constituencies. Rather, all Colombian voters could vote for candidates running for these reserved seats (Htun 2016: 94). There were no rules about verifying that candidates had connections to marginalized groups or activist groups that advocated on the behalf of Afro-Colombians. The 2014 election led to two non-Afro-descendants being elected to hold seats reserved for Afro-descendants. In areas where there were concentrations of Afro-descendants, many of them voted for traditional parties rather than voting for representatives of the reserved seats (Htun 2016: 94). Afro-descendants may not identify as one group and, thus, may not view themselves as having similar interests. This discussion is important when thinking about political representation because it demonstrates that even when there is formal institutionalization of inclusion, Afro-descendants remain outside of the political arena.

POLITICAL REPRESENTATION

It is necessary to give background on understandings of political representation before the analysis of how Afro-Brazilians discuss political underrepresentation. Descriptive representation means that a politician shares physical characteristics, such as race or ethnicity, or cultural characteristics with their constituents. Substantive representation means that, in the US case, a person represents the interests of a particular group. Claudine Gay (2002) finds that descriptive representation is more important for white voters than blacks in the US case. While blacks are more likely to contact black representatives, white constituents are more likely to give favorable assessments of and contact representatives who are white. On the other hand, Katherine Tate (2003) finds that African Americans believe black politicians will represent them better than non-blacks. Tate believes that discussions of representation should include descriptive and substantive representation. Mitchell et al. (2009) discuss coherent representation as a subset of descriptive representation that they believe is more appropriate to the Brazilian case, as officials may feel an obligation to respond to their constituency (232). In Brazil, both Afro-Brazilian and non-Afro-Brazilian politicians have represented issues of marginalized groups, including women and Afro-Brazilians. There is evidence that some Afro-Brazilian politicians seek a racial vote, although this is not common (Mitchell 2009a). There is also evidence that Afro-Brazilians who self-identify as *negro* or *preto* are more likely to vote for black candidates (Mitchell 2010; Aguilar et al. 2015). Despite this finding, most Afro-Brazilians do not vote along racial lines and most Afro-Brazilians do not identify as black. In other words, it is not true that only Afro-Brazilian politicians represent issues relevant to Afro-Brazilians and marginalized people. Workers Party political leaders such as former presidents Luis Inácio "Lula" da Silva and Dilma Rousseff have championed the issue of racial policies, such as quotas for Afro-Brazilians, and social class policies, such as *Bolsa Família*, that have benefited and lifted many Afro-Brazilians out of poverty. In addition, Afro-Brazilian politicians have been essential in advocating for racial policies and some politicians have a black activists background (Johnson 2006).

Negro representation must be understood in the context of black social movements throughout Latin America, which gained momentum in the 1980s and 1990s with transitions to democracy. Social and political movements occurred domestically and transnationally. Since the 1970s, there have been conferences that brought together Latin American Afro-descendants. The Congress of Black Culture in the Americas was held in Colombia in 1977, Panama in 1980, São Paulo in 1982, and Ecuador in 1984 (Johnson 2014). Abdias do Nascimento was a Brazilian black movement activist, scholar, and politician who advocated a Pan-African ideology and did not limit black activism to Brazil (Nascimento 1989). Tanya Hernandez (2013a) finds that Brazil, Ecuador, and Colombia instituted university affirmative action programs, while in Honduras and Ecuador, a certain percentage of university scholarships are set aside for Afro-descendants. These affirmative action programs are all the product of pressure from Afro-descendant activists on government officials. Activists challenged the dynamics of race relations, were engaged actions that led to more inclusion whether through opening space for more public discourse about racism, sought an increase in the presence of blacks in electoral politics (Johnson 2012), or advocated for public policies to democratize certain spheres in society in an inclusionary way (Hernandez 2013).

Activists and organizations outside of Latin America have also advocated on the part of Afro-descendants in collaboration with Afro-descendants in Latin America. Institutions such as the Ford Foundation, Inter-American Development Bank, and global organizations such as the United Nations have also played a role in supporting and serving as a platform to display the concerns of Latin American Afro-descendants (Johnson 2007). The 2001 United Nations World Conference against Racism and Xenophobia, held in South Africa, played a critical role as a site where Afro-Brazilians and others were able to voice their concerns about racism and exclusion in their countries (Telles 2004).

In summary, political representation of Afro-descendants in Latin America can be analyzed by examining the number of Afro-descendants in politics. Despite Afro-descendant underrepresentation, some Latin American countries have implemented racial policies that benefit Afro-descendants. Politicians have responded to pressure from black activists. Considering, descriptive political representation is important to consider in Latin American countries with substantial Afro-descendant populations because black movement activism has promoted ideas of racial group-ness and advocated for racial policies. Despite black activism, Afro-descendants continue to be underrepresented, so I am most interested in how Brazilian Afro-descendants explain political underrepresentation.

UNDERREPRESENTATION IN BRAZIL

Turning to Brazil specifically, Afro-Brazilians continue to be significantly underrepresented in electoral politics. Afro-Brazilians make up 53 percent of the population but are not represented as such in the National Congress. Twenty percent of federal deputies are Afro-Brazilian (*pardos* and *pretos*), and 9 percent of the Senate is Afro-Brazilian (Johnson 2015). Descriptive representation does not ensure that issues relevant to Afro-Brazilians will be addressed. Nonetheless Afro-Brazilian activists-turned-politicians, such as Abdias do Nascimento, fought for racial policies such as affirmative action. By appointing Afro-Brazilians to prominent positions, both Lula and Rousseff signaled that prestigious national political offices could be held by Afro-Brazilians who were capable of occupying these positions. In a country where blackness is often seen as inferior and dark skin is stereotyped negatively, this was a powerful symbolic gesture that challenged dominant ideologies of Afro-Brazilians. In this way, they contributed to descriptive and substantive representation.

Of course, the change in racial discourse is not top-down but rather bottom-up. Black movement activists such as Abdias do Nascimento, Paulo Paim, and Benedita da Silva all served in the National Congress. They advocated for policies that would address the needs of Afro-Brazilians even during a time when such policies were not popular and the myth of racial democracy was popularly accepted by most Brazilians. The myth of racial democracy is not as prevalent as it was in the past and research on underrepresentation finds evidence of racial voting.

AFRO-BRAZILIANS AND VOTING

In terms of voting, Mitchell (2010) finds that Afro-Brazilians that identify as black (*negro* or *preto*) are more likely to vote for *negro* politicians than those identifying in non-*preto/-negro* categories. The survey question employed the term *negro* to indicate *preto* and *pardo* politicians. Similarly, relying on an experimental design, Aguilar et al. (2015) find evidence of racial voting when considering the number of candidates on a ballot. When ballots are short, whites and *pardos* show no preference for candidates of the same color. However, when there is a long ballot, whites and *pardos* show a preference for candidates of the same color. Self-identifying *pretos* (blacks) show a preference for black candidates regardless of the number of candidates on the ballot.

Stanley Bailey (2009c) found in a Rio de Janeiro based survey that when considering a list of disadvantageous conditions to being elected to political office, most Brazilians believe low education and lack of resources are greater factors than race; therefore, race is secondary to class as an explanation of underrepresentation. However, when considering prejudice as a reason for a lack of underrepresentation, whites, *pretos*, and *pardos* overwhelmingly believe it explains why blacks are underrepresented in politics. When examining voting preferences for Benedita da Silva, Bailey finds that *pretos* were significantly more likely to cite color as a reason for their vote choice compared to whites and *pardos*.

Current research on voting demonstrate that *negros* or *pretos* politically behave differently than *pardos* and whites. *Negros* or *pretos* show a preference for voting for *negro* candidates (Mitchell 2010; Aguilar et al. 2015). These findings are based on research including survey data and experimental research. Most Afro-Brazilians do not identify as *preto*, which extrapolating from these findings would explain why Afro-Brazilians do not overwhelmingly vote for *preto* or *negro* candidates and that political underrepresentation remains an issue. In addition, more educated and younger people readily identify as *negro* (Bailey and Telles 2006). This is extremely important to note when considering the changing state of racial politics in Brazil. It indicates that although there is underrepresentation of *negros* in politics, changing self-identification as *negro* along with a *negro* preference for *negro* politicians may lead to an increase in *negro* political representation.

SOURCES OF UNDERREPRESENTATION

As mentioned earlier in this chapter, a lack of resources may also account for *negro* underrepresentation. Scholars studying underrepresentation in Brazilian politics have found that differences in resources for campaigns (Bueno and Dunning 2014) and political party recruitment (Oliveira 1997) partially account for Afro-Brazilian political underrepresentation. Oliveira

(1997) finds an increase in the number of Afro-Brazilians elected to city council from 1988 to 1992 in Salvador. Afro-Brazilians elected to the city council tended to come from working-class backgrounds, while white Brazilians tended to come from high- and middle-income backgrounds. Oliveira believes that a change in political recruitment by political parties aided this increase. Ollie Johnson (1998, 2007, 2015) traced underrepresentation of Afro-Brazilians in Congress over time and found that despite their low numbers, they were essential players in advocating for racial policies and gaining allies to support such policies.

Marcelo Paixão studied underrepresentation in some of the highest spheres of government, such as federal cabinet member appointees. Paixão and Carvano (2008) found that from 1985 to 2008, only seven of 350 cabinet members were Afro-Brazilian. President Lula appointed five of these cabinet members. As Johnson (2015) believes, Paixão and his team of researchers have found that "socioeconomic racial inequality contributed to political racial inequality" (19). What is made clear when researching the appointed members is the link between the white elite, prestigious positions of power, and the absence or exclusion of Afro-Brazilians. Andrew Janusz (2017) focuses on electoral outcomes in the Federal Chamber of Deputies and finds that even when adjusting for differences in education, occupation, and campaign resources, race accounts for differences in electoral outcomes. Scholars find that underrepresentation is due to resources and racial discrimination when resources and socioeconomic status do not explain underrepresentation. I am most interested in how Afro-Brazilians explain political inequality. This chapter examines the link Afro-Brazilian respondents make between underrepresentation and what I term "racial spatiality."

RACE, SPACE, AND UNDERREPRESENTATION IN BRAZIL

Theories of race and place are not new, and anthropologists, critical geographers, and critical race theorists have discussed race and place (Shabazz 2015; Alves 2014; Price 2012; Tyner 2012; Crenshaw 1991; McCallum 2005). My theory is distinct from scholarship on race and place where there is a focus on how marginalized spaces are racialized (Buras 2011; Lipman 2011; McCallum 2005; Moldonado 2009; Perry 2013 Vargas 2004). Some of the spaces that are racialized in this work are neighborhoods and communities. Brooke Neely and Michelle Samura's (2011) analytical framework of racial space bridges theories of race and space. Their theory of racial space is marked by four elements. The four elements of their theory, which are all characteristics of race and space, are that race and space are contested, fluid and historical, relational and interactional, and are marked by difference and inequality. I contribute to theories of race and place in these fields offering a comparative lens for US-based research, and my work complements research focused on Brazilian race relations and inequality. The focus of many researchers is on how dominant groups shape these spaces. Like Sansone's (2004) work, which addresses how Afro-Brazilians think about "black spaces," I also focus on how Afro-Brazilians experience and interpret exclusion in public spaces such as the space of politics.

"Though race is a malleable social formation, it is never divorced from place and is therefore never entirely divorced from the frictions of place, nor place from the frictions of race. Race, like place, is never totally fluid" (Price 2012). My research focuses on how Afro-Brazilians understand political underrepresentation as another facet of inequality whether it is based on race or class. Respondents articulate exclusion in a profoundly "Brazilian" way in which questions of race are sometimes classed and political spaces are viewed similarly to public spaces where Afro-Brazilians are informally excluded. I use the theory of racial spatiality to explain the results of 76 in-depth interviews of Afro-Brazilians in the cities of Salvador, São Paulo, and Rio de Janeiro.

Most scholarship examining social and racial spaces in Brazil comes from anthropologists. In these studies, dark-skinned bodies have been naturalized as occupying certain social positions in society (McCallum 2005). For example, dark-skinned women's bodies define them as domestic workers. When Afro-Brazilians occupy prestigious and higher-paid positions of employment (Silva and Reis 2011), they do not occupy "natural" positions. The Brazilian elite try to limit the interaction of lower-income, dark-skinned people from lighter-skinned, high-income individuals. This is highlighted in the urban revitalization projects in Salvador, Bahia (Perry 2013). In the city of Salvador, homes have been destroyed and families expelled from land they occupied for generations in the name of development. Underlying these "development" projects are ideas of value and marking space. Beautiful places with access to the beach where land is highly valued are seen as "white" spaces. Developers aid wealthy white Brazilians and foreigners in occupying such spaces while discouraging poor darker-skinned people.

A more extreme case of limiting Afro-Brazilians' movement can be found in the form of police violence and the police execution of Afro-Brazilians (Smith 2016; Vargas 2004; and Alves 2014). The Brazilian state, through its agents, the police, continuously harass and executes innocent young Afro-Brazilians. This practice is perpetrated by both Afro-Brazilian and non-Afro-Brazilian police officers as well as elite specialized squad units that are not part of standard police units. As Jan French (2013) notes, agents of the state and military police are often stigmatized and stereotyped because most of the rank-in-file officers are black. Even within the institution of law enforcement, Afro-Brazilians are stigmatized. More importantly, is that both Afro-Brazilian and non-Afro-Brazilian police officers stereotype Afro-Brazilians and sometimes seek to restrict their movement. Afro-Brazilian respondents discuss political inequality in terms of racial spatiality.

RACE, SPACE, AND BLACKNESS

Respondents were asked why *negros* are underrepresented in politics. In the survey question we use the term *negro* in the same way as mainstream media to include the census categories *pretos* and *pardos*. In this chapter, I use the terms "Afro-Brazilian" and *negro* interchangeably. When reporting responses, I use the terms that interviewees use, which is most often *negro*. Responses were grouped into five main categories, most of which deal with space or spatiality. As Lefebvre (1991) notes, social relations exist within social space. Within physical spaces, social relations exist and it is these relations of power and domination that are mirrored in society. My concept of racial spatiality refers to physical and social spaces where blacks are excluded, and relationships of subordination and domination are perpetuated. Certain social and political spaces are deemed white while others are deemed *negro*.

What explains this significant gap in political underrepresentation?[1] In the 76 in-depth interviews conducted in Salvador, São Paulo, and Rio de Janeiro, respondents overwhelmingly believe racism explains underrepresentation. Their responses fall into five categories: racism, social exclusion, slavery, faulting blacks, and political parties (listed in the order to which they are discussed in the chapter). Racism, social exclusion, and slavery all fit into a similar narrative wherein *negros* are excluded from society and

---

[1] The interview question asked about *negro* representation, referring to descriptive representation. However, some respondents discuss the fact that they prefer politicians who will promote policies in which they are interested, which is more of an issue of substantive representation.

limited to certain physical and social spaces. The notion of racial spatiality explains the relationship between racial inequality, social inequality, and political inequality.

RACIAL SPATIALITY

I define racial spatiality as the existence of boundaries created for the specific purpose of maintaining and limiting the movement of certain racial groups and for the maintenance of power of dominant groups. Lefebvre's (1991) notion of social space confirms the concept of racial spatiality when he emphasizes that social relations exist in a social space. Similarly, I am referring to physical spaces that also tend to be social spaces. In the Brazilian case, constraining the physical movement of Afro-Brazilians is practiced both socially and politically. The everyday occurrence of marking public spaces as white or black is common such as the case of the young woman and her friends at the bakery discussed at the beginning of this chapter. Although Jim Crow laws do not exist in Brazil, and never have, the marking of common spaces as white or black does exist. The devaluation of Afro-Brazilian people and the maintenance of non-black and non-brown spaces by restricting Afro-Brazilian movement in the public sphere serve as both a metaphor and a real life experience in the political arena.

A theory of racial spatiality acknowledges that various forms of violence are used to maintain boundaries that exclude marginalized people. Violence in Brazil can be manifested as physical violence, exclusionary discourse, and microaggressions that accept stereotypes about low-income and/or dark-skinned people. Blacks are made to feel unwelcome in public spaces such as high-end shopping malls, restaurants, and neighborhoods. Although this is changing, historically blacks were virtually invisible in the media except in stereotypical roles. In common discourse, blacks are not associated with positions of power. Many responses to the question about political underrepresentation articulate the fact that underrepresentation in politics is a result of the limitation or exclusion of *negros* in everyday public spaces, similar to "white" political spaces where *negros* are not welcome. In this way, political inequality becomes the result of social and racial inequality.

RACIAL SPATIALITY AND INTERSECTIONALITY

From my analysis of the impact of race, gender, and class, it is clear that racial spatiality is intersectional. Afro-Brazilian women's racialized and gendered experiences, along with their varying class positions, may lead to different ways of thinking and viewing the world. In my analysis I consider skin color along with factors such as gender, class, race, and age. These identities fundamentally shape how respondents experience the world and in turn how these experiences affect their political opinions. Brazil is highly violent against dark-skinned people and lower-income people. Experiences of exclusion, which characterize racial spatiality should be understood in the context of violence. Although Neely and Samura do not include violence as a way of maintaining space, it is important to consider the maintenance of space through violence (Tyner 2012). Exclusion should be understood as a form of violence because it is meant to maintain the status quo of limiting power to whites and most often men. Exclusion is not merely an inconvenient experience. Dark-skinned Brazilians, women, and low-income people are made to feel devalued and unworthy of being part of the nation state. An example of devaluation and exclusion has occurred through openly violent acts against Afro-Brazilians such as land expulsion, military police and secret police squads that target them, the harassment and killing of Afro-Brazilian youth, and everyday microaggressions from those in dominant positions who seek to maintain their status over marginalized people. Interviews took place in three of the most violent states for Afro-Brazilians. As Christen Smith (2016) notes, Bahia, where the city of Salvador is located, has the third highest rate of death squad murders in Brazil. São Paulo has the highest number of people killed by the police, followed by Rio de Janeiro, and subsequently Bahia.[2] Understanding this context of violence reveals why Afro-Brazilian respondents mention racial and class exclusion in response to explaining political inequality. Understanding that everyday exclusion, racism, and classism are forms of violence is important and aids in understanding how Afro-Brazilian respondents discuss *negro* political underrepresentation.

BACKGROUND ON PRESENT DAY BLACK ACTIVISM AND ELECTORAL POLITICS

Knowing the background of city demographics, information on present-day activism and the history of electoral politics as they affect Afro-Brazilians in the three cities selected is important to the discussion at hand. Knowledge of the contemporary context is also necessary as it sheds light on the environment in which Afro-Brazilians in these major cities live. Salvador's black

[2] "Bahia tem 3º maior número de mortes por policiais do País." 2014. ATarde.com.br http://atarde.uol.com.br/bahia/noticias/1637992-bahia-tem-3o-maior-numero-de-mortes-por-policiais-do-pais (accessed on July 29, 2017).

activism has centered on cultural rights. Although culture remains a prominent means of organizing, there are groups that focus on racialized experiences in Salvador. In São Paulo, where Afro-Brazilians are a numeric minority, activists have focused on rights for Afro-Brazilians while simultaneously trying to create unity and a black identity, although this was regularly challenged because of the racial democracy myth. In Rio de Janeiro, some early efforts focused on the issue of racism. However, activism also focused on culture rooted in African tradition with the intent of empowering Afro-Brazilians. Embracing African culture was certainly not countercultural in a nation that had always acknowledged its African roots. Historically, organizing around black culture did not challenge the popularly held notion of racial democracy (Hanchard 1994).

In all three cities, it is evident there are efforts in the black movement to unify around a *negro* identification, which is seen as necessary in the struggle against racism. However, these three cities are different in terms of their demographics and politico-social environments. Despite these differences, they share similar issues that are relevant to Afro-Brazilian communities, such as discrimination, inequality, violence, police brutality and increased costs of living. The following sections discuss economic, social, political demographics, and black activism in these three cities.

Salvador

Salvador (2014 pop. 2,902,927) is the third largest city in Brazil. According to the 2010 Brazilian Institute of Geography and Statistics (IBGE), Salvador is 75 percent Afro-Brazilian (*pardos* and *pretos*) and is often referred to as "Black Rome" because it has maintained African traditions through the practice of African-derived religions and cultural forms such as *capoeira*, an Afro-Brazilian martial art and dance created during slavery. Despite this rich history, economic inequality persists. The average salary of Afro-Brazilian workers in Salvador is 36.1 percent less than the average salary of non-Afro-Brazilian workers (Bancarios Rio 2013). The state of Bahia, where Salvador is located, is 76.3 percent Afro-Brazilian. Seventeen percent of the Bahian population identify as *preto*, but *pretos* only represent 4.7 percent of the State Assembly. The current city council is about 42 percent Afro-Brazilian.[3] In Salvador it is common for residents to say *negros não*

---

[3] This is an approximation because, until 2016, there were no available data on self-classification for political candidates. Beginning in 2016, the Superior Electoral Court (*Tribunal Superior Eleitoral*) began collecting information on candidates' color or race. I looked at photos of

votam em negros or "blacks don't vote for blacks" and that there is no racism in the city because it is mostly *negro*. Afro-Brazilians in Salvador are not in agreement about the existence of racism, nor are they a unified group with unified interests. The idea that Salvador is a city free of racial prejudice is in contradiction to lived realities. Many scholars have shown that even Afro-Brazilians believe that lighter skin is more valued than darker skin and that African features are less attractive than European ones (Twine 1998; Sheriff 2001; Hordge-Freeman 2015). Afro-Brazilians in Salvador do not tend to vote for each other. This can be interpreted in two ways. It can mean that race is not salient for Afro-Brazilians and that they do not vote based solely on color, or, that race *is* salient and that Afro-Brazilians *intentionally* do not vote for Afro-Brazilian candidates.

Since the 1970s, despite popular beliefs about the nonexistence of racial discrimination in Salvador, activists and cultural groups have embraced blackness and African culture. Carnival groups such as Ilê Aiyê were formed because Afro-Brazilians were excluded from white Carnival groups. The group embraces blackness through a focus on Africa. Pinho (2010) believes their notions of blackness are oftentimes body-centric in that they believe African descendants have an innate ability to dance and that there are certain physical qualities and capabilities that African descendants have. This group also provides activities for children in the community and tries to empower blacks with positive messages about blackness and African culture. Olodum is another Carnival group that embraces blackness, although in a more diasporic sense with its use of reggae music and drums. Both groups seek to positively embrace blackness, and both have programs geared toward Afro-Brazilian youth.

In Salvador, black activism comes in the form of local grassroots organizing and formal organizations. There are a number of organizations specifically designed to fight against racism and some are designed to challenge the effects of racism through their organizations. The Steve Biko Cultural Institute offers free vestibular preparation classes (for the college entrance test) to Afro-Brazilian and low-income youth. This has played a positive role on its students' self-esteem, as they have role models in the form of professionally successful Afro-Brazilian teachers and former students.

Keisha-Khan Perry's (2013) work in the *Gamboa de Baixo* neighborhood in Salvador highlights the importance of local grassroots organizing. Black women leaders, many of them young, organized to stop revitalization

current council members to determine if they were Afro-Brazilian and verified these classifications with native Brazilians.

efforts that would have resulted in expulsion from land on which their families had lived for generations. The importance of examining grassroots organizing is that only considering formal organizations overlooks local organizing, which is often the work of women. Some of the women interviewed discussed the racism and sexism they faced as they challenged government and political leaders face to face when striving to gain access to water for their communities and stop expulsion from familial land. In sum, black activism in Salvador involves embracing blackness through cultural groups, organizations such as *Reaja ou Será Morto* that fight police brutality, and fighting racism and sexism through local grassroots organizations. Salvador is unique because it demonstrates that even in a city that is mostly Afro-Brazilian, black activism and promoting positive images of Afro-Brazilians continue to be key elements of mobilization.

Electoral Politics and Afro-Brazilians in Salvador

Brazil, like most Latin American countries, has a long history of corruption and patron-client relations between elected officials and the electorate. Patron-client relations are those in which politicians exchange gifts or services for votes. Politicians give individuals' foodstuffs or other material goods or services. Afro-Brazilians' reflect the skepticism that Brazilians in general have of politicians. Some scholars believe there is less clientelism in Brazil today than in the past (Sugiyama and Hunter 2013). Nonetheless, the recent corruption scandal between members of the Workers Party and the state-run oil company, Petrobras, only strengthens Brazilian skepticism of politicians. The current president, Michele Temer, has also been accused of corruption. In northeastern Brazil, many politicians still benefit from name recognition and the wealth of family members who belong to the white political elite since Brazil was a non-democratic country.

Salvador also has a long history of corrupt politicians and patron-client relations. Now deceased, Antonio Carlos Magalhães (often referred to as ACM) held political office in the city of Salvador, the state of Bahia, and in national politics from 1954 to 2007. He was first elected as a state deputy and then became a leader of the Democratic National Union (UDN) (Terra 2007). He was elected mayor of Salvador in 1967 and was subsequently elected as governor and senator of the state. His last political position was serving in the state senate of Bahia from 2003 to 2007. Affiliated with the Party of the Liberal Front (PFL), now known as the *Democratas*, his time in office was marked with corruption. Although known as a corrupt politician, a common phrase used among Bahians when speaking about Magalhães was "*Ele rouba mas ele faz*" (He steals, but he gets things done).

Historically the PFL had a stronghold in politics in Bahia. However, in the 2004 mayoral election, João Henrique from the Democratic Workers Party (PDT) defeated Cesar Borges who was from the PFL. Henrique held office from 2005 to 2008, was re-elected and held office from 2009 to 2012. In 2013, ACM's grandson, known as Antonio Carlos Magalhães Neto (ACM Neto) of the *Democratas* party came into office. He signed a decree for the creation of the Working Group for the Program to Combat Institutional Racism (PCRI) in the Municipal Government of Salvador (Bancarios Rio 2013). This initiative started in 2005 with the Municipal Secretary of Reparations (Semur). Semur is a government-supported agency that holds workshops and panels addressing issues relevant to the Afro-Brazilian population. The decree prohibits institutional racism. If a public servant is found guilty of racism, he/she can be fired. It is not evident whether this decree will be successful. Most people who suffer from discrimination do not bring these cases to court (French 2013). ACM Neto was re-elected as mayor in 2016 and his vice mayor is Célia Oliveira de Jesus Sacramento. During the 2016 election, four of the seven candidates for mayor declared they were *pardo* or *preto* including ACM Neto. ACM Neto, Alice Portugal from the Communist Party of Brazil, Pastor Isidório from the Democratic Workers Party, and Claudio Silva from the Progressive Party registered as *pardo*, while Fabio Nogueira de Oliveira of the Socialism and Freedom Party, a leftist party, registered as *preto*. João Jorge Rodrigues, a black activist and president of Olodum, criticized the trend of very light-skinned people registering as *pardo* as a political maneuver. Changing identification is not uncommon in Brazil, so it is no surprise it happens among political candidates. Yet the fact that 57 percent of mayoral candidates claimed an Afro-Brazilian identification demonstrates the saliency of race and the perception that one must make a connection to voters through racial identification.

As noted earlier, Cloves Oliveira (1997) finds that political party recruitment has played a significant role in increasing the number of Afro-Brazilian city councilors. An increase in Afro-Brazilian politicians does not mean candidates commit themselves to addressing racial issues. Mitchell (2009a) finds that most Afro-Brazilian candidates for city council in Salvador and São Paulo in her study do not address racial issues. Olivia Santana, who at the time of her study was a city councilor, used Afro-Brazilian cultural cues in her advertisements for city council, and drew on blackness as it relates to Brazilian culture rather than in the diasporic sense that is common in São Paulo. In Salvador, Afro-Brazilians are underrepresented in politics, yet there is evidence that race is salient in politics. Some Afro-Brazilian politicians appeal to voters based on cultural cues, and some believe it necessary to change their racial identification to black or brown.

São Paulo

São Paulo (2014 pop. 11,895,893) is the largest city in Brazil. Although the city is 33 percent Afro-Brazilian, they hold less than 10 percent of the city council positions. The average salary of whites is 2.5 times more than that of Afro-Brazilians. Afro-Brazilians are most concentrated in the periphery, which makes transportation farther into the city, where there are more employment opportunities, difficult.

São Paulo continues to serve as a main site for activism. In 2003, Zumbi of Palmares University was created by the non-governmental organization *Afrobras* (*Sociedade AfroBrasileiro de Desenvolvimento Socio Cultural*) in São Paulo. The university, created with the goal of educating Afro-Brazilian students, became the first university in Latin America created with a focus on educating people of African descent.[4] São Paulo is also home to current black movement activity led by groups such as *Educafro*. *Educafro* is a non-governmental organization that prepares Afro-Brazilian and low-income youth for the *vestibular*. The organization also offers citizenship classes where students learn about race and racism. *Educafro* students have been involved in protest activity, advocating for affirmative action in universities and for the hiring of Afro-Brazilians in prestigious shopping malls. There are a number of other non-profit organizations that focuses on black women such as *Geledes*.

There are also organized local groups such as the Mothers of May (*Mães de Maio*), a group of Afro-Brazilian women, most of them mothers, who honor sons who died at the hands of São Paulo's secret death squads (Alves 2014). This group was formed in, but is also responding to, a very harsh reality Afro-Brazilians face. An illustration of the violence perpetuated by state agents against Afro-Brazilians is the 2004 case in which an Afro-Brazilian dentist, Flávio Ferreira Sant'Anna, was mistaken for a thief and was killed by Military Police. Black activists respond to racism and racial inequalities through organizations and less formal means.

Hip hop has served as a way of mobilizing Afro-Brazilian youth in both formal and informal ways. Pardue (2004) finds that Afro-Brazilian hip hop artists and participants in São Paulo understand the relationship between color and marginalization. While some artists' main focus is on finding

---

[4] "Universidade Para Negros." Raça Brasil. November 2005, no. 92, p.72.

ways for the voice of marginalized people to be heard, many recognize the intersection of race and poverty. Derek Pardue (2004) finds that youth who became involved in hip hop activities began to embrace blackness. The Center for the Cultural Formation of Cidade Tiradentes (*Centro Formação Cultural Cidade Tiradentes*) hosts shows, workshops, and seminars that attract Afro-Brazilian youth. These hip hop groups and grassroots organizations challenge repression and inequality.

Electoral Politics and Afro-Brazilians in São Paulo

In the current 55th Legislature of the Federal Chamber of Deputies, four of the 103 Afro-Brazilian Federal Deputies were elected from São Paulo. The State of São Paulo elects 70 representatives to the Federal Chamber of Deputies. This means that of those elected, only 6 percent are Afro-Brazilian. The state of São Paulo is 35 percent Afro-Brazilian (Melo 2012). The city council is approximately 11 percent Afro-Brazilian.[5] São Paulo city politics can be characterized as machine politics, and it was actually this structure that played a role in getting Celso Pitta, São Paulo's first Afro-Brazilian mayor, elected in 1996. He was the handpicked successor of Paulo Maluf.

Focusing only on Afro-Brazilian candidates and voters, Ana Valente (1986) examines the 1982 São Paulo elections. Political parties such as the Democratic Labor Party, the Party of the Brazilian Democratic Movement, and the Workers Party, all leftist parties, supported Afro-Brazilian candidates and were dedicated to minority issues. Black movement activists encouraged Afro-Brazilians to vote for Afro-Brazilian candidates. Despite their desire for an ethnic vote, of the 54 Afro-Brazilian candidates running for office, only two were elected. These two were not tied to the black movement and did not explicitly discuss racial issues. Valente's survey data of Afro-Brazilians reveal that most Afro-Brazilian voters did not know the Afro-Brazilian candidates that ran or were not concerned with the racial background of candidates. For these reasons, they did not vote for them. Ideological differences within the black movement were also contributing factors. Valente concludes that black movement activists prematurely expected an ethnic vote.

To highlight the lack of ethnic voting and the complexity of Afro-Brazilian politicians in São Paulo, I focus on the election of Celso Pitta. Despite the

---

[5] There was no available data on self-identification of city council candidates, so the author identified Afro-Brazilian politicians using photos available on the Municipal Council of São Paulo's website.

lack of ethnic voting in São Paulo, Michael Mitchell (1997) claims that at one point, while embroiled in numerous scandals, Pitta asserted that racism was the reason he was singled out. According to Cloves Oliveira (2007), although Pitta was de-racialized in television, the print media cast him as a representative of the Afro-Brazilian community. Pitta actively sought to de-racialize his identity and wanted to distance himself from blackness and Afro-Brazilian people. A significant number of Afro-Brazilians supported Luiza Erundina in the first and second rounds of mayoral voting in 1996. Mitchell contends that Pitta's claim that he was singled out due to his race was relevant given that during the campaign, Luiza Erundina, a Workers Party candidate and his rival, directed a racially insensitive comment at Pitta. Erundina, a white Brazilian woman, criticized him for not being black enough (Oliveira 2007).

Pitta used implicit racial appeals in his campaign after being attacked for his failure to address race. This kind of criticism forced him to appeal to the Afro-Brazilian community. He chose to do so through implicit appeals in his campaign. Oliveira (2007) gives an example of Erundina's advertisement where she states the following:

Despite being a black person, he has a mind like a white thief (*safado*). After the demand for a black representative of their radio and television programs, now a *petista* candidate decided herself to deal with the real political causes of the black race in São Paulo. Unfortunately, he only has black skin but internally has a mind and behavior like that of a white person; a white thief, a white thief. Of a white person who does not make promises with workers – who are the majority of the population. You all think you will vote for a mayor that is ordered around by another person? (Oliveira 2007: 289, my translation).

As Oliveira points out, the expression, "behavior and a mind of a white thief" is an inversion of popular derogatory phrases in Brazil against blacks: "*preto safado*" ("black thief") and "*preto sem-vergonha*" ("a black with no shame"). In response to this attack, Pitta posted an advertisement of black families as some of the beneficiaries of a housing program. Another advertisement showed whites and blacks benefiting from the *Leve-Leite* program, which distributes milk to children. Nonetheless, Pitta continued to be adamant that he was not a representative of the Afro-Brazilian community. Oliveira quotes an interview in the *Folha de São Paulo* newspaper, wherein Pitta insists that he is not a representative of the Afro-Brazilian community. Still if elected, reporters promulgated the idea that he could serve as a role model to Afro-Brazilian children (Oliveira 2007: 391). Further, he responded to people who criticized him for not addressing the racial question in the following manner: "I am not the candidate of this segment (blacks) of society. I will do all I can to bring prestige to this segment, but this election is not a racial election. I'm not a leader of any black movement. It would be false to incorporate this discourse" (Oliveira 2007: 391).

As Oliveira notes, despite distancing himself from the Afro-Brazilian community, Pitta still felt the need to use racial cues in his campaign. Most Afro-Brazilians who supported Pitta were conservative.

Pitta's election demonstrates the difficulties Afro-Brazilian politicians face in elections where their rivals can place expectations on them because of their racial identification even if they do not feel connected to the racial group. The media can also place pressures on these politicians due to their race. At the same time, black activists do not support candidates simply due to their race; they are also interested in politicians' commitment to progressive policies especially those that will benefit Afro-Brazilians.

Mitchell (2009a) finds that although seeking a racial vote is not a tactic commonly used by Afro-Brazilian politicians in São Paulo it has been viable for both local politicians and those elected to serve in the Federal Congress. At the time of her study, in 2006, there were only two Afro-Brazilian city council members in São Paulo, both of whom she interviewed. One member, Claudete Alves, relied on a racial vote and specifically discussed racial and gender issues. The other, Agnaldo Timóteo, denied the existence of racism against Afro-Brazilians and disagreed with racial policies aimed at this group. Much of Alves' campaign material addressing black mobilization drew on foreign black movements, such as those in the United States and South Africa, despite the fact that São Paulo has been at the forefront of black mobilization. Janete Pietá admitted in her 2007 interview that she seeks a racial vote and teaches racial consciousness during her campaigns to potential voters. She dresses and wears her hair in a style she believes embraces Africa and blackness. In this way she is a visible symbol of black empowerment. In São Paulo, there is evidence among elected politicians that appealing to Afro-Brazilian voters is a political strategy for some Afro-Brazilian politicians.

In sum, like in most political campaigns, an individual's political party, resources, and popularity are all components that determine the success of one's election. For Afro-Brazilian candidates in São Paulo, black movement activists also play an important role in a candidate's success because they shape racial discourse. A recent example is an Educafro-sponsored political debate between Afro-Brazilian political candidates running for city council held in September 2016 in São Paulo. They discussed some of Temer's proposals and their individual political agendas. This political debate of *negro* political candidates highlights the saliency of race in São Paulo.

Rio de Janeiro

The city of Rio de Janeiro (2014 pop. 6,453,682), the second largest city in Brazil, is nearly 50 percent Afro-Brazilian. Rio is known for the shanty-towns or *favelas* that dot the city in close proximity to very wealthy neighborhoods. While the *favelas* are mainly composed of Afro-Brazilians, the neighboring wealthy areas are mainly white. It is home to some of the most famous Samba schools in the country, and these schools often have a rich history of blacks creating them and maintaining this tradition. In addition, tourists from the world over flock to Rio to witness the beautiful "*mulata*," an image the Brazilian state promotes to the world of a racially mixed woman who is sexually available to men (Caldwell 2007). Rap artist Snoop Dogg's well-known song "Beautiful" was filmed in Rio de Janeiro. While this stereotype draws many foreigners to Brazil, it is damaging to Afro-Brazilian women. Despite the tourist appeal of Rio de Janeiro, it has historically served as a site for black movement activism, which continues until the present day.

Rio de Janeiro's black movement activists include the now deceased Abdias do Nascimento, who was arguably one of the most well-known Afro-Brazilian activists, scholars, and politicians. Rio de Janeiro is also home to Benedita da Silva, a well-known black woman activist and politician who began her early career as a champion for the rights of poor black women. Not only is Rio de Janeiro home to some of the most well-known black activists, it also has a number of organizations dedicated to Afro-Brazilian rights and the improve-ment of Afro-Brazilian lives. *Criola* is a non-profit organization that focuses on Afro-Brazilian women's issues. As is the case in São Paulo, *Educafro* is also in Rio de Janeiro and was involved in protest work in support of quotas. The fruits of Rio de Janeiro's black activism are present not only in racial policies enacted at the national level, but also because Rio de Janeiro is where the first Brazilian state university enacted an affirmative action policy by initiating the first student enrollment quotas in 2002.

Afro-Brazilian students have organized on university campuses, creat-ing black spaces to encourage embracing one's blackness. Penha-Lopes (2013) discusses a black student organization during the early stages of affirmative action at the State University of Rio de Janeiro where Afro-Brazilian students discussed racism. Many Brazilian universities, have *negro* student research groups that focus on the study of *negros* in and in which the dynamics of race are discussed and researched. In these groups Afro-Brazilians can join together to challenge the hegemonic belief that they are incapable and intellectually inept.

Another type of mobilization was popularized around the time of preparation for Brazilian mega events. *Rolêzinos* were announced on social media in 2013 near the time of the World Cup and led to disruptions of public spaces, such as prestigious shopping malls. Large crowds of usually dark-skinned and often poor Brazilian young people gathered in prestigious shopping malls. In most cases they were just hanging out, dancing, and listening to music, and they believed they should have the freedom to do so despite being poor and black. This everyday act of resistance occurred in Rio at a very important time when people around the world were paying attention to the city. This action proved that seemingly inconsequential, simple acts can serve as acts of resistance. While poor and Afro-Brazilian young people were not legally barred from these spaces, they are informally excluded because of social norms that make them feel unwelcome.

A 2013 case in Rio de Janeiro exemplifies that Afro-Brazilians are unwelcome in elite white spaces. A music event for *funkeiros* (those who listen to Brazilian funk music) took place near a mall. Police officers were told that youth in the mall were about to commit a robbery. The innocent youth were humiliated as the police officers forced them to get on the ground and partially undress. The youth were Afro-Brazilian. The incident was filmed and displayed on YouTube. Mall shoppers applauded the police officers. This is an example of Afro-Brazilian bodies being associated with criminality, especially since they were in a "white space," (a prestigious mall) rather than in a "black space" (the funk party) where darker-skinned people are *expected* to be. Another atrocious example was in March 2014 when Cláudia Silva Ferreira, an Afro-Brazilian woman, was killed by military police in the Morro da Congonha neighborhood in Madureira, a suburb of Rio de Janeiro. She was carrying a cup of coffee and bread after going to the supermarket. Police claimed they thought she was involved in drug trafficking by bringing coffee to drug dealers. In reaction to the killing, community members protested and blocked traffic. Mobilization around police brutality and executions are another form of activism.

In sum, a significant proportion of the population in Rio de Janeiro are Afro-Brazilian, and Afro-Brazilians have been involved in mobilization for cultural and racial rights. Today, despite the fact that the city has developed due to the World Cup and Olympics, racial inequalities continue to exist. A consequence of these mega-events is police repression and Afro-Brazilians continue to mobilize against the torture and killing of innocent people.

Electoral Politics and Afro-Brazilians in Rio de Janeiro

The state of Rio de Janeiro is 51.7 percent Afro-Brazilian. Rio de Janeiro is represented in the Federal Senate with three senators and 46 representatives in the Chamber of Deputies. Considering whites, blacks, and browns elected from the state of Rio de Janeiro, Afro-Brazilians were only 18.2 percent of federal deputies elected in 2014. In the 2012–2016 term, approximately 12 percent of Rio de Janeiro city council members are Afro-Brazilian.[6]

There have been studies of voting patterns in the state of Rio de Janeiro according to racial groups. Soares and do Valle Silva (1987) examine Rio de Janeiro's 1982 governor election of Leonel Brizola. Although their focus is on the effects of urbanization, social class, and party organization on the Brizola vote in various *municipos*, they are also interested in the role of race. They find that the higher the proportion of non-whites, the more votes Brizola received. *Morenos* or those claiming a brown (*moreno*) identity, tended to vote for Brizola more than whites and blacks. Afro-Brazilians who claim a brown identity may be light- or dark-skinned. Telles (2004) claims that dark-skinned Afro-Brazilians who claim a *moreno* identity may be expressing a form of whitening and believes it is an ambiguous term allowing people who may not be able to call themselves white to avoid stigmatized non-white categories (98). Soares and do Valle Silva (1987) propose three possible reasons blacks did not support Brizola as much as browns. One is that Brizola made an explicit appeal for *socialismo moreno* to attract Afro-Brazilian voters; however, it is possible that he isolated black voters, as the appeal was for *moreno* socialism, not black socialism. Second, blacks live outside of metropolitan Rio in areas where the party's organization was not very strong. Third, illiteracy could have played a role in voter access and blacks had the highest illiteracy rate of all color groups.

---

[6] Information on racial identification was not available, so the author viewed photos of council members of the Rio de Janeiro Municipal Council and verified classification with native Brazilians. As noted earlier, information on candidate's color or race became available in 2016.

There have also been studies of electoral politics at the city level. Benedita da Silva is an important political figure in Rio de Janeiro. Cloves Oliveira (2007) examines the role of the media in the election campaign of Silva. Oliveira compares Silva's campaign to Pitta's campaign. Unlike Pitta, Silva did not shy away from addressing racial issues during her campaign. She is a black activist who is concerned with marginalized groups including Afro-Brazilians, the poor, and women. She is known for addressing race, gender, and class issues and is affiliated with the Workers Party. In Rio de Janeiro, she was first elected to the city council in 1982, and was elected as a Federal Deputy in 1994. She ran for mayor in 1992 and lost. She was elected to the Senate in 1994, becoming the first woman senator in Brazil. She was vice governor under Anthony Garotinho, and when he ran for president in 2002, she become governor of Rio, making her the first Afro-Brazilian and woman to serve as governor. She was appointed by President Lula to serve as the minister of Social Welfare from 2003 to 2007. She is currently a federal deputy.

Other important politicians who address racial issues are Edson Santos and Jean Wyllys. Santos has been a long-time advocate of Afro-Brazilian rights. Jean Wyllys is an Afro-Brazilian federal deputy from Rio de Janeiro and addresses intersectional issues such as Afro-Brazilian rights and LGBTQ rights. While many Afro-Brazilian politicians have advocated for rights based on intersectional identities based on race and class, and for some gender, it is noteworthy that Brazil's first openly gay Afro-Brazilian politician comes from Rio de Janeiro.

In sum, in all three cities, Afro-Brazilians are underrepresented at state and city levels. Income inequality between whites and Afro-Brazilians also exists in these cities. Violence against Afro-Brazilians from the police and secret squads shape the Afro-Brazilian experience in these cities. Black activism continues to play a role in challenging racial, economic, and political inequality in these cities. In electoral politics, most Afro-Brazilian candidates do not mobilize voters based solely on race, although some have done so and been successful. Rather than focusing on politicians as a way of explaining Afro-Brazilian political inequality, I rely on voters.

IN-DEPTH INTERVIEW SAMPLE DEMOGRAPHICS

In 2012, my research team and I conducted 76 interviews in Salvador (27), Rio de Janeiro, (26) and São Paulo (23). Respondents were asked in which monthly family income bracket they belonged. The brackets were as follows: up to two minimum salaries, two to five minimum salaries, five

Table 1.1 *Monthly Family Income (USD) by City*

Monthly Family Salary	Salvador	Rio de Janeiro	São Paulo
Up to $813.08	14	4	9
$813.08–$2,032.68	10	8	7
$2,032.68–4,065.36	2	8	1
$4,065.36–$8,130.72	0	2	0
No Information	1	4	6
Total	27	26	23

to ten minimum salaries, or ten to twenty minimum salaries. I convert salaries based on purchasing power parity of $1.53 in 2012, relying on data available from the World Bank. In 2012, the minimum salary was $622 Brazilian *reais* or US$406.54 per month. I report monthly salaries in US Dollars. Most respondents in Salvador and São Paulo belong to the lowest family income bracket of up to US$813.08 per month. In Rio de Janeiro, there is an equal split between respondents in the US$813.08–$2,032.68 income range and the US$2,032.68–$4,065.36 range. Clearly, the Rio de Janeiro sample is wealthier than the Salvador and São Paulo samples.

For an idea of the cost of living, I report the cost of basic household products, referred to as a *cesta basica* or basic basket of goods. This includes essential products such as beans, milk, bread, oil, and tomatoes. Based on data from the Interlabor Department of Statistics and Socioeconomic Studies (Deese), the monthly cost of purchasing these items in Salvador is US$108.96, US$138.64 in São Paulo, and US$126.02 in Rio de Janeiro. The average rent for an apartment of 60 square meters is US$1,016.24 in Rio de Janeiro, US$1,077.59 in São Paulo, and US$585.56 in Salvador (Fign 2017).

Fourteen respondents in Salvador earn up to US$813.08 per month, while this number falls to four in Rio de Janeiro (Table 1.1). In São Paulo, of those reporting their incomes, nine respondents earn up to US$813.08 per month. In São Paulo, seven respondents reported family incomes from US$813.08 to US$2,032.68 per month. Eight respondents in Rio de Janeiro and ten respondents in Salvador earned US$813.08 to US $2,032.68 per month. Only one respondent in São Paulo reported a family income of US$2,032.68–$4,065.36 per month. Eight respondents in Rio de Janeiro and two respondents in Salvador reported family incomes of US$2,032.68–$4,065.36 per month.

Of those reporting their educational levels, in Salvador eleven respondents have less than a high school diploma (Table 1.2). In São Paulo, four have less

Table 1.2 *Education by City*

Educational level	Salvador	Rio de Janeiro	São Paulo
Did not complete middle school	6	4	1
Completed middle school	2	0	3
Did not complete high school	3	1	0
Completed high school	8	6	7
In college	5	4	7
Completed college	3	4	0
Some level of graduate education	0	4	0
No Information	0	3	5
Total	27	26	23

than a high school diploma and in Rio de Janeiro five have less than a high school diploma. In Salvador, eight respondents completed high school and in São Paulo seven respondents completed high school. In Rio de Janeiro, six respondents completed high school. In Salvador eight respondents are in college or have a college degree. In São Paulo, seven respondents have some college education or a college degree. Rio de Janeiro has the most number of highly educated respondents. Twelve respondents have at least some college education or a college degree.

INTERVIEW RESULTS

The following open-ended question about underrepresentation of Afro-Brazilians was posed to respondents: "*Negros* make up more than half the Brazilian population. Why are there few *negro* politicians at the federal, state, and municipal level? In your opinion, why does this happen? In other words, why is there such a low number of *negro* politicians in this country?" Most responses fall into one or more of five categories: racism, social exclusion, blaming blacks, slavery, and political parties.[7] In terms of racial spatiality, social exclusion, racism, and slavery are all examples in which these practices are used to maintain "social spaces," Some interviewees' responses fall into more than one category. For example, a respondent might have mentioned both racism and social exclusion. The interview responses better illuminate the maintenance of social space as well as the connection between racial and economic inequality and political inequality.

[7] Some responses did not fit into these categories.

The connection between responses and racial spatiality is that racism occurs in social interactions, whether when simply walking on the street or being in elite spaces unofficially deemed to be for whites. Tanya Hernandez's (2013b) notion of racial regulation is a way of explaining that societal practices are basically customary laws or rules that, although not actually legal, are supported and regulated by the state. There is a cultural history of placing Afro-Brazilians in certain spaces in Brazilian society. This was articulated in the interviews. Thus customary laws regulate racial subordination of Afro-Brazilians and reinforce the notion that certain spaces in Brazil are deemed to be for non-Afro-Brazilians. "Customary law is particularly relevant to the examination of state racial projects because of the way customary law often arises from the need for social coordination in the reinforcement of social conventions" (Hernandez 2013b: 11). These customs continue even now and extend to the realm of politics.

RACISM AS A CONTRIBUTION TO UNDERREPRESENTATION

In this section I discuss the findings with a focus on comparing Afro-Brazilian women and men. More than half (32 responses) of the 63 responses refer to racism, racial exclusion, or racial prejudice against Afro-Brazilians. I refer to responses rather than respondents because some responses elicited responses that fall in more than one category of responses Despite differing racial demographics in these cities, many respondents believe that racial stratification and the stereotyping of Afro-Brazilians have an impact on their daily lives and that methods of controlling and regulating Afro-Brazilians consequently bar them from politics.

I first discuss general trends concerning underrepresentation then follow with an intersectional analysis. Thirty-two responses about underrepresentation involve racism (Table 1.3). Fifty-nine percent of Afro-Brazilian men and 41 percent of Afro-Brazilian women cite racism as a cause for underrepresentation. Twelve of these respondents reside in Salvador, 11 reside in Rio de Janeiro and nine in São Paulo. Most respondents self-identify as *negro* or *preto*, and 12 respondents fall into the dark-skinned color continuum in the categories five or six. The scale is from one to six, with one representing the lightest color and six the darkest skin color. Fourteen respondents self-identify as *negro*, three as *preto*, and one as black (stated in English). Eight respondents identified as *pardo*, two as *moreno*, one as *mulato*, and one as *cafuso*. Racial or color information is missing for two respondents. It is revealing that even Afro-Brazilians identifying in non-*negro* and non-*preto* identifications note

Table 1.3 *Respondents Who Referred to Racism as a Cause for the Underrepresentation of Negros in Politics*

City	Gender	Educational Level	Family Income (USD)	Age	Skin color	Racial or Color Identification	Hairstyle
Salvador	Male	In college	Up to $813.08	20	3	*Negro*	Twist-out
Salvador	Male	In college	Up to $813.08	30	5	*Negro*	Two-strand twists
Salvador	Male	Completed college	$813.08–$2,032.68	30	5.5/6	Black (in English)	Low cut
Salvador	Male	Completed middle school	Up to $813.08	43	2	*Pardo*	Low cut
Salvador	Male	Incomplete middle school	Up to $813.08	58	5–6	*Moreno*	Low cut curly hair
Salvador	Male	Completed middle school	Up to $813.08	30	5	*Preto*	Cornrows
Salvador	Male	Incomplete middle school	Up to $813.08	34	6	*Negro*	Cornrows
Salvador	Male	Incomplete high school	Up to $813.08	59	5	*Pardo*	Low cut
Salvador	Male	Incomplete middle school	$813.08–$2,032.68	46	5	*Cafuso*	Low cut
Salvador	Male	Completed high school	$813.08–$2,032.68	30	5	*Negro*	Low cut
Salvador	Female	Completed high school	$813.08–$2,032.68	27	2	*Parda*	Curly
Salvador	Female	Incomplete middle school	$813.08–$2,032.68	59	5	*Parda*	Relaxed
Rio de Janeiro	Male	Incomplete middle school	NI	69	5	*Pardo*	Low cut
Rio de Janeiro	Male	Completed high school	$2,032.68–$4,065.36	35	3	*Pardo*	Straight hair
Rio de Janeiro	Male	Incomplete high school	Up to $813.08	18	3	*Negro*	Low cut
Rio de Janeiro	Male	completed high school	$813.08–$2,032.68	26	3	*Negro*	Dreads
Rio de Janeiro	Male	PhD Student	$813.08–$2,032.68	32	4.5	*Negro*	Twist-out
Rio de Janeiro	Female	Master's degree	$4,065.36–$8,130.72	31	3	*Preta*	Relaxed hair
Rio de Janeiro	Female	Incomplete high school	NI	19	3	*Parda*	Relaxed hair

(continued)

Table 1.3 *(continued)*

City	Gender	Educational Level	Family Income (USD)	Age	Skin color	Racial or Color Identification	Hairstyle
Rio de Janeiro	Female	Incomplete middle school	Up to $813.08	35	4	*Negra*	Relaxed hair
Rio de Janeiro	Female	No information	NI	29	5	*Preta*	Wavy
Rio de Janeiro	Female	In college	$2,032.68–$4,065.36	27	3	*Negra*	Relaxed
Rio de Janeiro	Female	Master's degree	$4,065.36–$8,130.72	28	2	*Negra*	Curly
São Paulo	Male	In college	Up to $813.08	25	2	*Negra*	Low cut
São Paulo	Male	NI	NI	NI	NI	NI	NI
São Paulo	Male	Completed high school	$813.08–$2,032.68	49	NI	*Pardo*	NI
São Paulo	Male	Completed middle school	Up to $813.08	51	6	*Negro*	Low cut
São Paulo	Female	In college	$2,032.68–$4,065.36	30	4.5/5	*Negra*	Tight curly[8] (Crespo)
São Paulo	Female	Completed high school	$813.08–$2,032.68	24	1	*Morena*	Straight
São Paulo	Female	NI	NI	64	NI	*Mulata*	NI
São Paulo	Female **	NI	NI	NI	NI	NI	NI
São Paulo	Female	Incomplete college	Up to $813.08	29	NI	*Negra*	NI

* NI= No information given
** Interview ended before demographic data was collected.

8 Naturally curly hair in Portuguese is referred to as *crespo*, which can be translated as kinky hair.

racism as an impediment to political representation. Research has shown differences in political opinion between *negros* and non-*negros*. Afro-Brazilians who identify as *negro* or *preto* are more likely to support *negro* politicians (Mitchell 2010; Aguilar et al. 2015); however, these data show that both *negro* and non-*negro* Brazilians believe racism is linked to political inequality.

In terms of citing racism and skin shade, twelve respondents citing racism belong to the five and six color categories, seven belong to the color category of three, four to the category of two, and one to the category of one. Three respondents were classified as a four or 4.5. The respondent classified as a 4.5/5 was counted in this category. There was no skin color information for five respondents. The pattern shown is that if we consider one to three as lighter skin colors and four to six as darker skin colors, 56 percent of respondents citing racism were in the dark skin color categories. Because of Brazil's skin color pigmentocracy, it is possible that those with darker skin are more likely to cite racism when considering political inequality because they are so acutely aware. Yet as noted before, it is not simply dark skin color or racial identification as *negro* or *preto*, as those in lighter skin color categories also noted racism.

Afro-Brazilian Women Citing Racism as a Cause for Underrepresentation

Thirteen Afro-Brazilian women cited racism as a reason for political underrepresentation. Six of them reside in Rio de Janeiro, two in Salvador, and five in São Paulo. Seven of them identify as *negra* or *preto* while five identify in non-*preto* or non-*negro* categories. Racial or color information is not available for one respondent. Three identify as *pardo*, one as *moreno*, and one as *mulato*. Six of the women have relaxed or straightened hair, two have hairstyles in which their hair was curled (*enrolado*), one has curly or *crespo* hair, and one has wavy hair. Information on hair texture is not available for three respondents. Skin color information was not available for three respondents. Considering skin colors, six respondents belong to the category one to three, which are the lighter skin colors, and four in the dark skin color categories four to six. Body politics is part of the experience of Afro-Brazilian women. In Brazil, kinky hair is referred to as bad hair not only among Brazilians in general but also among Afro-Brazilians (Caldwell 2007; Hordge-Freeman 2015). While this is changing due to more women embracing naturally

, hair, straight hair is still seen as more acceptable than curly hair. For this reason, it is noteworthy that many Afro-Brazilian women, citing racism, have relaxed or straightened hair. One way of altering one's appearance as more "acceptable" is to chemically relax curly hair to make it straight. Rather than view this act as one of not accepting blackness, another way to think about it is as a form of survival in a patriarchal society that puts even more weight on women's appearance. Half of the dark-skinned women had relaxed hair, while 67 percent of those in the light-skinned category had relaxed or straightened hair. In his study on plastic surgery in Brazil, Alexander Edmonds (2010) makes the point that some clinics offer surgeries to low-income women, so plastic surgery is not marked by the same inequality that persist throughout Brazil. In other words, women across class and race have similar access to beauty manipulation. Similarly, being able to manipulate one's appearance through changing one's hair is a means of accessing beauty standards set forth by society.

In terms of education and income, Afro-Brazilian women citing racism tend to be well educated and middle class. Two women have graduate degrees, three are in college or have completed college, and two have completed high school. One has not completed high school, and two did not complete middle school. Information is missing for three respondents. All of the women with graduate degrees and who are in college or have completed college self-identify as *negra* or *preta;* despite that, there is variance among skin color. In fact, most of them fall into the lighter skin-color categories. Consistent with Mitchell-Walthour and Darity's (2014) findings, education predicts identification as *preta/negra*. They also find that those who identify as such are more likely to admit they have experienced racial discrimination. These highly educated *negra* and *preta* women may be more likely to have experienced or more readily identify racism despite their skin tone. This finding shows that Afro-Brazilian women with higher education may be acutely aware of racism in various spheres of life, and this is articulated in their reason for political inequality.

Negra and *Preta* Women Citing Racism as a Cause for Underrepresentation

Three of the *negra* and *preta* women have relaxed hair, one has curly (*crespo*) hair, one has wavy hair, and the other has curled hair. Hair information is not available for one *negra* respondent. Considering skin colors, the respondents are evenly divided between light and dark. Skin color information is missing for one *negra* respondent. In terms of the socioeconomic status of *negra* women, they tend to be highly educated. Five have some college education, with two of these four having master's degrees. Educational information is missing for one respondent and the other respondent has not completed middle school. Only two *negra* respondents belong in the low-income categories, up to US$813.08 USD and US$813.08–$2,032.68. Two belong to the medium-income category of US$2,032.68–$4,065.36, and two to the high-income category of $4,065.36–$8,130.72. Income data is not available for one respondent. These findings are in line with previous studies showing the link between self-declared blacks and income (Telles 2004). In this case, Afro-Brazilian women who identify as *negra* or *preto* are those most likely to cite racism as a reason for underrepresentation, and most of them have medium and high incomes and are well-educated. In this sub-sample, the average age is 30 years old. In addition, 71 percent of self-identified *negra* and *preta* women are from Rio de Janeiro, while 29 percent are from São Paulo. It is interesting that none of these self-identified *negra* and *preta* women come from Salvador, which is known as having a large population of Afro-descendants. Crenshaw's notion of structural intersectionality is useful, as it allows us to think about how these multiple identities via class, city, skin color, identification, and hairstyle lead these women to cite racism as a cause for underrepresentation. The very dynamics of spatial segregation in Rio de Janeiro and informal racially exclusionary spaces create an environment where middle- and high-income and well-educated Afro-Brazilian women may not feel welcome, which gives them insight into how racism works in Brazilian society and in particular in these cities in which they live. João Costa Vargas (2006) compares spatial segregation of neighborhoods in Rio de Janeiro to Apartheid era segregation in South Africa and segregation in the US. *Favelas* are clearly occupied by Afro-descendants and are stigmatized and racialized as black and criminal. Similarly, in São Paulo, many neighborhoods that are predominantly Afro-Brazilian are spatially segregated, as they are located in the periphery. Context matters. The cities in which these women live matter because the local racial dynamics have an impact on their locations within structures of marginality and/or privilege relative to their intersecting identities.

To gain more insight into how they explained political inequality, I examine some of their responses.

I think part [of underrepresentation] is [due to] racial prejudice and the other is a lack of opportunity. *Negros* don't have as much knowledge and education than those with more education and knowledge who are mostly white. Prejudice still exists [against *negros*. For example,] whites look behind themselves [when walking] because they think blacks will rob them. (30-year-old, dark-skinned *preta* female who is a college student in São Paulo)

First because of racism that impedes *negros* . . . Second is the issue of access to enter campaigns. Most *negros* don't have money to finance campaigns . . . (28-year-old light-skinned self-identified *negra* female in Rio de Janeiro with a master's degree).

Not only is it prejudice but also a lack of opportunity to study. In the first place is prejudice and second a lack of opportunity. A lot of people do not have the same education that white people have. (31-year-old light-skinned self-identified *negra* female, who holds a master's degree and resides in Rio de Janeiro)

As explained in the theory of racial spatiality, public spaces are where discomfort and racialization occur. The first respondent relates the common act of walking as a site where whites feel threatened by blacks. In this public space, whites believe Afro-Brazilians are trying to violate their possessions by trying to rob them. In this context of fear, racial prejudice happens every day and in the realm of politics. While the second respondent does not describe an act of prejudice or racism, she believes racism serves as an impediment to *negro* political representation. This same respondent also acknowledges that *negros* lack the financial resources to make them competitive contenders for political office. This resource argument is similar to Bueno and Dunning's (2017) findings that Afro-Brazilians have fewer resources to effectively compete in political campaigns. The third respondent mentions prejudice and a lack of opportunity and notes that whites have different opportunities from others. In this way, she has both a class and race analysis of underrepresentation. Two respondents do not give specific details as to why racism or prejudice impedes blacks. In all three responses they mention social or class inequality but prioritize racism, and they specifically identify inequality between *negros* and whites. These respondents believe that inferior levels of education and racial prejudice lead to an inferior position in society, including in politics.

Non-*Negra* and Non-*Preta* Women Citing Racism as a Cause for Underrepresentation

On the other hand, considering the non-*negra* and non-*preta* women who claim racism is a reason for underrepresentation, none of them have any college education; however, two have completed high school. One has not completed middle school, and the other has not completed high school. Educational information is missing for one respondent. Income information is missing for two of these respondents. Three of them have low family incomes of US$813.08–$2,032.68. Three are light-skinned, one is dark-skinned, and skin color information is not available for one respondent. For those with hairstyle information, all but one have relaxed or straightened hair. One has curled hair. What we can see from this profile is that most non-*negra* and non-*preta* women have light skin, low incomes, and are not well educated. Two are from Salvador, two from São Paulo, and one from Rio de Janeiro. In this sub-sample, the average age is 39 years old, which is older than those identifying as *negra* or *preta*. While there are more *pretas* and *negras* that discuss racism as a reason for underrepresentation, non-*negras* and non-*pretas* discuss racism as well. However, their overall profile is distinct. Bailey and Telles (2006) find that less-educated Brazilians are more likely to identify in ambiguous color categories. *Moreno* is an ambiguous color category. *Mulato* translates as racially mixed, and *pardo* is a census category that denotes racial mixture. These identifications are ambiguous in this case, as two *parda* women are light in skin tone and one is dark in skin tone. The two oldest respondents, ages 64 and 59, both identify in non-*negra* and non-*preta* categories. Two are from Salvador, which is a context where the population is mainly Afro-Brazilian yet most of them identify as *pardo*. One quote by a *parda* woman in Salvador reveals how prejudice intersects based on race and class. The respondent states

I think that it is prejudice . . . prejudice is not only against the *negro* but against] the poor population as well. (27-year-old, light-skinned *parda* female in Salvador who has a high school education)

The finding that even non-*negra* and non-*preta* women believe racism is a cause for political inequality is significant because it demonstrates that across city, they believe race plays a significant role in politics. Racial discourse focusing on racism has an impact on Afro-Brazilian women's understandings of the political world, regardless of the level of their educational attainment.

Afro-Brazilian Men Explain Citing Racism as a Cause for Underrepresentation

Ten men explaining racism as a cause for *negro* political underrepresentation are from Salvador, five are from Rio de Janeiro, and four from São Paulo. Ten have low family incomes of up to US$813.08, and six have incomes of US$813.08–$2,032.68. Only one respondent has a middle income of US$2032.68–$4065.36. Income data is missing for two respondents. Five respondents have some education, four have finished high school, and nine have low education, meaning they completed middle school, did not complete high school, or did not complete middle school. Sixty-one percent or 11 Afro-Brazilian men identify as *negro* or *preto*, including one who identifies as black in English. In my analysis I include the self-identified black in the *negro/preto* category. Five identify as *pardo*, one identifies as *moreno*, and one as *cafuso*. Information is not available for one respondent. Eleven respondents are dark-skinned, six have a light skin tone, and information is not available for two respondents.

Thirty-two percent of Afro-Brazilian men citing racism wear hairstyles that are culturally marked as black (two-strand twists, a twist-out, dreads, and cornrows [a braided hairstyle].[9] The significance of these hairstyles in a city such as Salvador is that they are associated with blackness. Members of cultural groups such as Ilê Aiyê and Olodum often wear braided hairstyles, dreads,[10] or other styles associated with Africanness and blackness. While everyday citizens can also wear these hairstyles, they are popularized by cultural groups.

Negro/Preto Men Citing Racism as a Cause for Underrepresentation

Fifty-five percent of *negro/preto men* citing racism wore their hair in natural hairstyles. All *negro/preto* men citing racism as a reason for *negro* underrepresentation have low family incomes; seven have incomes of up to US$813.08 per month, and four have family incomes of US$813.08–$2,032.68 per month. Six respondents reside in Salvador, three in Rio de Janeiro, and two in São Paulo. Five *negro/preto* men have some college education, two have completed high school, and three have a low level of education, which is less than a high school education. Forty-five percent have high education, but all respondents have low family incomes. This could be because some of these respondents are in college. As noted earlier, because of stigmatization of black culturally marked hair, it is likely that these *negro/preto* respondents with natural hair are aware of racism based on the experiences they face because of physical characteristics and class.

---

[9] Two-strand twists are a hairstyle achieved by gathering portions of hair and twisting them together. This is different from braids, which involve gathering three portions of hair to braid. A twist-out hairstyle is achieved by simply untwisting two-strand twists.

[10] In Brazil, dreadlocks are referred to as "dreads" or "rasta." I use the terminology used in Brazil. However, I note that in the United States there is a debate about the use of the term "locs" rather than "dreadlocks."

An example of the way racism is articulated as an explanation for under-representation is made by an Afro-Brazilian man who believes whites intentionally impede *negro* progress through white supremacy and control. In this respondent's analysis, one of the areas of control is through politics.

[*Negros* are underrepresented in politics because of] white supremacy. Salvador is a city with a [large] *negro* population in relation to the number of [*negros* in other] cities in Brazil . . . but there is still a sense of supremacy from the white race. They watch and control us. They do not give opportunities to *negro* people to arrive, to get what they have so they try to do the most they can to impede *negro* people from getting more . . . ." (30-year-old dark-skinned self-identified black man in Salvador with a college degree)

Another male interviewee claims there is less opportunity in politics due to discrimination. However, this respondent also claims that *negros* discriminate against whites and that there is *racism* against women. Even though this respondent first says *negros* discriminate against whites, his comment about being marked by showing one's origins is important. Although this respondent realizes wearing a black hairstyle marks him, he wears his hair in cornrows.

I think there is a lack of opportunity because of discrimination. There is a lot [of discrimination] not only against *negros* but . . . [against] others. *Negros* discrimi-nate against whites ..in this region where *negros* are the majority . . .. There is also racism against women . . ... People are human no matter what their color is, whether they are black or blue . . . A lot of people are discriminated against, like *negros* or people with curly hair like those that play in reggae bands. You are marked . . . if you show your origin, or culture. (34-year-old, dark-skinned, self-identified *negro* male who has not completed middle-school and wears cornrows)

When wearing black culturally marked hairstyles, Afro-Brazilians can be negatively stereotyped and suffer from racism. In March 2015, Thatiane Santos da Silva, an Afro-Brazilian woman doctor suffered from racist insults made about her hair, which she wears in dreads. Chemically altering one's natural hair may not so much be about avoiding blackness, but about alleviating racist insults. These *negro* and *preto* men are acutely aware of discrimination that *negros* with African features face and believe this discrimination leads to political inequality.

Non-*Negro*/Non-*Preto* Afro-Brazilian Men Citing Racism as a Cause for Underrepresentation

Seven Afro-Brazilian men citing racism identify in non-*negro*/non-*preto* categories. Five respondents identify as *pardo*, one as *cafuso*, and one as *moreno*. Four respondents reside in Salvador, one in São Paulo, and two in Rio de Janeiro. Five non-*negro*/non-*preto* men have low incomes. Three have family incomes of up to US$813.08, and two have family incomes of US$813.08–$2,032.68. One has a middle income of US $2,032.68–$4,065.36.

Similar to non-*negra*/non-*preta* Afro-Brazilian women citing racism, most non-*negro* and non-*preto* men have a low socioeconomic status. This means that despite that a lower number of non-*negro*/non-*preto* men compared to *negro* and *preto* men, both groups believe that political inequality is the result of racial discrimination. In this way, Degler's escape hatch is less prominent as Afro-Brazilians in ambiguous racial identifications are aware of racial discrimination making them similar to *negros* and *pretos* rather than different.

Social Exclusion as a Cause for *Negro* Underrepresentation

Racial spatiality is exemplified in the idea that blacks are excluded and marginalized in society. Although racism was the most cited reason for underrepresentation, respondents also believe that social exclusion, in the form of a lack of schooling or few opportunities, serves as a reason for underrepresentation. Fourteen of 63 respondents cited social exclusion, lack of schooling, or no opportunities as a reason for underrepresentation of *negros* in politics. Seven respondents are from Salvador, five reside in Rio de Janeiro, and two are from São Paulo (Table 1.4). Of those reporting incomes, 71 percent belong to low-income categories of up to US$813.08 and US$813.08–$2,032.68. Twenty-one percent belong to the medium-income category of $2,032.68–$4,065.36, and only 8 percent belong to a high-income category of US$4,065.4–$8,130.72. Forty-three percent of respondents have a medium level of education, which means they completed high school; 36 percent have some college education; and only 21 percent have low education or less than a high school level of education. Ninety-three percent of respondents self-identify as *negro* or *preto*, and only 7 percent identify as *moreno*. In terms of physical appearance, considering those with available information, 54 percent wear black culturally marked hairstyles such as Afros, cornrows, or tightly curled or twist-out hairstyles; 31 percent have cropped hairstyles; and 15 percent have relaxed hair. Of those with skin color information, 46 percent of respondents have light skin tones and 54 percent have dark skin tones.

Table 1.4 *Respondents Who Referred to Social Inequality in Answer to Underrepresentation of Negros in Politics*

City	Gender	Education	Family Salary (USD)	Age	Skin color	Racial Identification	Hairstyle
Salvador	Male	In college	Up to $813.08	20	3	*Negro*	Twist-out
Salvador	Male	Completed high school	$813.08–$2,032.68	25	5–6	*Preto*	Low cut curly hair
Salvador	Male	Incomplete high school	Up to $813.08	49	6	*Negro*	Low cut
Salvador	Male	Incomplete middle school	Up to $813.08	34	6	*Negro*	Cornrows
Salvador	Male	Completed high school	Up to $813.08	31	4	*Negro*	Low cut
Salvador	Male	Completed high school	$813.08–$2,032.68	31	6	*Negro*	Low cut
Salvador	Female	In college	$2,032.68– $4,065.36	21	5	*Negra*	Afro
Rio de Janeiro	Male	Completed high school	$2,032.68– $4,065.36	25	2	*Negro*	Afro
Rio de Janeiro	Female	Master's degree	$4,065.40–$8,130.72	31	3	*Negra*	Relaxed hair
Rio de Janeiro	Female	Completed High school	$813.08–$2,032.68	46	1	*Negra*	Afro
Rio de Janeiro	Female	Completed High School	$813.08–$2,032.68	19	2	*Negra*	Afro
Rio de Janeiro	Female	In college	$2,032.68- $4,065.36	27	3	*Negra*	Relaxed hair
São Paulo	Male	Incomplete middle school	Up to $813.08	74	6	*Moreno*	Tight curly hair (*crespo*)
São Paulo	Male	Incomplete college	Up to $813.08	29	NI	*Negro*	NI

Afro-Brazilian Women Believe Social Exclusion Causes *Negro* Underrepresentation

Five Afro-Brazilian women cite social exclusion as a reason for political inequality, and they all self-identify as *negra*. Sixty percent of them have at least some college education and 40 percent have completed high school. Sixty percent have black culturally marked hairstyles while 40 percent have relaxed hair. Forty percent have medium level incomes, another 40 percent have low-level incomes and 20 percent have a high level of income. These demographics demonstrate that these respondents perceive social exclusion as a reason for political inequality even though they generally have higher levels of education. They are equally split between low and medium income levels.. Historically exclusion has been viewed as based on class, therefore it is common that most Brazilians readily accept the existence of class inequality. In this case, Afro-Brazilian women, despite varying class levels, acknowledge class-based inequality as a contribution to political inequality. Interviews reveal how class works along with race to exclude *negro* politicians.

One respondent makes a direct parallel with *favelas* as places where *negros* are located and chic or fancy places where they have little presence and representation. As explained in the theory of racial spatiality, the prestigious realm of politics is not viewed as a space Afro-Brazilians have the opportunity to occupy. Occupying physical and social locations at the bottom rung of society has an impact on the opportunity to enter prestigious places. This argument is made below.

[*Negros*] don't have the education [to be in politics]. Most *negros* are in the *favelas*, they are not in chic places. They are still in the *favela*. It is difficult for people from the hill to go to Brasília. (Self-identified light-skinned, 46-year-old *negra* female who completed high school and wears an Afro hairstyle in Rio de Janeiro.)

Her reference to Brasília is telling, as it is the capital of Brazil and is where the president and Congress are located. By mentioning Brasília, she references the highest level of power and believes that it is impossible that people in the *favelas* can occupy such prestigious positions. One of the appeals of Lula was that he had a low level of education and had come from humble backgrounds yet was able to hold the office of the presidency. Yet for this *negra* woman respondent, social mobility is impossible for *negros*.

Afro-Brazilian Men Believe Social Exclusion Causes *Negro* Underrepresentation

Nine Afro-Brazilian men cited social exclusion as key to political underrepresentation. Many respondents discuss Afro-Brazilian underrepresentation as a result of *negros* not having the opportunity to gain education and that *negros* generally lack opportunities. Sixty percent of these respondents have some college education, 44 percent have a high school education, and 34 percent have a low level of education. Sixty percent have low income and 40 percent have medium income. Eighty-nine percent of Afro-Brazilian men self-identify as *negro* or *preto*, and only 30 percent as *moreno*. Considering respondents with available skin tone information, 80 percent of Afro-Brazilian men are dark-skinned and 20 percent are light-skinned. Eighty percent are from Salvador to Rio de Janeiro and 20 percent are from São Paulo.

In many ways, respondents discuss class inequality as a challenge for *negros* to enter politics, but they do not view class equally as a *negro* problem. Thus some are not making the argument that class inequality is due to racism or racial inequality. Most of these respondents are from Salvador. Some may be more likely to believe that because Salvador is predominantly Afro-Brazilian, inequality is due to class rather than race. Two examples are in the following quotes.

It is not easy for *negros* to study ... Perhaps the *negro* does not have as much [educational] development as the white. (*preto* male who is 25-years-old with short curly hair, is dark-skinned, and completed high school in Salvador)

I think it is a social question and also a racial question not only for the *negro* population but for many people of the lower class ... You need a college education. (31-year-old dark-skinned *negro* male with a short haircut who has finished high school and resides in Salvador)

There is at least one respondent who does not separate race and class. The older respondent is 74-years-old and, views blacks as a class. The word "class" could refer to an economic class but can also be used to simply mean a group of people. It is likely that he uses it to refer to a group. However, it is common for Afro-Brazilians to refer to *negros* and *poor* people interchangeably (Lamont et al. 2016). He states the following:

The black class ... our low class and the *negro* class are not valorized ... people of the high class don't invite people of the [lower] class. (74-year-old dark-skinned self-identified *moreno* male with an incomplete level of middle school education in São Paulo)

In this way he views *negros* as similar to low-income people. *Negro* people and low-income people are marginalized he believes, not invited to elite places, politically barring them from prestigious political positions. Another respondent mentions the *favelas* or shantytowns stating:

Social exclusion. The *favelas* are mostly composed of *negros* . . . ." (Light-skinned self-identified *negro* male, 25 years of age in Rio de Janeiro with a completed high school level of education.)

Rio de Janeiro was the only city where respondents mentioned *favelas*. This is not surprising considering that it is well known for *favelas*, which stand in stark contrast to very wealthy areas, although these neighborhoods are within visible distance from one another. What is telling is that even when explaining political inequality as a result of class inequality, by acknowledging that *favelas* are mainly composed of *negros*, respondents are explaining political inequality by relying on the intersection of racial and class inequality.

EXPLAINING *NEGRO* UNDERREPRESENTATION
BY FAULTING *NEGROS*

Fourteen respondents believe *negros* are to blame for underrepresentation in politics. Nine Afro-Brazilian women blamed *negros*, while five Afro-Brazilian men blamed *negros* (Table 1.5). Five of these respondents reside in Salvador, eight in Rio de Janeiro, and one in São Paulo. One way *negros* were blamed for underrepresentation was shown in the claim that they lacked interest in education, which is required to run for office. Some claimed that *negros* discriminate against other *negros*, or that *negros* lack culture. Seventy-nine percent of these respondents are dark-skinned and 21 percent are light-skinned. Ninety-three percent self-identify as *negro* or *preto*, and 7 percent as *pardo*.

Afro-Brazilian Women Fault *Negros* for *Negro*
Underrepresentation

In their perceptions, there are no impediments to voting, and people who choose *not* to vote for *negro* politicians are making a conscious decision not to vote for *negros* based on prejudice against *negros*. This is exemplified in the quotes below:

Because of prejudice right? And also I think it is prejudice by *negros* in this case. They are free to vote, so I think that *negros* themselves have this prejudice. (Dark-skinned *negra* woman of 76 years of age with naturally curly hair and an incomplete middle school education)

Table 1.5 *Respondents Who Fault Negros for Negro Underrepresentation in Politics*

City	Gender	Education	Family Salary (USD)	Age	Skin color	Racial Identification	Hairstyle
Salvador	Female	Incomplete middle school	Up to $813.08	76	5.5	*Negra*	Curly (*Crespo*)
Salvador	Female	Completed College	$2,032.68–$4,065.36	48	6	*Preta*	Cornrows
Salvador	Female	Completed college	NI	32	4	*Negra*	Cornrows
Salvador	Female	In college	$813.08 –$2,032.68	27	6	*Negra*	Straight
Salvador	Female	In college	$2,032.68–$4,065.36	21	5	*Negra*	Afro
Rio de Janeiro	Male	In college	$2,032.68–$4,065.36	27	6	*Negro*	Afro
Rio de Janeiro	Male	Completed middle school	Up to $813.08	69	5	*Pardo*	Low cut
Rio de Janeiro	Male	Completed high school	$813.08–$2,032.68	29	4	*Negro*	Low cut
Rio de Janeiro	Male	Completed college	$2,032.68–$4,065.36	28	4	*Preto*	Dreads
Rio de Janeiro	Female	Incomplete college	$813.08 –$2,032.68	39	4	*Negra*	Relaxed hair
Rio de Janeiro	Female	NI	NI	29	5	*Preta*	Wavy
Rio de Janeiro	Female	In college	$813.08 –$2,032.68	21	2	*Negra*	Chemically relaxed
Rio de Janeiro	Female	NI	$2,032.68–$4,065.36	64	3	*Negra*	Braids
São Paulo	Male	In college	Up to $813.08	25	2	*Negro*	Low cut

It seems that *negros* do not have a lot of interest [in politics]. I don't see a lot of blacks interested [in politics] like whites. (21-year-old, light-skinned *negra* college student with relaxed hair who resides in Rio de Janeiro)

One respondent believes *negros* are not "politically prepared." She thinks *negro* voters are not sophisticated in the sense that they do not make informed decisions when voting and are simply voting *against negro* candidates because of prejudice. She states the following:

Negros themselves are prejudiced and they do not have a political education, you understand? So I think that the *negro* is not politically prepared. (Dark-skinned self-identified *preta* woman in Salvador who is forty-eight years of age and has completed college.)

As mentioned in the background section, perhaps these dark-skinned *negra* women have experienced, or are aware of, *negros'* disdain for blackness. As previously noted, Elizabeth Hordge-Freeman's (2015) work in Salvador demonstrates that darker-skinned children receive less affection within families. In this sense, some respondents believe anti-black attitudes are manifested when *negros* do not support *negro* politicians.

Afro-Brazilian Men Fault *Negros* for *Negro* Underrepresentation

Afro-Brazilian men believe *negros* are not interested in education and thus are not prepared to run for political office. A 29-year-old self-identified *negro* male with a medium complexion who has a high school level education stated the following:

. . . I also don't see an interest by the *negro* population . . . The *negro* does not have this preoccupation to study, to change their life, this is not a preoccupation of the poor. The question of the *negro* in politics is a historical factor with the whites from Portugal, but I also think that *negros* are a little at fault because they do not want to study.

While the previous respondent believes *negros* are not oriented toward education, he also believes underrepresentation is historical. Ultimately he reiterates that *negros* do not want education. He also conflates race and class as he states *negros* or the poor are not interested in education. The respondent below thinks *negros* are not interested in politics, and one respondent believes that it does not make strategic sense to vote for *negros* because they are less likely to be elected. The following quotes are examples of respondents who believe *negros* are not interested in politics.

I think this occurs because of a lack of interest from *negros*. If you have a *negro* political candidate there is a low probability that he will be elected and there is a lack of interest from the *negro* population … A *negro* candidate does not represent our interests and will not resolve our problems. (dark-skinned 27-year-old self-identified *negro* male college student who resides in Rio de Janeiro and wears his hair in an Afro)

Negros do not know who they are … they have fewer opportunities and there is a lack of self-esteem from the *negro* population. They don't feel capable of studying to have a good level of education and to occupy political seats. (light-skinned twenty-five-year-old self-identified *negro* male college student in São Paulo)

The respondent believes *negros* are not interested in running for office. This respondent believes that descriptive representation does not lead to representing Afro-Brazilian interests.

In sum, most Afro-Brazilian men who fault *negros* for political inequality are highly educated and most live in Rio de Janeiro. The line of argument that political inequality is due to *negros* lack of interest in education is similar to the argument in the US that economic inequality is the result of African American children not being interested in education. The idea by some scholars and even politicians, including President Barack Obama, is that African American students underperform to avoid stigmatization. In contrast, studies have shown that African American students do not intentionally underperform and that underperformance is not an effort to avoid being viewed as "acting white." Tyson et al. (2005) find that black students seek achievement and there is no overwhelming evidence of racialized peer pressure. Regardless of race, high achieving students are stigmatized and this is due to school structures not racialized peer pressure. Similarly, I believe that these pathological explanations that *negros* in Brazil are not interested in education do not explain political inequality. Rather, they divert attention from structural inequalities in society that may lead to lower educational outcomes of Afro-Brazilian students compared to white students.

In sum, many higher-educated Afro-Brazilians are critical of other Afro-Brazilians, believing they do not want to study. This negative stereotype of *negros* could be the result of these Afro-Brazilians gaining or pursuing college degrees, therefore believing that education is attainable despite obstacles in society. For this reason, they stereotype *negros* as not wanting an education rather than point to structural inequality that is a result of racial discrimination. They pathologize *negros*, believing that Afro-Brazilians are inherently uninterested in gaining an education.

Afro-Brazilian women were more likely to believe *negros* themselves were at fault for *negro* underrepresentation. Afro-Brazilian men and women in all three cities make a link between social or class inequality and political inequality. Yet these respondents do not have a narrative about institutional racism as a contributing factor to low levels of education among Afro-Brazilians. These respondents believe that Afro-Brazilians lack self-esteem or the will to further their education so they do not perceive underrepresentation to be part of institutional racism. Rather, they believe it is *negros'* lack of willpower that is to blame for social inequality. In Salvador, some respondents actually said *negros* were prejudiced against *negros* and that *negros* did not believe *negro* political candidates are capable of holding office. The claim of "*negro* prejudice" is unique to Salvador, perhaps due to it being a predominantly Afro-Brazilian city.

Like Jan French's (2013) research demonstrating that some Afro-Brazilian police officers hold prejudice against Afro-Brazilians, some of the general citizenry also holds prejudice against Afro-Brazilians. Not all Afro-Brazilians have power to act on these prejudices; but non-Afro-Brazilians who hold powerful and prestigious positions can act on these prejudices to exclude *negros*. However, the political process gives Afro-Brazilian citizens a unique opportunity to exercise power and influence the composition of the political elite. These respondents believe some *negros* forego this exercise of power because of a lack of interest, or some vote in *favor* of whites because of their personal biases against *negros*. These responses are particularly insightful since in Salvador and Rio de Janeiro *negros* are either the majority or nearly half the population, and highly educated *negros* and *pretos* make up a significant proportion of these respondents. Afro-Brazilian women who are dark-skinned and highly educated are critical of Afro-Brazilians believing they lack interest. In a way some of these respondents exemplify respectability politics that focus on faults of the individual rather than institutions within society. Critics of respectability politics (Cohen 2010; Taylor 2016) acknowledge that institutional racism, sexism, and homophobia better account for inequality than the inadequacy of African Americans. In a similar vein, Afro-Brazilians explanations of political inequality as due to *negro* inadequacy exemplifies respectability politics that claim that if people gain an education they will be integrated into society and will gain opportunities.

SLAVERY AS A CAUSE FOR *NEGRO* UNDERREPRESENTATION

Nine respondents mentioned slavery or the abolition of slavery as an explanation for the underrepresentation of *negros* in politics (Table 1.6). All but one identify as *negro* or *preto*. Four of these respondents were from Salvador, four from Rio de Janeiro and one from São Paulo. These respondents are

Table 1.6 *Respondents Citing Slavery as a Reason for Political Underrepresentation*

City	Gender	Education	Family Salary (USD)	Age	Skin Color	Racial Identification	Hairstyle
Salvador	Male	In college	Up to $813.08	20	3	*Negro*	Twist-out
Salvador	Male	In college	Up to $813.08	29	3	*Negro*	Cornrows
Salvador	Male	Incomplete middle school	$813.08–$2,032.68	46	5	*Cafuso*	Low cut
Salvador	Female	Completed college	$2,032.68–$4,065.36	32	4	*Negra*	Cornrows
Rio de Janeiro	Male	Completed high school	$2,032.68–$4,065.36	25	2	*Negro*	Afro
Rio de Janeiro	Male	Completed high school	$813.08–$2,032.68	26	3	*Negro*	Dreads
Rio de Janeiro	Male	Completed college	$4,065.36–$8,130.72	63	5	*Negro*	Low cut
Rio de Janeiro	Female	Completed College	$2,032.68–$4,065.36	67	4	*Negra*	Relaxed
São Paulo	Male	In college	$813.08–$2,032.68	26	2–3	*Preto*	Afro

overwhelmingly male (78 percent). Twenty-two percent are female. While slavery is historical in nature, it is an example of spatiality as the practice of slavery relegated Afro-descendants to certain positions in society. It is noteworthy that Salvador served as the main port of entry for enslaved people. However, Rio de Janeiro also had a large number of enslaved Africans.

Afro-Brazilian Women Citing Slavery as a Reason for Political Underrepresentation

Both Afro-Brazilian women identify as *negro* and are highly educated. One lives in Salvador and the other in Rio de Janeiro. One of these respondents states the following:

I think it is a historical consequence. *Negros* were brought from [Africa] and since slavery . . . blacks have not been seen as qualified. (Self-identified *negra* female who is 32 years old with a light complexion and resides in Salvador.)

She is stating that inequality is a consequence of slavery and that persistent negative stereotypes lead people to believe *negros* are not qualified for political office.

Afro-Brazilian Men Citing Slavery as a Reason for Political Underrepresentation

Afro-Brazilian men stating political inequality is a result of slavery are overwhelmingly highly educated and light-skinned and wear their hair in black culturally marked hairstyles. One example an interviewee gives is that Afro-Brazilians are now mentally enslaved. In his response, he also mentioned racism against *negros*. It is not clear how he believes *negros* are mentally enslaved, but he views political inequality as a result of racial inequality that existed since slavery. Linking racial inequality or racism to slavery is different from most respondents, who do not link slavery as a racially discriminatory institution to present racial inequality. They link slavery to class inequality. The second response quoted below is typical of respondents who view class inequality as a remnant of slavery. In this way, class inequality has an impact on political inequality.

This is the result of a racial process in Brazil beginning from slavery. *After probing by the interviewer about the connection between slavery and today, he answered* [Negros] have passed from physical slavery to mental slavery. (Self-identified *negro* male who is 29 years old with a light skin complexion and resides in Salvador.)

Four respondents discussing slavery believe the historical past of slavery has an impact on inequality today, one factor being inequality in education. In this way, a lack of opportunity to gain a high level of education has been passed down since slavery. Just as enslaved people did not have an opportunity to study, opportunities for *negros*, especially poor *negros* are extremely limited, these respondents conclude. This is seen in the quote below:

In the era of slavery, the Golden Law made [*negros*] free . . . but without education we ended up in *favelas* . . . There is a big difference in schooling. Those who study in private schools have it easier because they have a better education and the majority of people who study in public schools are poor and they come from communities that are *favelas*, that are mostly made up of *negros*. (25-year-old *negro* male of light complexion with a high school education who resides in Rio de Janeiro)

Another respondent claims that although laws have changed, the situation of *negros* have not. Presumably he is referring to the social situation of *negros*, as a way to explain political inequality.

Since the beginning of slavery, laws have changed but the situation [of *negros*] has not changed a lot. (26-year-old male who has completed high school who wears his hair in dreads and lives in Rio de Janeiro)

Like most other respondents, he links slavery to class inequality. He does so by claiming that post-abolition, Afro-Brazilians had to work lower-class jobs and had an inferior education; these things were passed down to the present day, making it difficult for Afro-Brazilians to become politicians. The respondent's quote is below:

It is all a reflection of history. After the abolition of slavery, *negros* worked inferior jobs, had inferior education . . . it is impossible to access other things so it is difficult for *negro* politicians. (Light-complexioned, self-identified *preto* male college student who is 26 years of age from São Paulo.)

In sum, even though 67 percent of respondents citing slavery have at least some college level education, they do not articulate that slavery was a racist institutional system in which African descendants were viewed as inferior. In today's society, white supremacy is practiced in schools, where teachers are more likely to give less attention to darker–skinned children. In addition, Afro-Brazilians' employment opportunities are greatly limited when employers prefer lighter-skinned employees. Even when employed, Afro-Brazilians are paid less than their white counterparts. As Elise Nascimento (2007) states in her idea of the *sorcery* or magic of color, focusing on discrimination as a product of slavery allows people to ignore how white supremacy has been maintained over time, causing discrimination and inequality to be viewed as class issues. In this way, as Nascimento claims, as if by magic, class inequalities and by extension political inequality exist between whites and Afro-Brazilians due to slavery.

POLITICAL PARTIES EXCLUDE *NEGROS*

Four respondents mentioned political parties as an obstacle for *negro* politicians because they do not receive enough financial support from these parties (Table 1.7). All respondents self-identify as *negro*. Three of the respondents are *negro* women: one has a master's degree; one is still in high school. Educational information was not available for the other respondent. The male respondent is in college. Those for whom income data is available all have incomes of US$2,032.68–$4065.36 monthly salaries. An 18-year-old *negra* female in high school states that "There is a low number [of blacks in politics] because the leaders of political parties do not give *negros* a chance." It is likely she is referring to the fact that political parties first choose candidates to run then these parties support certain candidates.

A resource argument to explain Afro-Brazilian underrepresentation is in line with Bueno and Dunning's (2014) findings, except that one respondent also cites racism as a reason for *negro* underrepresentation. In this way, these respondents are acknowledging the fact that political campaigns are expensive and that *negros* do not have personal financial resources to make running for office a possibility. The lack of financial support from political parties, according to them, makes it impossible for Afro-Brazilians to participate in electoral politics as candidates.

Respondents are also concerned that political parties do not lend financial support to *negro* candidates. In one response, the interviewee mentions a lack of financial support from political parties and racism in society. The following quotes are from two respondents in Rio de Janeiro.

... Political parties welcome *negro* candidates but do not financially support *negro* candidates. For example, I knew six candidates for city council but they could not get financial support and without support they could not win. (64-year-old light-skinned *negra* woman in Rio de Janeiro who wears her hair in braids)

First because of racism that impedes *negros* ... Second the issue of access to enter campaigns is an issue because most *negros* don't have money to finance campaigns and third is the issue of political education. (28-year-old light-skinned *negra* woman with a master's degree who resides in Rio de Janeiro)

Table 1.7 *Respondents Citing Political Parties as a Cause for Afro-Brazilian Underrepresentation*

City	Gender	Education	Family Salary (USD)	Age	Skin color	Racial Identification	Hairstyle
Salvador	Female	In high school	No information	18	6	*Negra*	Curly
Rio de Janeiro	Male	In college	$2,032.680–$4065.36	30	1	*Negro*	Afro
Rio de Janeiro	Female	NI	$1,555–$3,110	64	3	*Negra*	Braids
Rio de Janeiro	Female	Master's degree	$2,032.680–$4065.36	28	2	*Negra*	Curly

Rio sample, perhaps due to the visibility of high profile Afro-Brazilian candidates, *cariocas* (residents of Rio de Janeiro) are aware that Afro-Brazilians are significantly underrepresented and are politically savvy in their knowledge that candidates need support from political parties. The respondent who says racism is an impediment to *negros* also believes that political inequality is the result of both racism and inequality in resources to enable competition in campaigns. Financial support from a political party could help potential Afro-Brazilian candidates overcome the financial barrier to entry into politics.

SUMMARY

Afro-Brazilian men and women commonly cited five reasons for *negro* underrepresentation in Brazilian politics: racism, social inequality, *negros* themselves, slavery, and political parties. Considering racial identification, gender, and city of residence, there are some differences among respondents. For example, in the sample of those who found *negros* at fault for *negro* underrepresentation, in Salvador only Afro-Brazilian women believe it was *negro* people's fault. In some cases, respondents' believe that *negros* are prejudiced against each other. When referring to social inequalities as a cause for *negro* underrepresentation, there are equal numbers of Afro-Brazilian men and women. The problem with explaining political inequality based on class inequality, is that many respondents do not acknowledge the impact of racism on creating class inequalities. Like those citing slavery, discussing class inequality often ignores the harmful impact of racism to perpetuate inequality. With the exception of one respondent, those citing political parties as a hindrance to *negro* participation in politics do not discuss *why negros* lack the financial resources in the first place. It is not simply that class inequalities or unequal opportunities for good quality education have hindered the prospects for education and, by proxy, higher levels of income that would then allow one to be a competitive politician in costly campaigns. Racism shapes and informs *negro* people's location in society, whether they have high or low levels of education, are politically savvy or have a *political education*. The current day racism that exists in society leads *negros* to occupy specific spaces in society and limits or excludes the spaces they can physically occupy, much like the example presented at the beginning of this chapter. Political space simply becomes another space where Afro-Brazilians are actively excluded because all facets of their lives are shaped by the experience of race via racism.

2

Blackness and Racial Identification in Contemporary Brazil

Little Black Girl (*Menina Pretinha*)

Little black girl[1]
Exotic is not cute
You are not a little cutie
You are a little queen
I will have fun while I am small
Barbie is cool, but I prefer African Makena
like the story of the Grio
I am black
And I am proud of my color
My hair is curled without needing a curling iron
I rap with love and this is my way
I am a black child, I am also resistance
MC Soffia

Valorizing blackness by embracing African physical features, such as curly hair and dark skin, is a form of resistance. Messages of black empowerment are manifested in music such as hiphop. MC Soffia is a 13-year-old female hiphop artist who produces music that embraces blackness and encourages Afro-Brazilian children, especially girls, to embrace their natural hair texture and dark skin. Valorizing blackness in music is not new. Afro-Brazilians have openly shared views of blackness in music since at least the 1970s. The soul music of the 1970s, which included African American soul, was consumed by Afro-Brazilians. The notions of blackness associated with this music were

[1] Menina pretinha Exótica não é linda. Você não é bonitinha. Você é uma rainha. Vou me diverter enquanto sou pequena. Barbie é legal, mas eu prefiro a Makena Africana. Como história de grio. Sou Negra. E tenho orgulho da minha cor. O meu cabelo é chapado, sem precisar de chapinha. Canto rap por amor essa é minha linha. Sou criança sou negra, também sou resistência. – MC Soffia

embraced by black Brazilian youth and used to forward Brazil's black movements (Hanchard 1994). Hiphop music has also had an impact on modern conceptions of blackness in Brazil (Santos 2014; Pardue 2008; Sansone 2004). Blackness is still denigrated in the larger society so hiphop artists challenge negative stereotypes of blacks, and some Afro-Brazilians embrace blackness through their identification as *negro* or *preto*.

The purpose of this chapter is to examine why Afro-Brazilians choose a *negro* identification. This is important because past research shows that there is a relationship between the identification one chooses and political preferences (Soares et al. 1987; Mitchell 2010; and Aguilar et al. 2015). With the introduction of affirmative action policies for blacks and browns, one critique has been that no one knows who is black in Brazil and that race is ambiguous and fluid. Black activists and scholars such as Sales Santos (2006), Hélio Santos (2015), and Hédio Silva (1998) believe that agents of the state know how to identify who is black, especially when punishing and excluding blacks. In response to opponents of affirmative action claiming race is too ambiguous to direct a policy at a racial group, activists and scholars often respond that it is not very difficult to identify who is black because they are those who are marginalized and who are often targeted by police officers; they are also those who make up the majority in low-income neighborhoods. Francis and Tannuri-Pianto (2012) find that some Brazilians misrepresented their racial identification to apply for university quotas seats. What is lost in this discussion is an explanation about who would identify as black in non-policy contexts. What would motivate an Afro-Brazilian to identify as *negro* or *preto* in a country that negatively stereotypes *negros* and where race is supposedly ambiguous?

Racial identification has been an important aspect of research on Afro-Brazilian voting. While I believe it is important to consider racial identification, I also believe researchers should unpack the concept of racial identification. Claiming blackness is not always a passive act in a racialized context such as is found in Brazil. Yet I acknowledge that sometimes blackness is simply understood as something naturally inherited. In Brazil, one may claim a non-black color category but believe oneself to be racially black (*negro*) (Sheriff 2001). Mitchell-Walthour and Darity (2014) use statistical analyses to show that in Brazil, racial identification is an endogenous variable. They find that the racial identification one chooses depends on having experienced racism, one's skin color, and whether one feels linked to blacks as a racial group. In some cases, one's education has an impact on the racial identification one chooses; in other cases, it is income. Analysis relying on one dataset shows that the more education a person has, the more likely they will claim a *negro* or *preto* identification. The other dataset shows the more income a person has, the higher the likelihood that they will claim a *negro* or *preto* identification. A person who has experienced racism is more likely to claim a *negro* or *preto* identification. Likewise, those who identify as *negro* or *preto* are more likely to have experienced racism. As many black activists have noted, people who claim a black identification became black *after* the experience of racism and exclusion (Hanchard 1994; Caldwell 2007).

Rather than simply include the variable "racial identification" as an independent variable, scholars must be mindful of the experiences this identification entails. For this reason, in my statistical analyses I use the experience of discrimination along with racial identification, when possible. A discussion of racial identification, as it pertains to blackness, is necessary because it is not simply one's physical characteristics to which I refer when examining political behavior but also the *experience* of race as a factor influencing political behavior and opinion.

In this chapter I first develop the meaning of blackness within the framework of racial identification, relying on 76 in-depth interviews conducted in 2012 in Salvador, Rio de Janeiro, and São Paulo. Why do Afro-Brazilians choose a black identification? What do Afro-Brazilians think about blackness? The interview questions are as follows: Do you identify as *negro*? If so, why? Why do not some Afro-Brazilians identify as *negro*? Second, I examine *preto* racial identification, relying on the LAPOP survey, which includes a national survey in Brazil. I analyze these in-depth interviews through an intersectional lens, considering color, gender, and education. Statistical limitations make it difficult to provide an intersectional analysis for my quantitative analysis. Rather I focus on general trends to examine motivating factors for identifying as *preto*.

IDENTIFYING AS *NEGRO*

In response to the open-ended question of whether and why respondents identify as *negro*, I grouped responses into five categories: skin color or physical features, ancestry, family or community, political consciousness, and the *negro* struggle.[1] In some cases, respondents elicited responses that fell into more than one of these categories. A total of 60 respondents out of 76 interviewed said they identify as *negro*. Eight respondents said they do

[1] Other responses include "ethnicity," "race," "born this way," and "*negro* is pretty." Some respondents said yes but did not answer the question of why they identify as such, and some simply repeated they identify as *negro*.

not identify as *negro*, and there was no information for eight respondents. Even though race in Brazil is often characterized as ambiguous and fluid, for those who identify as *negro*, it is essentialized and seen as unalterable. This is extremely telling, as social scientists view race as a social construct. As stated earlier in the book, skin color is different from race, but both are racialized such that light skin is viewed as superior to dark skin, and African features are viewed negatively. Yet 23 responses to the question about identification demonstrate that racial identification is fixed because identity is based on physical characteristics or ancestry. Nine women and four men say they are *negro* based on their skin color or other physical characteristics. Six women and four men say they are *negro* based on ancestry. This is similar to Sheriff's (2001) findings that most Afro-Brazilians living in the shantytown where she conducted research in Rio de Janeiro identified Afro-Brazilians of various skin shades as *negros* indicating a *"negro"* race. Depending on which measure social scientists use, racial demographics change (Silva and Paixão 2014). This interview question is telling because it highlights respondents' choice as to why they identify as such. In the first part of my analysis, I explain several findings combining men and women. In the second part I examine men and women separately.

Thirteen of 60 respondents, or 22 percent, identify as *negro* based on their skin color or physical features. These respondents tend to be highly educated and believe their identification is restricted to their physical features. Unlike the popular myth that highly educated and high-income Afro-Brazilians become white, these highly educated respondents identify as *negro*. Ten respondents out of 60, or 17 percent, identify as *negro* because of their ancestry, most often citing their parents. These responses point to the unambiguous nature of race. An interesting response was that eight respondents noted they identify as *negro* because of their family or the community in which they live. Many researchers have found there are color differences within families in Brazil and those with dark skin are treated less favorably (Twine 1998; Hordge-Freeman 2015) and even within communities (Sheriff 2001). Yet as Hordge-Freeman finds, there are some families that embrace blackness. However, in cities with class segregation, some neighborhoods may be viewed as poor and *negro* (Vargas 2006).

Five respondents (8 percent) say they identify as *negro* because of political consciousness. The political consciousness referred to is that they became aware of racial issues or identified as a non-*negro* identification in the past but now identify as *negro*. Four men and one woman identify as *negro* based on political consciousness. They have finished high school and most are in or have completed college. Scholarship on black identification has shown that respondents that identify as *negro* tend to be more educated and young (Bailey and Telles 2006), or involved in black movement activism (Burdick 1998; Caldwell 2007). Caldwell's book focuses on Afro-Brazilian women and how they become *negra* through their activism. Noteworthy in these findings across three different cities is that becoming *negro* through a racial political consciousness is more characteristic of highly educated and relatively young Afro-Brazilian men.

SKIN COLOR AND PHYSICAL FEATURES

Twenty-five percent of respondents identify as *negro* because of physical reasons such as skin color, and nose and lip size. This is the most popular response. Of these respondents, 64 percent are women and 36 percent are men. Twenty-nine percent are light-skinned (colors one to three) and 64 percent are dark-skinned (colors four to six); skin color information is missing for 7 percent of the sample. Twenty-nine percent of respondents are from Salvador, 21 percent from São Paulo, and 50 percent from Rio de Janeiro. Seventy-seven percent have some college education, 15 percent have less than a high school education, and 8 percent have completed only high school. Sixty-nine percent of those with available income information belong to low-income households that make up to US$813.08 per month or US$813.08–$2,032.68 per month. Twenty-three percent belong to middle-income households, which are those that bring in US$2,032.68–$4,065.36 per month and 8 percent belong to a high-income household of $4,065.36–$8,130.72 per month. Of those with available information, 31 percent have a black culturally marked hairstyle, 54 percent have relaxed or curled hair, and 15 percent have low cut hair. In general, what we learn is that of those believing *negro* identification is based on skin color, they tend to be women, dark-skinned, highly educated, have relaxed or curled hair, and are from low-income households. Because most of these respondents are in college, their household incomes are low despite their education. Examining these characteristics in an intersectional way reveals why Afro-Brazilians at the intersection of skin color, class, and hair type choose or feel limited to identify as *negro* or *preto*. Highly educated Afro-Brazilian women who are dark-skinned may feel more restricted in their identification despite the supposed choice they have in identification. I now turn to an analysis of Afro-Brazilian men and Afro-Brazilian women choosing a *negro* identification.

Afro-Brazilian Women Who Identify as *Negra* Based on Skin Color and Physical Features

Nine Afro-Brazilian women identify as *negro* based on skin color or physical features (Table 2.1). Of these women, 78 percent wear their hair relaxed or curled and only 22 percent wear black culturally marked hairstyles. As stated earlier I define black culturally marked hairstyles as Afros, locked hair, very curly natural hair (*crespo*), or braided hair. Fifty-six percent of them are dark-skinned and 44 percent are light-skinned. Of those with available income information, 62 percent of them come from low-income households, 25 percent from middle-income households, and 12.5 percent from high-income households. Seventy-eight percent have some college education and 22 percent have less than high school education. The sample is highly educated but family income is low, which is likely due to many of the respondents being in college. Fifty-six percent of respondents reside in Rio de Janeiro, 22 percent reside in Salvador, and 22 percent reside in São Paulo. In this sub-sample, the average age is 28. In general, Afro-Brazilian women that identify as *negro* based on skin color or physical features wear their hair relaxed or curled, are dark-skinned, come from low-income households, and are highly educated. As mentioned earlier, it is possible that chemically relaxing one's hair is done strategically because Afro-Brazilians who wear their hair naturally, face discrimination and these women are aware of the values society places on people with straight hair. All of the women residing in Rio de Janeiro have relaxed hair which may tell us more about the racial politics of the city. Rio de Janeiro exemplifies class and color residential divisions (Vargas 2001). Ribeiro et al. (2010) find that one impact of residential segregation is that Brazilians living in low-income neighborhoods have less access to labor market participation. These communities have lower levels of "social capital" such as education. In addition, research discussed previously also shows that Afro-Brazilians are more likely to be unemployed than whites with the same level of education. For this reason, it is possible that hairstyle is one attempt to alleviate the effects of racial discrimination, which is so visible where blacks are racialized as poor, independent of class status.

While Afro-Brazilian women can manipulate their appearance by altering their hair, it does not appear this is an option when considering other physical features. In fact, some respondents explicitly say because of their physical features they cannot identify as anything else but *negro*. An example is below:

Table 2.1 *Afro-Brazilian Women Who Identify as Negra Based on Skin Color/Physical Features*

City	Gender	Education	Family Salary (USD)	Age	Skin color	Racial Identification	Hairstyle
Salvador	Female	Completed college	NI	32	4	*Negra*	Cornrows
Salvador	Female	Incomplete high school	Up to $813.08	18	6	*Negra*	Curly
São Paulo	Female	In college	$813.08–$2,032.68	19	2	*Negra*	Relaxed
São Paulo	Female	In college	$2,032.68–$4,065.36	30	4.5/5	*Negra*	*Crespo*
Rio de Janeiro	Female	Master's	$4,065.36–$8,130.72	31	3	*Negra*	Relaxed
Rio de Janeiro	Female	Incomplete college	$813.08–$2,032.68	39	4	*Negra*	Relaxed
Rio de Janeiro	Female	Incomplete middle school	Up to $813.08	35	4	*Negra*	Relaxed
Rio de Janeiro	Female	In college	$2,032.68–$4,065.36	27	3	*Negra*	Relaxed
Rio de Janeiro	Female	In college	$813.08–$2,032.68	21	2	*Negra*	Relaxed

Yes (laughing) . . . You look at me and see my features, nose, and skin color. I do not have anywhere to run, to deny this But for a time . . . I had tried to deny [this]. Because I grew up in a white school with this idea of white beauty so you try to look [white], to straighten your hair. Today I am not like this. I've already passed through all these crises. (32-year-old self-identified *negra* female with medium skin tone and cornrows who completed college in Salvador)

This respondent highlights the issue of hair. In her opinion, Afro-Brazilian women straighten their hair to uphold a white beauty standard. Physical features such as one's nose and hair play a significant role in determining how one identifies. Interestingly, some of these respondents draw on stereotypes of *negros* as a reason they identify as *negra*. For example, they discuss having a big nose or a flat nose as if these were innate characteristics of *all negros*. Below is an example of an Afro-Brazilian woman who relies on stereotypical features of *negros* as the reason she identifies as *negra*.

Yes . . . I think white, *negro*, albino exists . . . [There are] differences in skin color. I am *negra* because I have crespo (tightly curled) hair . . . my skin is darker than others. I have big lips [and] a flat nose. My characteristics are the characteristics of my ancestors . . . . (30-year-old self-identified *negra* woman college student who is dark-skinned with tight curly (*crespo*) hair who resides in São Paulo)

Another female respondent relies on her skin tone as the basis of her identification. While relying on skin tone, she uses diminutives to discuss color. Sheriff (2001) discusses the role of diminutives of racial terms. They are used to soften the term or to display affection. The most common are *pretinho, escurinho,* and *neguinho.* "The term *pretinho* usually means a "little black," and indeed it is sometimes used to describe a child or an adult of diminutive stature. Far more often, however, its meaning is closer to "a little bit black" (2001: 52). One of her respondents told her it is better to call someone *escurinho* rather than *preto.* In the case of this interview respondent, she uses a diminutive to describe herself. Although this respondent is talking about her own identification, using diminutives allows her a "softer" way of discussing her color.

I am *negro* because I am a little bit dark (*escurinha*). I am not a little bit light (*clarinha*). (35-year-old dark-skinned negra woman with relaxed hair and an incomplete level of middle school education living in Rio de Janeiro)

In sum, Afro-Brazilian women who believe they are *negra* due to skin color or physical features are highly educated, and although they tend to be dark-skinned are not exclusively so. Two women wear their hair in black culturally marked hairstyles. One has braided hair and the other has naturally tight curly (*crespo*) hair. They are both dark-skinned and both have some college education. Both of these women have accepted their blackness by wearing their hair naturally and they both identify as *negra*. Nonetheless, like the others in the sample, this identification is restricted to their physical appearance. Other women in the sample have altered their appearance by chemically relaxing their hair and many of these women reside in Rio de Janeiro.

Men Who Identify as *Negro* Based on Skin Color and Physical Features

Fifty percent of Afro-Brazilian men that identify as *negro* based on skin color reside in Salvador, 25 percent live in Rio de Janeiro, and 25 percent in São Paulo (Table 2.2). Of those with hairstyle information, 50 percent wear black culturally marked hair and 50 percent wear low cut hair. Considering skin color information, they are all dark-skinned. Seventy-five percent are highly educated, and 25 percent have mid-level education (have completed high school). Seventy-five percent are low income and 25 percent are middle income. In this sub-sample, the average age is 29.5. Overwhelmingly, Afro-Brazilian men that claim a *negro* identification based on skin color are highly educated and dark-skinned. It is possible that they believe they are restricted to this identification due to their skin color. Despite their education level, it does not appear that they have "whitened." Rather, their skin color restricts them to the *negro* identification. A 30-year-old dark-skinned man with a college education in Salvador says he identifies as black simply because it is his color. Another example is a 31-year-old dark-skinned *negro* man with low cut hair and a middle school level of education. He states, "By my origins [and] skin color. There is no way to escape this." One respondent claimed he identified as *negro* because of physical traits and said that *negros* have big lips and noses, but he denied he has these traits. As stated earlier, some respondent's responses fell in multiple categories. Like most of the male respondents, the quote from a respondent below points to his physical features or "traces."

This thinking in Brazil is that Brazil is mixed. My [physical] traces are those of my ancestors who suffered a lot and who suffered from some of the same things [we suffer today such as] prejudice and racism. Also [my identity] is an issue of pride. I have a lot of pride not only in this country but all of those in the African Diaspora. (28-year-old dark-skinned male with dreads and a college education residing in Rio de Janeiro)

Table 2.2 *Afro-Brazilian Men Who Identify as Negro Based on Skin Color and Physical Features*

City	Gender	Education	Family Salary (USD)	Age	Skin color	Racial Identification	Hairstyle
Salvador	Male	Completed college	$$813.08–$2,032.68	30	5.5/6	Black (in English)	Low cut (*crespo*)
Salvador	Male	Complete high school	Up to $813.08	31	4	*Negro*	Low cut
São Paulo	Male	In college	Up to $813.08	29	NI⁻	*Negro*	NI
Rio de Janeiro	Male	Completed college	$2,032.68–$4,065.36	28	4	*Preto*	Dreads
Rio de Janeiro	Male	Completed high school	$$813.08–2,032.68	29	4	*Negro*	Low cut

In sum, similar to Afro-Brazilian women, most men who identify as *negro* based on physical attributes are dark-skinned, highly educated, and come from low-income households. The high education and low-income distinction is likely due to most of this sample being college students. Men are just as likely to wear black culturally marked hairstyles as they are to keep their hair very cropped. Women more often chemically relax their hair. Women were more likely to compare their color to others, saying they were a little dark but not a little white or saying their skin color is darker than others. Whereas men made no comparisons, simply stating they are *negro* because of skin color.

ANCESTRY

Eighteen percent of respondents say they identify as *negro* because of their ancestry. This is in contrast to Nogueira's (2007) claim that identification is not based on ancestry, such as racial identification in the United States, but that it is based on how one looks. Forty percent of these respondents have some college education, and 60 percent have completed high school. Half are dark-skinned and half are light-skinned. Thirty percent have black culturally marked hair; 40 percent have relaxed, straightened, or curled hair; and 30 percent have cropped hair. One man identified as *mulato*, and one woman identified as *parda* – but both claim they are *negro* due to ancestry. Identification can change depending on one's context in Brazil. In the cases of the *mulato* man and *parda* woman, they claim both *negro* and mixed-race identifications. Bailey et al. (2013) show differences in racial inequality when racial schemes such as census categories, ascribed census categories, black-white binary, photo comparisons as a white-black dichotomy, and ancestry are varied. Quantitative results on inequality can lead to differing results depending on the way in which racial identification is operationalized. This mixed-methods scholarship on political inequality and identification interrogates the motivations of identification and contribute to such studies

Afro-Brazilian Women Who Identify as *Negra* Based on Ancestry

Sixty-two percent of Afro-Brazilian women that identify as *negra* based on ancestry have completed high school, and 38 percent have some college education (Table 2.3). Sixty-two percent are light-skinned and 38 percent are dark-skinned. Sixty-two percent reside in Rio de Janeiro, 19 percent reside in Salvador, and another 19 percent reside in São Paulo. Thirty-eight percent wear black culturally marked hair and 62 percent have curled, relaxed, or straightened hair. In this sub-sample, the average age is 29.6

Table 2.3 *Afro-Brazilian Women Who Identify as Negra Based on Ancestry*

City	Gender	Education	Family Salary (USD)	Age	Skin Color	Racial Identification	Hairstyle
Salvador	Female	Completed High school	$813.08–$2032.68	27	2	*Parda*	Curly
São Paulo	Female	Completed high school	Up to $813.08	19	4	*Preta*	Straight
Rio de Janeiro	Female	Completed high school	$813.08–$2,032.68	46	1	*Negra*	Afro
Rio de Janeiro	Female	In college	$813.08–$2,032.68	39	4	*Negra*	Relaxed
Rio de Janeiro	Female	Completed high school	$813.08–$2,032.68	19	2	*Negra*	Afro
Rio de Janeiro	Female	Master's degree	$4,065.36–$8,130.72	28	2	*Negra*	Curly

years old. One of the light-skinned Afro-Brazilian women in the open-ended question on racial identification identifies as *pardo;* yet in response to the question of *negro* identification, she responds that in a certain way she is *negro* because of ancestry. Both women with black culturally marked hair reside in Rio, have completed high school, have low incomes and are light-skinned. They claim a *negra* identity due to ancestry. They demonstrate their blackness to society through their hair despite having light skin. Some light-skinned respondents do not have black culturally marked hair but still identify as *negra*. Respondent's state the following:

I don't care if a person is *negro* or white. However, I feel offended when people act despairingly toward *negros*. I am a descendant, so in a certain way I am *negra*. Do you understand? (27-year-old self-identified *parda* woman with curly hair and a light skin tone in Salvador who has a high school education)

Yes clearly. First I am a daughter of *negros* . . . all my family is *negro*. Blacks are not just those who are darker than others. (19-year-old light-skinned *negra* woman with an Afro who has a high school education and resides in Rio de Janeiro)

My mother and father were *negro*, so I am *negra*. (46-year-old light-skinned *negra* woman with an Afro who has a high school education and resides in Rio de Janeiro)

While many of these women are light-skinned, they believe they are *negra* because of ancestry, which is unalterable. Both women with Afro hairstyles are light-skinned. Wearing such a hairstyle allows them to visibly show their "blackness" or African ancestry, and one defensively says that *negros* are not only those with dark skin. Most of the women claiming blackness due to ancestry have a medium level of education, and most have a low income.

Afro-Brazilian Men Who Identify as *Negro* Based on Ancestry

Four Afro-Brazilian men identify as *negro* based on ancestry (Table 2.4). In this sub-sample, the average age is 27 years old. Seventy-five percent of them identify as *preto* or *negro*. Twenty-five percent are *mulato*. Like the sample of women where one respondent identified as *pardo*, this is an example of Afro-Brazilian men who in the open-ended question say they identify as *negro* based on ancestry but in answer to the question about the race or color they identify as one respondent identifies as *mulato*, a non-*negro* category. Identification is contextual (Racusen 2010), but we can also understand that one may identify their color in one way but racially identify as *negro*. Considering those with available income data, 66 percent of these men come from low-income households and 34 percent from high-income households.

Table 2.4 *Afro-Brazilian Men Who Identify as* Negro *Based on Ancestry*

City	Gender	Education	Family Salary (USD)	Age	Skin color	Racial Identification	Hairstyle
Salvador	Male	Completed high school	$813.08–$2,032.68	25	5.5	*Preto*	Short curly hair
São Paulo	Male	In college	NI	36	2	*Negro*	Low cut
São Paulo	Male	Completed high school	$813.08–$2,032.68	18	4	*Mulato*	Low cut
Rio de Janeiro	Male	Completed college	$4,065.36–$8,130.72	28	4	*Preto*	Dreads

Seventy-five percent wear their hair in low cuts, and 25 percent have a black culturally marked hairstyle. Half have some college education, while the other half have completed high school. Seventy-five percent are dark-skinned, and 25 percent light-skinned. Fifty percent are from São Paulo, 25 percent from Salvador, and 25 percent from Rio de Janeiro. Interestingly the respondent with the highest income and highest education wears his hair in dreads and lives in Rio de Janeiro. He is a systems analyst (*analista de sistema*). This hairstyle may be seen as "unprofessional" in some workplaces. Despite the "elite profile" of discrimination that Afro-Brazilian professionals encounter, this respondent wears a hairstyle that would further racialize him.

One of the male respondents identifies as *mulato* in the open-ended question about identification, yet in response to the survey question about identifying as *negro*, he says yes because of his heritage. Another respondent identifies as *negro* because of ancestry but also invokes history as he jokingly says he is the son of the *senzala*, or plantation. In this way, he is marking blackness in a particular way by mentioning the plantation where enslaved people worked during slavery.

Because I am *negro* (laughing). I am the son of a *negro*, the son of the plantation (*senzala*) (laughing). (25-year-old *preto* male with a dark complexion, short curly hair, and who has a high school level of education and resides in Salvador)

Yes because of my heritage; my father. I don't have dark skin, but I am *negro*. (self-identified *mulato* male with dark skin who completed high school and resides in São Paulo)

Afro-Brazilian men identifying as *negro* due to ancestry also view racial identification as unalterable because of parentage. In fact, one respondent laughs as if questioning why he identifies as *negro* is ridiculous due to the unchanging aspect of identification. In sum, many of the Afro-Brazilian women identify as *negra* due to ancestry are light-skinned, whereas most men are dark-skinned. Connected to this ancestry is history and current-day racism. A man alludes to the history of slavery. Rather than deny this history, he lays claim to it. In the case of the woman, she indicates that she is aware of negative perceptions of *negros* and remarks she is offended by these negative perceptions. This awareness demonstrates that these respondents are aware of negative stereotypes of *negros* but that, due to their ancestry, they identify as such.

FAMILY/COMMUNITY

Thirteen percent of respondents identify as *negro* based on their family or community. Eighty-eight percent of these respondents are Afro-Brazilian women, and 12 percent are men. Twenty-five percent come from São Paulo, 37.5 percent come from Salvador, and 37.5 percent from Rio de Janeiro. Of those with available hairstyle information, 57 percent of respondents have relaxed or straightened hair, and 43 percent have black culturally marked hair. In terms of income, 37.5 percent have a low family income, and 57 percent have a middle family income. Twelve-and-a-half percent have a high family income. In terms of education, for those with available information, 71 percent have a high level of education, 14.5 percent have completed high school, and 14.5 percent have not finished high school. Fifty-seven percent are dark-skinned, and 43 percent are light-skinned. In sum, most of those citing family or community are highly educated women.

Afro-Brazilian Women That Identify as *Negra* Due to Family/ Community

In these responses, women believe the racial composition of one's community defines one's individual racial identification. Gender differences in identification as *negro* is an unexplored area of research. Fifty-seven percent of Afro-Brazilian women identifying as *negra* due to family or community are dark-skinned and 43 percent are light-skinned (Table 2.5). Sixty-seven percent have some college education, 11.5 percent have completed high school, and 11.5 percent did not complete high school. Forty-three percent of these women have a medium income, 28.5 percent have a low income, 28.5 percent have a high income.

Table 2.5 *Afro-Brazilian Women Who Identify as Negra Based on Family/Community*

City Neighborhood	Gender	Education	Family Salary (USD)	Age	Skin Color	Racial Identification	Hairstyle
Salvador Santa Cruz	Female	In college	$813.08–$2,032.68	27	6	*Negra*	Straight
Salvador Parque São Cristovão	Female	In college	$2,032.68–$4,065.36	21	5	*Negra*	Afro
Salvador Boca do Rio	Female	Incomplete high school	Up to $813.08	15	5	*Negra*	Relaxed
São Paulo Cidade Tiradentes	Female	Completed high school	$2,032.68–$4,065.36	20	4	*Negra*	Braided
Rio de Janeiro	Female	NI	$2,032.68–$4,065.36	64	3	*Negra*	Braids
Rio de Janeiro Cidade de Deus	Female	In college	$2,032.68–$4,065.36	27	3	*Negra*	Relaxed
Rio de Janeiro Meier	Female	Master's Degree	$4,065.36–$8,130.72	31	3	*Negra*	Relaxed

These respondents claim they are *negro* due to family or community composition. This is different from parentage because respondents discuss location and family rather than a parent such as a mother or father. An example is a 15-year-old[2] dark-skinned self-identified *negra* high school student in Salvador who states "Yes, I am *negra* because my community is made up of *negros.*" This respondent resides in Boca do Rio. This neighborhood has middle-class and low-income areas. Similarly, a respondent in Rio de Janeiro says she identifies as *negra* based on her neighborhood. This respondent lives in Cidade de Deus, or City of God, a predominantly *negro* neighborhood in Rio de Janeiro. Many people recognize City of God, because of the 2002 movie that detailed police corruption and gangs in this neighborhood. When accompanying my research assistant on her interviews conducted in Cidade de Deus, I saw mixed-income housing in the sense that some homes looked less developed, while others were very middle-income homes. Some were even wired with Wi-Fi. With the exception of a funk party that night, the neighborhood was relatively quiet. Most recent, in December 2016, a military police airplane crashed in Cidade de Deus. This resulted in increased police harassment of community members, as police claimed they were looking for drug dealers. It is important to consider this context when thinking about respondents in Rio de Janeiro, especially those living in the City of God. Responses that mention community and family are below:

Yes. I think I identify by my color and where I was born . . . in Rio. Being *negro* is also where you live . . . and where you arrive. People say you are *preto* or you have hard hair . . . that you don't know anything. If you know a little English, [people say] a *preta* in the favela knows a little English! (27-year-old light-skinned self-identified *negra* college student who resides in Rio de Janeiro)

Yes I consider myself *negra*. I am from a *negro* family. I am not white. I declare it even if people do not see it in my color. I declare it. (27-year-old dark-skinned *negra* college student with straightened hair who resides in Salvador)

The concept that individual identity is connected to a group is more common among women than men. Only one man claims he is *negro* due to his family.

Afro-Brazilian Man That Self-Identifies as *Negro* Based on Family

Only one Afro-Brazilian man identifies as *negro* based on family (Table 2.6). He is a college student with a low income. He states that he identifies as *negro*

---

[2] All respondents in the sample were of voting age with the exception of this respondent.

Table 2.6 *Afro-Brazilian Men Who Identify as* Negro *Based on Family*

City	Gender	Education	Family Salary (USD)	Age	Skin color	Racial Identification	Hairstyle
São Paulo	Male	In college	Up to $813.08	29	NI	*Negro*	NI

"because I have dark skin and my family is of African descent. It is a fact." This respondent views no flexibility in racial identification because his family is *negro*. This is very different from findings that purport that Brazilian families have different racial identifications within families (Twine 1998; Hordge-Freeman 2015). In this respondent's opinion, family composition as *negro* determines individual identification. Unlike many Brazilians who will acknowledge they have family members who are *negro* or white, this respondent claims his family is entirely *negro*.

In sum, the notion that one is *negro* because of belonging to a *negro* family goes against the Brazilian common sense that typical of Brazilian family is that they are multiracial. The idea that one is *negro* because they are from a black community also goes against the idea of multiracial neighborhoods. In the case of the respondent from the City of God, she acknowledges that there are stereotypes about people in *favelas*, such as surprise if a *negro* person can speak a little English. Although she is light-skinned, she identifies as *negra* based on community. Because there are more women there is more variance in education although the majority are very educated just like the male respondent. However, women are more likely to derive a *negro* identity based on family and community.

POLITICAL CONSCIOUSNESS

Eight percent of respondents claim a *negro* identification based on political consciousness. Considering those with available data, 60 percent of these respondents come from low-income households, and 40 percent have high incomes. Of those with available data, 60 percent have some college education, and 40 percent have completed high school. Of those with available data, 60 percent are light-skinned, and 40 percent are dark-skinned. Only 20 percent of respondents wear black culturally marked hair.

Afro-Brazilian Women and Men Who Identify as *Negro* Due to Political Consciousness

Only one Afro-Brazilian woman identifies as *negra* due to political consciousness (Table 2.7). She is dark-skinned and is well educated. She has a doctoral degree and also has a high family income.

I identify as *negra*. I learned [this] in the family … with a family in the *favela*. I have a brother. At thirteen years old, I wore my hair in an Afro. We had a lot of racial consciousness through culture … heard black music from Brazil, Afro-American music and African music … I learned that being black is good. (45-year-old dark-skinned *preta* woman who has a doctoral degree and resides in Rio de Janeiro)

She discusses that she gained racial consciousness through the diasporic notion of blackness that her family embraced. Although she says she grew up in a *favela*, this experience is not marked by negative experiences or stereotypes of *negros*. In her recollection, it is a site where she became conscious of blackness.

Seventy-five percent of Afro-Brazilian men who say they are *negro* because of political consciousness are highly educated, and 25 percent completed high school (Table 2.8). Seventy-five percent have a low family income, and 25 percent have a middle income. Considering those with skin color information, 75 percent are light-skinned and 25 percent are dark-skinned. One respondent says that he is *negro* because of his "political vision" and that he is aware of racial issues. Along with other reasons such as dark skin and family, this respondent also says he identifies as *negro* due to his consciousness. Of those with available information, 50 percent of these men have low-cut hair, 50 percent have a black culturally marked hairstyle.

These men discuss consciousness, not through learning in their families but through individual awareness or through institutions such as the Steve Biko Cultural Institute in Salvador, Bahia. Biko prepares high school students for college entrance exams. However they also host workshops where racial issues are discussed. The three responses below illustrate that

Table 2.7 *Afro-Brazilian Women Who Identify as* Negra *Based on Political Consciousness*

City	Gender	Education	Family Salary (USD)	Age	Skin color	Racial Identification	Hairstyle
Rio de Janeiro	Female	PhD	$4,065.36–$8,130.72	45	5	*Preta*	Curly

Table 2.8 *Afro-Brazilian Men Who Identify as Negro Based on Political Consciousness*

City	Gender	Education	Family Salary (USD)	Age	Skin Color	Racial Identification	Hairstyle
Salvador	Male	In college	Up to $813.08	20	3	*Negro*	Twist-out
São Paulo	Male	In college	Up to $813.08	29	NI	*Negro*	NI
Rio de Janeiro	Male	Completed high school	$813.08–$2,032.68	29	4	*Negro*	Low cut
Rio de Janeiro	Male	Completed college	NI	34	1.5/2	*Negro*	Low cut
Rio de Janeiro	Male	In college	$2,032.68–$4,065.36	30	1	*Negro*	Afro

two men from Rio de Janeiro and a man from Salvador embrace blackness due to racial consciousness:

In my case today, I identify as *negro*. If I had to put my [identification] on a document, I would openly say I am *negro*. Today I am almost thirty years old, so I have already lived a lot. I have a lot of experience: I'm already a father; I've already lived a lot. I'm still young but when I was seventeen or eighteen years old I would not have said that I was *negro*. I would have said *moreno*. And today I understand that *moreno* is a person a lot lighter than me. I don't identify as *moreno*. I identify as *negro* because today I know what is white, white is a color for me that has European characteristics, a fine nose, little eyes, light skin color, and straight hair. I know that [*negros* have] *crespo* (tightly curled) hair, big lips, and big eyes. My nose is not like a [*negro*] nose but I have [*negro*] characteristics. We are *negros*, my father is *negro*, my mother is not white; my mother is *mulata*, so today I know that I am *negro*. (29-year-old dark-skinned *negro* male with low-cut hair who has a high school level education and resides in Rio de Janeiro)

Because of the type of education I have had, I thank the Biko [Institute for me having] a political vision of the world. Before I came to the [Biko] Institute, I had no idea of the racial discussion. (20-year-old male college student with a twist-out hairstyle in Salvador)

Yes ... There was consciousness in my family ... also the difficulties I have day to day because I suffer ... It is a difficulty only *negros* have. Someone with blonde hair does not have [these difficulties] ... but I identify as *negro and* not only because of my physical features." (30-year-old light-skinned self-identified *negro* male with an Afro hairstyle who is in college and lives in Rio de Janeiro)

These men have developed a political consciousness about blackness. Some of this awareness comes with a better understanding of the meaning of racial categories and the manipulations people make in an effort to avoid identifying as *negro*. Additionally, identifying as *negro* is also an acknowledgment that there are certain struggles or "difficulties" that *negros* have in Brazilian society.

Many of the men in the sample and the one woman in the sample have some college education. Although they do not talk about experiences in college, the university is another site where Afro-Brazilian students come into contact with black movement discourse (Penha-Lopes 2013). As the 20-year-old college student notes, it was in an educational site (the Steve Biko Cultural Institute), where he learned about racial issues. Those that do not learn about racial consciousness through institutions, may learn about it through maturity. In this sample, Afro-Brazilian men are more likely to claim blackness due to racial consciousness.

THE *NEGRO* STRUGGLE

Eight percent of respondents (five) identify as *negro* because they want to identify with a group that struggles because of discrimination. Of those with available skin color information, they are all light-skinned. Considering available data, 75 percent have some college education, and 25 percent have completed high school. The average age is 27.5. Seventy-five percent have black culturally marked hairstyles, and 25 percent have curly hair. In some cases, respondents discuss their personal difficulties as *negros*. Sixty percent are from Rio de Janeiro, and 40 percent are from São Paulo.

Afro-Brazilian Women and the *Negro* Struggle

Half of the women (Table 2.9) are from Rio de Janeiro, and the other half are from São Paulo. Income information is only available for one respondent. This respondent has a high income and a high level of education and is from Rio de Janeiro.

Yes, I identify with this group [of people] who have suffered since slavery. My mother is *negra* and my father is *negro*. (28-year-old light-skinned woman with curly hair and a master's degree who resides in Rio de Janeiro)

The second respondent states,

I identify as *negra*. I do not have a great explanation for this, but I live as a *negra*; [and] the experience of racism. (Woman from São Paulo.)

These Afro-Brazilian women are from different cities in Brazil, but both identify as *negra* because of the experience of suffering and racism *negros* face. One also adds that her parents are *negros*. The highly educated light-skinned woman from Rio does not point out an individual experience of suffering but acknowledges that, since slavery, *negros* have suffered. There is no demographic or physical data on the respondent from

Table 2.9 *Afro-Brazilian Women Who Identify as* Negra *Based on the* Negro *Struggle*

City	Gender	Education	Family Salary (USD)	Age	Skin Color	Racial Identification	Hairstyle
São Paulo	Female	NI	NI	NI	NI	NI	NI
Rio de Janeiro	Female	Master's degree	$2,032.68–$4,065.36	28	2	*Negra*	Curly

São Paulo. However, she identifies as *negra* because of the experience of racism. These two instances capture the idea that identification is a set of experiences, and in their interpretation, these experiences are difficulties *negros* face post-abolition.

Afro-Brazilian Men and the *Negro* Struggle

Men who identify as *negro* based on the *negro* struggle do so because of difficulties they faced. All of these men have low incomes, are light-skinned and wear their hair in black culturally marked hairstyles (Table 2.10). Sixty-six percent have some college education, and 34 percent completed high school. Sixty-six percent reside in Rio de Janeiro, and 34 percent live in São Paulo. In this sub-sample, the average age is 27.3.

As was seen earlier in the text, even light-skinned Afro-Brazilians are aware of stereotypes of *negros*. In the case of the male respondent below, identifies as *negro* because he is aware of and has experienced the struggles that *negros* face. Rather than shy away from a *negro* identity he claims it. His response is below.

I am completely *negro*. Each one of us will feel it in some way when people say that the *negro* is dirty and my hair is bad and hard. Despite this, I demonstrate [I am *negro*] in all my posture. (26-year-old light-skinned *negro* male who is from São Paulo and wears an Afro)

This respondent asserts himself as *negro* as a form of resistance. He is light-skinned and wears his hair in an afro, which is in line with his remark that he demonstrates his identity in his posture. The 30-year-old respondent below also remarks on the difficulties *negros* face. He states the following:

Table 2.10 *Afro-Brazilian Men Who Identify as* Negro *Based on the* Negro *Struggle*

City	Gender	Education	Family Salary (USD)	Age	Skin Color	Racial Identification	Hairstyle
São Paulo	Male	In college	$813.08–$2,032.68	26	2.5	*Preto*	Afro
Rio de Janeiro	Male	In college	$2,032.68–$4,065.36	30	1	*Negro*	Afro
Rio de Janeiro	Male	Completed high school	$813.08–$,2032.68	26	3	*Negro*	Dreads

Yes. . . . First because of what I talked about such as the consciousness I had inside
. . . . . .in my family, also difficulties I have day today because I suffer and suffered
to be *negro* in my community. It is a difficulty only *negros* have. Someone with
blonde hair doesn't have this . . . but I identify as *negro* not just because of my
physical features. (30-year-old *negro* male college student who wears an Afro and
resides in Rio de Janeiro)

Yes I identify as *negro* because this is where the struggle starts and because I
struggle. (26-year-old light-skinned *negro* male with a high school level education
who wears his hair in dreads and resides in Rio de Janeiro)

In the case of these Afro-Brazilian men, despite that they are all light-skinned,
they all discuss the struggle or suffering *negros* experience, and they all
say they have suffered. This goes against the idea that Afro-Brazilians with
light skin suffer less prejudice or racism in Brazil. Despite their suffering,
they wear their hair in black culturally marked hairstyles. Because some of
them are college students, they may have more freedom to wear these
hairstyles.

In sum, comparing men and women, we see that Afro-Brazilians who
identify as *negro* based on the history or experience of suffering and racism
come from Rio de Janeiro and São Paulo. All of these respondents are
light-skinned, which fundamentally goes against the idea that one's light
skin protects one from discrimination. Social scientists making such claims
should also take into account differences among lighter-skinned Afro-
Brazilians, which include gender and hair texture. Respondents with
black culturally marked hairstyles may face or acknowledge discrimination
more than those without such hairstyles. The men take on an active role in
embracing their blackness by wearing their hair in black culturally marked
hairstyles.

SUMMARY

In sum, 79 percent of Afro-Brazilians say they identify as *negro*. Some of
the reasons they identify as such are based on skin color or physical
features, ancestry, family or community, political consciousness, and the
negro struggle. Even though race in Brazil is often characterized as ambiguous and fluid, for those who identify as *negro*, they often do so because
they view identification as unalterable. This is even the case of highly
educated Afro-Brazilians. While women tend to be those that identify
based on family or community, men tend to be those that identify as
negro due to political consciousness. This gendered component of *negro*
identification is one that should be explored by future researchers.

NOT IDENTIFYING AS *NEGRO*

The previous section explored why Afro-Brazilians identify as *negro*. In this section, I explore why Afro-Brazilians believe other Afro-Brazilians do not identify as *negro*. One limitation of the interviews is that we did not ask non-*negro*-identifying respondents why they do not identify as *negro*. However, respondents were asked in an open-ended question why some Afro-Brazilians do not identify as *negro*. This question is important because it captures common understandings of blackness and allows respondents to express how blackness is perceived by others. They did not feel pressured to discuss why they personally might think negatively of blackness. These interviews offer a rich view of how Afro-Brazilians explain the negation of blackness. Considering the most common responses, I created six categories: racism, shame, *negros* are viewed negatively, lack of consciousness, avoidance of blackness as strategy, and whitening or miscegenation. A total of 45 respondents answered this question. However, some of those interviewees gave responses that fall into more than one category. When calculating the percentage of respondents under each category, I use the total number of respondents (45) in this calculation. Percentages do not equal 100 percent because seven respondents have responses that fall into more than one category.

SHAME

The most popular response was that Afro-Brazilians do not identify as *negro* because of shame. Thirteen respondents, or twenty-nine percent, believe that Afro-Brazilians do not identify as *negro* because they are ashamed. These responses, along with responses about negative perceptions of *negros*, really bring home the point that being *negro* in Brazil remains a stigmatization despite recent political gains, such as the implementation of affirmative action policy. This underscores the fact that, even in cities with high percentages of Afro-Brazilians, blackness remains stigmatized.

Fifty percent of sample respondents have some college education. Forty-two percent have finished high school. Eight percent have less than a middle-school education. Of those with available information, 55 percent of the sample have low incomes, 36 percent have middle incomes, and 9 percent have high incomes. Fifty-eight percent of the sample is dark-skinned, and 42 percent are light-skinned, of those with skin color information.

Afro-Brazilian Women Who Believe Afro-Brazilians Do Not Identify as *Negro* Because of Shame

Many women who believe Afro-Brazilians do not identify as *negro* because they are ashamed, come from Rio de Janeiro. Fifty-seven percent of these women reside in Rio de Janeiro, 29 percent reside in Salvador, and only 14 percent reside in São Paulo (Table 2.11). Considering those with skin color information, 50 percent are dark-skinned, and 50 percent are light-skinned. Twenty-nine percent come from low-income households, 57 percent come from middle-income households, and 14 percent come from high-income households. Overall, these women are highly educated. For those with education data available, 83 percent have at least some college education and 17 percent have only completed high school. Only 17 percent of women wear their hair in a black culturally marked hairstyle. In this sub-sample, the average age is 37. They also believe that one reason some Afro-Brazilians are ashamed to say they are *negro* is that they do not accept their color. Half of the respondents for whom skin color information is available are dark-skinned, and half are light-skinned. Eighty-six percent identify as *negra*, and 14 percent identify as *morena*.

Although women believe Afro-Brazilians are ashamed of being *negro* in all three cities, most of these respondents live in Rio de Janeiro, and the second highest number of respondents reside in Salvador. These are two cities where blackness is upheld culturally in music, dance, and cuisine. However, as Pinho (2010) notes, restricting blackness to stereotypical roles and notions of blackness functions to further stereotype *negros*.

A lot of times [people don't identify as *negro*] because of shame or for example, in work when identifying color [people know] if someone identifies as *negro* they will be eliminated [from the applicant pool]. [They] don't declare it for benefits. I think a lot [of denial is] because of shame. (27-year-old dark-skinned self-identified *negra* female with straightened hair who is in college in Salvador)

Because I think Brazil is still a country where a lot of people don't accept things and are ashamed to be *negro*. You are *marrom bom bom* . . . a lot of people want to be white. Even *negros* themselves will not say they are *preto* or *negro* . . . People don't respect themselves, even *negros* themselves. (27-year-old light-skinned woman who is in college, has relaxed hair, and resides in Rio de Janeiro)

They are ashamed of their color, of their race; to be *preto* or to be *negro* so they say they are *mulato* or *pardo*. However, for me I am *preta* and that's it (67-year-old dark-skinned *negra* woman with relaxed hair who has completed college and resides in Rio de Janeiro).

Table 2.11 *Afro-Brazilian Women Who Believe Afro-Brazilians Do Not Identify as Negro Because They Are Ashamed*

City	Gender	Education	Family Salary (USD)	Age	Skin Color	Racial Identification	Hairstyle
Salvador	Female	Incomplete college	$813.08–$2,032.68	27	6	*Negra*	Straight
Salvador	Female	Incomplete college	$2,032.68–$4,065.36	21	5	*Negra*	*Crespo/Afro*
Rio de Janeiro	Female	Master's degree	$4,065.36–$8,130.72	31	3	*Negra*	Relaxed
Rio de Janeiro	Female	In college	$2,032.68–$4,065.36	27	3	*Negra*	Straight/relaxed
Rio de Janeiro	Female	Completed college	$2,032.68–$4,065.36	67	4	*Negra*	Relaxed
Rio de Janeiro	Female	NI	$2,032.68–$4,065.36	64	NI	*Negra*	NI
São Paulo	Female	Completed high school	$813.08–$2,032.68	24	1	*Morena*	Straight

They are ashamed. (24-year-old light-skinned *morena* female who has completed high school and resides in São Paulo)

Afro-Brazilian women believe Afro-Brazilians deny being *negro* because they are ashamed. However, many of these women also acknowledge that the impact of being *negro* that job applications will be thrown away by prospective employers.

Afro-Brazilian Men Who Believe Afro-Brazilians Do Not Identify as *Negro* Because They Are Ashamed

Considering those with available income data, they are all low income (Table 2.12). Sixty-seven percent are dark-skinned, and 23 percent are light-skinned. Sixty-seven percent identify as *negro*, and 23 percent identify as non-*negro* or non-*preto* identifications. Some of their responses are below:

They are ashamed. They are ashamed to be *negro*. (18-year-old dark-skinned self-identified *mulato* and *marrom* male with low-cut hair who has completed high school, and resides in São Paulo)

Because they are ashamed to show their ethnicity; their racial class. (20-year-old dark-skinned man with curly hair who has completed high school and resides in Salvador).

These Afro-Brazilian men believe Afro-Brazilians do not identify as *negro* because they are ashamed, and as one respondent says, do not want to show their ethnicity. In their perception, shame of being *negro* continues even in cities with a high population of Afro-Brazilians.

In sum, Afro-Brazilian women who believe Afro-Brazilians do not identify as *negro* because they are ashamed are more educated than Afro-Brazilian men with similar opinions. Both are largely from Rio de Janeiro, although there are respondents from all three cities. Highlighting that feeling ashamed in these three cities where black movement activism has been significant is telling. While most of these respondents identify as *negro*, they are aware being *negro* is a source of shame for others. Afro-Brazilian women were more likely to say that Afro-Brazilians identify in other color categories because of shame over identifying as *negro*. In these cases, they did not say Afro-Brazilians want to identify as white, but they listed other color and racial categories such as *marrom* or *pardo*.

Table 2.12 *Afro-Brazilian Men Who Believe Afro-Brazilians Do Not Identify as Negro Because They Are Ashamed*

City	Gender	Education	Family Salary (USD)	Age	Skin color	Racial Identification	Hairstyle
Salvador	Male	Completed high school	$813.08 $2,032.68	20	5	*Preto*	Curly
Rio de Janeiro	Male	In college	NI	27	6	*Negro*	Afro
Rio de Janeiro	Male	Completed high school	$813.08 $2,032.68	29	4	*Negro*	Low cut
Rio de Janeiro	Male	Complete high school	NI	35	3	*Pardo*	Straight
Rio de Janeiro	Male	Incomplete middle school	Up to $813.08	18	3	*Negro*	Low cut
São Paulo	Male	Completed high school	$813.08 $2,032.68	18	4	*Mulato, Marrom*	Low cut

NOT IDENTIFYING AS *NEGRO* BECAUSE *NEGROS* ARE VIEWED NEGATIVELY

The second most-cited reason for Afro-Brazilians not identifying as *negro*, is that *negros* are viewed negatively. Twelve respondents (27 percent) cited this as a reason. Forty-two percent were Afro-Brazilian women, and 58 percent were men. All of these respondents self-identify as *preto* or *negro*. Of those with reported incomes, 64 percent are low income, 18 percent are middle income, and 18 percent are high income. Ninety-two percent are highly educated, and 8 percent have a low level of education. Fifty percent of these respondents have black culturally marked hair such as dreads and cornrows. Forty-two percent reside in Rio de Janeiro, 25 percent reside in Salvador, and 33 percent reside in São Paulo. The average age of female and male respondents in this sub-sample who believe Afro-Brazilians do not identify as *negro* because *negros* are viewed negatively is 35 years old.

Afro-Brazilian Women Who Believe Afro-Brazilians Do Not Identify as *Negra* Because *Negros* Are Seen Negatively

Afro-Brazilian women believe Afro-Brazilians do not identify as *negro* because it is seen negatively or because there are negative representations of *negros* in the media. All of these respondents identify as *negra* or *preta* (Table 2.13). Of those with identifying information, 25 percent have black culturally marked hair and 75 percent have curly or wavy hair. They are evenly divided in terms of skin tone. Twenty percent reside in Salvador, 40 percent reside in São Paulo, and 40 percent reside in Rio de Janeiro. They all have some college education, with 60 percent already having completed college, and of these, one has a doctoral degree and the other a master's degree. In this sub-sample, the average age is 31 years old. Their responses are below.

I think we have . . . a politics of whitening. It is bad to be *negro*, to have a relationship with Africa. To be *negro*, to be *preto* is bad. This is part of our social grammar. In Brazilian society whitening is in our history . . . . (45-year-old *preta* woman with curled hair who has a doctoral degree and resides in Rio de Janeiro)

[This is] the history . . . You always want to escape what is bad, and unfortunately what is bad is to be *negro*. [It is] a bad culture, *negro* culture you know? *Negro* culture is only valorized when it is part of folkloric dance, in *capoeira* [or] when we, we speak of religion. This is a little problematic, you understand? I will keep fighting against this. There are some people who obviously are a little light-skinned, [and] people tell them they are not *negro*, but they say "No, I am *negro*." Yes! But you have to try to do what is best for you . . . The other day [I was] with a friend and I said that I am *negra*, and she told me to stop being racist

Table 2.13 *Afro-Brazilian Women Who Believe Afro-Brazilians Do Not Identify as Negro Because Blacks Are Seen Negatively*

City	Gender	Education	Family Salary (USD)	Age	Skin Color	Racial Identification	Hairstyle
Salvador	Female	Completed college	Up to $813.08	32	4	*Negra*	Cornrows
Rio de Janeiro	Female	Master's degree	$2,032.68–$4,065.36	28	2	*Negra*	Curly
Rio de Janeiro	Female	PhD	$4,065.36–$8,130.72	45	5	*Preta*	Curly
São Paulo	Female	In college	$813.08–$2,032.68	23	3–4	*Negra*	Wavy
São Paulo	Female	Incomplete college	Up to $813.08	28	NI	*Negra*	NI

and that I am not *negra*, I am *morena*. There is music from Ilê [Aiyê] that being *negro* is not a question of pigmentation. It is a [question] of resistance. (32-year-old self-identified *negra* female with a dark skin tone and cornrows who has completed college and resides in Salvador)

Because no one wants to accept [the belief that] they are criminal and bad. It hurts. (28-year-old self-identified *negra* woman with some college education who resides in São Paulo)

In these women's accounts, there are negative stereotypes of *negros*, such as the notion that they are bad people. One woman admits that when she identifies as *negra*, her identity is questioned. However, she believes that identifying as *negra* is a form of resistance against stereotypes of *negros*. She has a college education and wears cornrows. Her educational level may be one reason her friend did not want to identify her as *negra*. More importantly is her comment that *negro* culture is valorized, but *negro* people are seen as bad. The fact that *negro* culture can be embraced while *negros* are stigmatized is related to the fact that Brazilian culture embraces its African cultural roots. Hanchard (1994) explains that black movement activists found it difficult to establish black culture separate from national identity, which includes African elements. Black culture and black bodies are exoticized at the same time that Afro-Brazilians are viewed as dangerous and criminal. This comment is also directly tied to Christen Smith's (2016) articulation of Salvador (the same city as this respondent's) Afro-Paradise where in Brazil, racism against dark-skinned people simultaneously exists with an acceptance of aspects of black culture largely understood as Brazilian culture.

Afro-Brazilian Men Who Believe Afro-Brazilians Do Not Identify as *Negro* Because *Negros* Are Seen Negatively

Seventy-one percent of these men have black culturally marked hair (Table 2.14). Eighty-six percent are dark-skinned, and 14 percent are light skin. Considering those with available income data, 67 percent have a low income, 16.5 percent have a medium income, and 16.5 percent have a high income. In this sub-sample, the average age is 37 years old.

Everything that is *negro* is seen as a bad thing. Because [of] racism ... [a] person with a darker skin tone [suffers] more [and a] *negro* suffers more racism. (30-year-old dark-skinned *negro* man with a twisted hairstyle).

Some men mention negative stereotypes of Afro-Brazilians in the media. These negative stereotypes confirm prevalent stereotypes of *negros*.

Table 2.14 *Afro-Brazilian Men Who Believe Afro-Brazilians Do Not Identify as Negro Because Negros Are Seen Negatively*

City	Gender	Education	Family Salary (USD)	Age	Skin Color	Racial Identification	Hairstyle
Salvador	Male	College	Up to $813.08	30	5	*Negro*	Twists
Salvador	Male	Completed college	$813.08–$2,032.68	30	5.5/6	Black	Low cut
Rio de Janeiro	Male	Completed college	$2,032.68–$4,065.36	28	4	*Preto*	Dreads
Rio de Janeiro	Male	Completed college	$4,065.36–$8,130.72	63	5	*Negro*	Low cut
Rio de Janeiro	Male	PhD student	NI	32	4.5	*Negro*	Twist-out
São Paulo	Male	In college	$813.08–$2,032.68	26	2.5	*Preto*	Afro
São Paulo	Male	Complete Middle school	Up to $813.08	51	6	*Negro*	Low cut

125

In sum, Afro-Brazilian men who believe Afro-Brazilians do not identify as *negro* because being *negro* is a bad thing, tend to be older than
Afro-Brazilian women with similar opinions. Most of these men wear
black culturally marked hairstyles, unlike the women in this sub-sample
who do not tend to wear black culturally marked hairstyles. They are
acutely aware of stigmatization. A higher percentage of Afro-Brazilian
men have low incomes. A higher percentage of Afro-Brazilian women
have higher educational levels. Some of these men reference stereotypes
of *negros* in the media. As many scholars have noted, Afro-Brazilians are
virtually absent in the media except for stereotypical roles, yet these
stereotypes have been challenged. Gillam (2016) argues that some of
these roles have actually empowered *negra* women. Afro-Brazilians are
also virtually absent in fashion magazines. The media reinforces predominant notions in society that beauty is not associated with blackness and
black people. Of course, there are numerous organizations that promote
black beauty – from Carnival groups such as Ilê Aiyê to Afro-Brazilian
bloggers such as Carla Fereirra of *Indeireitas Crespas*. Yet Brazilian
society is still riddled with stereotypes of blacks. According to those
interviewed, Afro-Brazilians choose not to identify as *negro* because of
these negative *negro* stereotypes.

RACISM

Eight respondents, or 18 percent of the sample, believe Afro-Brazilians do
not identify as *negro* because of racism. Seventy-one percent are male,
and 29 percent are female. Seventy-one percent are light-skinned, and 29
percent dark-skinned. Forty-three percent have some college education,
another 43 percent completed only high school, and 14 percent only
completed middle school. Only twenty-nine percent of the sample wear
their hair in black culturally marked hairstyles. Forty-three percent are
from Salvador, 28.5 percent from São Paulo, and 28.5 percent from Rio de
Janeiro. Eighty-six percent identify as *preto* or *negro*, and only 14 percent
identify as *moreno*. Forty-three percent wear their hair in black culturally
marked hairstyles.

Afro-Brazilian Women Who Believe Afro-Brazilians Do Not Identify as *Negro* Because of Racism

All Afro-Brazilian women who believe that Afro-Brazilians do not identify
as *negro* because of racism have some college education. Fifty percent have

Table 2.15 *Afro-Brazilian Women Who Believe Afro-Brazilians Do Not Identify as* Negro *Because of Racism*

City	Gender	Education	Family Salary (USD)	Age	Skin Color	Racial Identification	Hairstyle
Rio de Janeiro	Female	Master's degree	$2,032.68–$4,065.36	28	2	*Negra*	Curly
São Paulo	Female	In college	$813.08–$2,032.68	24	2	*Negra*	Straight

a middle income, and the other half have high income (Table 2.15). All are light-skinned and identify as *negra*. Half are from Rio de Janeiro, and the other half are from São Paulo. When referring to racism, they do not explain what they mean by racism. One respondent states racism and that being *negro* is seen as a bad thing. This respondent acknowledges that to view *negros* as bad is a form of racism, and she states the following:

Because of racism. Who wants to associate with someone bad . . . ? *Negro* is almost offensive . . . People [want to] avoid this stigma. (28-year-old light-skinned self-identified *negra* female with curled hair who has a master's degree and resides in Rio de Janeiro)

Afro-Brazilian Men Who Believe Afro-Brazilians Do Not Identify as *Negro* Because of Racism

Eighty-three percent of men identify as *negro* and *preto*, and 17 percent identify as *moreno* (Table 2.16). Fifty percent of these men wear their hair braided or in an Afro. Fifty percent are light-skinned, and 50 percent are dark-skinned. Fifty percent completed high school, 33 percent have at least some college education, and 17 percent have a low level of education. In this sub-sample, the average age is 27 years old. Some of their responses are below.

Because of racism based on color. Sometimes people say *pretos* steal (25-year-old *moreno* male who resides in Rio de Janeiro).

Because people do not see *negro* people as people; they see them as some type of object. (30-year-old dark-skinned self-identified black man in Salvador with a college degree)

Because of racism and racial segregation. Some people think if they identify as lighter such as *cabo verde* or *moreno*, they are escaping this word *negro* to have

Table 2.16 *Afro-Brazilian Men Who Believe Afro-Brazilians Do Not Identify as Negro Because of Racism*

City	Gender	Education	Family Salary (USD)	Age	Skin Color	Racial Identification	Hairstyle
Salvador	Male	Completed college	$813.08–$2,032.68	30	5.5/6	Black (in English)	Low cut
Salvador	Male	College	Up to $813.08	20	3	*Negro*	Twist-out
Salvador	Male	Completed middle school	Up to $813.08	30	5	*Preto*	Corn rows
Salvador	Male	Completed high school	Up to $813.08	31	4	*Negro*	Low cut
Rio de Janeiro	Male	Completed high school	$2032.68–$4065.36	25	2	*Negro*	Afro
São Paulo	Male	Completed high school	Up to $813.08	25	2	*Moreno*	Low cut

more opportunity or that it is better. (31-year-old dark-skinned *negro* male who has a middle-school level of education and lives in Salvador)

These respondents blame racism and provide examples of racism. One respondent demonstrates racism in his explanation that blacks are objectified. Another respondent admits that racism is due to one's skin color. The respondent residing in Salvador says Afro-Brazilians do not identify as *negro* because of racism. He also adds racial segregation. He is likely referring to informal racial segregation in Salvador, where *negros* are made to feel unwelcome. This respondent articulates a very different viewpoint that negates the idea that Brazil is free of racism and racial segregation. This idea that segregation is race-based and not class-based is also less common. It is common for Afro-Brazilians in Salvador to deny the existence of racism because they make up a significant amount of the population. However, as I explain earlier in the book, Salvador has the highest amount of income inequality between *negros* and whites. This respondent couples the answer with a response related to strategy. In order to alleviate racism, Afro-Brazilians identify in non-*negro* categories such as *moreno* or *cabo verde.*

In sum, Afro-Brazilian women who believe that racism serves as an impediment to Afro-Brazilians claiming a *negro* identification tend to be more educated than Afro-Brazilian men who state the same. Half of these Afro-Brazilian men wear black culturally marked hairstyles and live in Salvador and Rio de Janeiro, cities with significant proportions of Afro-descendants. Despite these large proportions, they express that racism prevents Afro-Brazilians from identifying as *negro.*

LACK OF CONSCIOUSNESS

Seven respondents, or 16 percent of Afro-Brazilians, say others do not identify as *negro* because they lack consciousness. Respondents say that *negros* have a lack of will and are racist against themselves. Focusing on failures of *negros* takes focus away from white supremacy and domination in society. The negativity associated with *negros* acknowledges that the lived experience of being *negro* makes embracing blackness difficult for some. However, only citing a lack of consciousness or ignorance does not acknowledge the role of racism. Thirty-four percent of these respondents have a college education, and 66 percent only completed high school. Eighty-six percent are light-skinned, and 14 percent are dark-skinned.

Afro-Brazilian Women Who Believe Afro-Brazilians Say They Are Not *Negro* Because of a Lack of Consciousness

All of these women are light-skinned and are low income. Sixty-six percent of these women have completed only high school, and 34 percent have some college education (Table 2.17). Sixty-six percent have afros, and 34 percent have relaxed hair. In this sub-sample, the average age is 29 years old. They are all from Rio de Janeiro. Even in a city such as Rio de Janeiro, which is rich with Afro-Brazilian culture, respondents say *negros* do not accept their blackness. Two examples are the quotes below:

A lot of people are scared to accept blackness . . . [Blacks are seen as] incompetent [and are] not valued. People do not have this consciousness. (19-year-old light-skinned self-identified *negra* female who has completed high school and wears an Afro hairstyle in Rio de Janeiro)

They have racism against their own color. They do not accept their color. (46-year-old light-skinned woman from Rio de Janeiro who wears her hair in an Afro and has a high-school education)

These women believe that Afro-Brazilians have not accepted their blackness, are not conscious, and one respondent believes they are racist against *negros*. The idea that *negros* harbor prejudice like many Brazilians is similarly discussed in terms of racism. However, racism implies that power can be used against a group of people to continue racial domination. This is not the case of most *negros* in Brazil, nor is it the case that as a group they can benefit from privileges bestowed upon the group.

Table 2.17 *Afro-Brazilian Women Citing Lack of Consciousness as the Reason Afro-Brazilians Do Not Identify as* Negro

City	Gender	Education	Family Salary (USD)	Age	Skin Color	Racial Identification	Hairstyle
Rio de Janeiro	Female	Completed High school	$813.08 $2,032.68	46	1	*Negra*	Afro
Rio de Janeiro	Female	Completed High school	$813.08 $2,032.68	19	2	*Negra*	Afro
Rio de Janeiro	Female	Incomplete college	$813.08 $2,032.68	21	2	*Negra*	Relaxed

Afro-Brazilian Men Who Believe Afro-Brazilians Say They Are Not *Negro* Because of a Lack of Consciousness

Seventy-five percent of the men in this sample are light-skinned, and 25 percent are dark-skinned (Table 2.18). Seventy-five percent identify as *negro*, and 25 percent identify as *pardo*. Only twenty-five percent have a black culturally marked hairstyle, and 75 percent have a low-cut hairstyle. Seventy-five percent are in college, and 25 percent have not finished middle school. The average age is forty. Of those with available information, 66 percent have a low income, and 34 percent have a middle income. Some of their responses are below:

Negros are ignorant. (69-year-old dark-skinned *pardo* male with low-cut hair who has not completed middle school and resides in Rio de Janeiro).

I think it is a lack of consciousness among them; not all families here accept that they are *negros*. My mother was a militant in the black movement and gave me the opportunity to become conscious, so I am *negro*. This is contrary to a lot of people. When *negro* or *preto* is pejorative, it is because they do not want to accept it … Why is it that in a lot of poor neighborhoods they straighten their hair? It is because they do not want to accept their blackness. Unfortunately, education is lacking. I studied in schools and went through and there was nothing about black history such as how we came here. There is always history of the Portuguese. (30-year-old light-skinned *negro* man who is in college, wears his hair in an Afro, and resides in Rio de Janeiro)

I believe that the *negro* does not know he is *negro*. I have been saying this since the beginning of the interview, right? (laughing) I am certain that the Brazilian *negro* does not know who he is. A lot of times he does not know because he has not learned [this]. He does not know. (25-year-old *negro* male college student with a low-cut hairstyle who resides in São Paulo)

Table 2.18 *Afro-Brazilian Men Citing Lack of Consciousness as the Reason Afro-Brazilians Do Not Identify as* Negro

City	Gender	Education	Family Salary (USD)	Age	Skin Color	Racial Identification	Hairstyle
Rio de Janeiro	Male	Incomplete middle school	Up to $813.08	69	5	*Pardo*	Low cut
Rio de Janeiro	Male	In college	$2,032.68–$4,065.36	30	1	*Negro*	Afro
São Paulo	Male	In college	Up to $813.08	25	2	*Negro*	Low cut
São Paulo	Male	Incomplete college	NI	36	2	*Negro*	Low cut

These men believe that Afro-Brazilians that do not identify as *negro* are ignorant, are ashamed to be *negro,* and lack consciousness. The consciousness one respondent refers to is one influenced by the black movement, as his mom was a black movement activist. He also believes consciousness is the result of learning black history. As this respondent claims, this is a history that was not taught in schools. Although many schools have not adequately implemented Law 10.639/03 which requires the teaching of African and Afro-Brazilian history, presumably Afro-Brazilian students who are taught black history will be more accepting of their blackness. At least, this is the line of thinking of this respondent. In this sense he is not simply saying that Afro-Brazilians are ignorant, but that this ignorance is rooted in a lack of education about their history, whereas, some respondents did not explain ignorance as rooted in Eurocentric education and simply stated that blacks were ignorant. Costa's (2014) work exemplifies how decolonializing thought and teaching Afro-Brazilian history can challenge Eurocentric and anti-black sentiments.

MISCEGENATION OR WHITENING

Brazil is known for its racially mixed population; thus it is no surprise that miscegenation was mentioned. Eight respondents, or 18 percent of the sample, explained that the denial of blackness is because Brazilians are racially mixed or because of whitening. This demonstrates that the phenomenon of whitening still exist. It also exemplifies the myth of racial democracy. In this sense, Afro-Brazilians deny being *negro* in favor of the idea that Brazilians are racially mixed, so they cannot identify as distinct racial groups. Half are men, and half are women. The average age is 33 years old. Fifty percent of these respondents reside in São Paulo, 25 percent reside in Salvador, and 25 percent reside in Rio de Janeiro. Fifty-seven percent identify as *negro* and *preto,* 43 percent identify as *pardo* or *mulato,* for those with available information. Fifty percent are light-skinned, and 50 percent are dark-skinned.

Afro-Brazilian Women Who Believe Afro-Brazilians Do Not Identify as *Negro* Because of Racial Mixture or Whitening

Considering those with available information, 33 percent of Afro-Brazilian women who believe Afro-Brazilians do not identify as *negro* because of racial mixture or whitening self-identify as *mulata* (Table 2.19). Sixty-seven percent identify as *negro* and *preto.* Considering available

Table 2.19 *Afro-Brazilian Women Who Believe Afro-Brazilians Do Not Identify as* Negro *Because of Racial Miscegenation or Whitening*

City	Gender	Education	Family Salary (USD)	Age	Skin Color	Racial Identification	Hairstyle
São Paulo	Female	In college	$2,032.68– $4,065.36	30	4.5/5	*Negra*	*Crespo*
São Paulo	Female	NI	NI	64	NI	*Mulata*	NI
São Paulo	Female	NI	NI	NI	NI	NI	NI
Rio de Janeiro	Female	PhD	$4,065.36– $8,130.72	45	5	*Preta*	Curly

income information, half of respondents have a middle income, and half have a high income. In this sub-sample, the average age is 46 years old. Women believe racial mixture, both past and present, makes it difficult for some Afro-Brazilians to identify as *negro*. Responses are below.

Because of racial mixture. My mother is white and my father is a lot darker, so we don't know because we are *mestiço*. (64-year-old *mulata* woman who resides in São Paulo)

On account of the Portuguese. We know the history. There was miscegenation between the Portuguese and people of African origin. Today I am *negro* but my daughter has lighter skin, so this creates doubts [for her] to say she is *negro*. (30-year-old dark-skinned woman in college who has tightly curled hair and resides in São Paulo)

I think we have . . . a politics of whitening. It is bad to be *negro*, to have a relationship with Africa. To be *negro*, to be *preto* is bad. This is part of our social grammar. In Brazilian society whitening is in our history . . . . (45-year-old *preta* woman with curled hair who has a doctoral degree and resides in Rio de Janeiro)

We suffer from the big problem of miscegenation, so no one identifies as *negro* or Afro-Brazilian because miscegenation is used as an excuse [and] so they consider other alternatives such as *pardo*. (woman in São Paulo; information on income, age, skin color, racial identification was not collected)

Afro-Brazilians are keenly aware of the historical dimension of racial mixing. As Anthony Marx (1998) confirms, the national myth is that racial miscegenation and whitening came about in a positive manner. However, he believes the process of racial mixture has been romanticized to fit the national myth rather than Brazilians acknowledging that, at the nation's outset, Portuguese men sexually violated Indigenous and African women. In addition, some black activists and scholars, such as Abdias do

Nascimento (1989), discuss whitening as a form of black genocide, because as the African descendant population began to outnumber whites, the idea was to rid Brazil of its Afro-Brazilian population. Some of the women in this sample discuss the national history as a way of explaining skin color and why it is difficult for some Afro-Brazilians to identify as *negro*. However, one woman believes miscegenation is used as an excuse to identify in a non-*negro* category such as *pardo*.

Afro-Brazilian Men Who Believe Afro-Brazilians Do Not Identify as *Negro* Because of Racial Mixture or Whitening

In this sub-sample, the average age of men is 41 years old. Seventy-five percent are light-skinned, and 50 percent identify as *pardo* (Table 2.20). Of those with available income information, they are all low income. Half of these men have some college education, 25 percent completed only high school, and 25 percent completed only middle school. Half are from Salvador, 25 percent from Rio de Janeiro, and 25 percent from São Paulo. Both respondents from Salvador identify as *pardo*. Responses are below:

Brazil was discovered by the Portuguese. The Africans worked as slaves. It was mixed, so we do not know how to really define ourselves. We are a mix. (43-year-old light-skinned *pardo* man with low-cut hair who has a middle school education and resides in Salvador)

I think it is because of people being mixed. For me, *preto* or *branco*, everyone is the same. (60-year-old dark-skinned *pardo* man with curly hair who has a high school education and lives in Salvador)

Table 2.20 *Afro-Brazilian Men Who Believe Afro-Brazilians Do Not Identify as Negro Because of Racial Miscegenation or Whitening*

City	Gender	Education	Family Salary (USD)	Age	Skin color	Racial Identification	Hairstyle
Salvador	Male	Completed middle school	Up to $813.08	43	2	*Pardo*	Low cut
Salvador	Male	Completed high school	$813.08–$2,032.68 USD	60	6	*Pardo*	Curly
Rio de Janeiro	Male	Completed college	NI	34	1.5/2	*Negro*	Low cut
São Paulo	Male	In college	$813.08–$2,032.68	26	2.5	*Preto*	Afro

Because of this issue of whitening. You will whiten if you have the possibility of escaping discrimination. *Preto* and *negro* are considered bad, but if you are lighter, to get employment, you will prefer not to identify as *negro*. You will not identify as *negro* because it will not help you personally. (34-year-old light-skinned *negro* man with low-cut hair who has a college education and resides in Rio de Janeiro)

Because in school and our society, [*negros*] are viewed as the downtrodden and it is difficult to accept this. The hair is seen as bad, and the *negro* is seen as dirty. When children become adults, they will associate and live with whites. It is still difficult for a child with lighter pigment. Whitening is physical and mental. (26-year-old light-skinned male college student who sports an Afro and resides in São Paulo)

Afro-Brazilian men discuss whitening and the history of racial mixture between the Portuguese and Africans as reasons Afro-Brazilians may not identify as *negro*. In the discussion of whitening, they both refer to examples of whitening by identifying differently or by associating with whites rather than whitening by choosing lighter spouses. One respondent says whitening is physical and mental, but he gives an example of someone who whitens by associating and living with whites. He also indicates that it is mental, which implies one can whiten through their way of thinking. This respondent also believes that even those with lighter skin face difficulties. Two men in Salvador who both identify as *pardo* do not discuss whitening but focus on the history of racial mixture.

In sum, Afro-Brazilian women and men who believe Afro-Brazilians do not identify as *negro* because of racial mixture or whitening do not acknowledge the violent history of whitening. Rather they speak about it as racial mixture between Africans and Portuguese. There is no discussion of the gendered dimension of the racial mixture that occurred between Portuguese men and African and Indigenous women in Brazil's early history. Women were more likely to refer to whitening as biological, whereas men referred to it as a strategic process, such as putting a lighter color on a job application or by living with whites.

STRATEGY

Four responses (9 percent) fall into the category of those who do not identify as *negro* in a strategic attempt to lessen racism or prejudice. Acknowledging identification as a strategy is important because some individuals choose to avoid a category because of prevailing stereotypes. The logic behind this idea is that, given the prevalence of stereotypes, Afro-Brazilians choose identifications that may be less costly and that might even benefit them. I note that perceived benefits do not actually mean that

Table 2.21 *Afro-Brazilian Women and Men Explain Afro-Brazilians Who Do Not Identify as* Negro *as a Strategy*

City	Gender	Education	Family Salary (USD)	Age	Skin color	Racial Identification	Hairstyle
Salvador	Female	Completed college	NI	32	4	*Negra*	Cornrows
Rio de Janeiro	Female	Master's degree	$4,065.36–$8,130.72	31	3	*Negra*	Relaxed
Salvador	Male	Completed high school	up to $813.08	31	4	*Negro*	Low cut
Rio de Janeiro	Male	Finished college	NI	34	1.5/2	*Negro*	Low cut

benefits are rendered. The average age of these respondents is 32. Half reside in Salvador and half reside in Rio de Janeiro. Similarly, half are men and half are women. Considering available data, half are low income and half are high income. Only 25 percent of this sample wear a black culturally marked hairstyle. Half are dark-skinned, and half are light-skinned. Seventy-five percent have completed college.

Afro-Brazilian Women and Men Explain Afro-Brazilians Who Do Not Identify as *Negro* as a Strategy

These Afro-Brazilian women reside in Salvador and São Paulo, and are all highly educated (Table 2.21). They both identify as *negra*. Both indicate that they believe Afro-Brazilians do not identify as *negro* as a means of escaping. One respondent believes Afro-Brazilians are trying to escape reality, while the other believes they are aware of negative stereotypes of *negros* and so they wish to escape these negative associations by identifying otherwise.

An example of strategy can be seen in the following quotes:

They do not see themselves as such. They end up calling themselves *morenos* or other things to escape reality. (31-year-old light-skinned *negra* woman with a master's degree and relaxed hair who resides in Rio de Janeiro)

The history. You always want to escape what is bad and unfortunately what is bad is to be *negro* (32-year-old dark-skinned *negra* woman with a college education who wears cornrows and resides in Salvador)

Half of the Afro-Brazilian men have college education, and the other half finished high school. Both men have low-cut hairstyles. Like the women, they admit that avoiding a *negro* identification in favor of other terms, such as *moreno*, is to avoid stigmatization and to gain opportunity. One of the male respondents quoted earlier believes it is a method to escape discrimination. One of the male respondents is quoted below.

Because of racism, racial segregation ... Some people think if they identify as lighter, *cabo verde, moreno* they are escaping this word *negro* so that they will have more opportunity or it will be better. (31-year-old self-identified *negro* male of medium complexion with low-cut hair who completed high school in Salvador)

In sum, Afro-Brazilians believe there are others who deny a *negro* identification to avoid stigmatization. Unlike respondents who discussed identification as something one cannot choose, these respondents believe some Afro-Brazilians make the choice to call themselves a different term, such as *moreno*, to avoid being associated with blackness. Women and men offer similar explanations when discussing the strategic use of identification.

QUALITATIVE INTERVIEW SUMMARY ON IDENTIFYING AS *NEGRO* AND DENYING A *NEGRO* IDENTIFICATION

Based on these qualitative interviews, it appears that a main feature of identifying oneself as *negro* is based on unalterable physical traits or one's ancestry. This applies even in the case of highly educated Afro-Brazilians. While women tend to identify based on family or community, men tend to identify as *negro* due to political consciousness. The most popular logic used for explaining why some Afro-Brazilians do not identify as *negro* is that Afro-Brazilians are ashamed and do not value themselves. Unfortunately, this undervaluation accepts stereotypes of *negros*. White aesthetics are not only upheld by whites but also by Afro-Brazilians. The next most popular response for not identifying as *negro* was that *negros* are seen as bad, which included stereotypes that *negros* are criminals. Afro-Brazilian women were more likely to say that Afro-Brazilians identify in other color categories because of shame over identifying as *negro*. Afro-Brazilian men believe Afro-Brazilians do not identify as *negro* because being *negro* is viewed negatively. These men tend to be older than the Afro-Brazilian women who hold similar opinions. Most of these men wear black culturally marked hairstyles unlike the women. Despite stigmatization, these men wear these hairstyles.

This shows that blackness is embraced by some people – and not simply because they were born *negro*. Some respondents acknowledge experiences such as racism or knowing about the experience of struggle and the history of *negros* as reasons for embracing blackness. Nearly 20 percent of responses focused on these life experiences or on the acknowledgment of such experiences as reasons for embracing blackness. Quantitative analysis will highlight some of the variables that explain the data about which Afro-Brazilians identify as the census category *preto* in the survey.

QUANTITATIVE ANALYSIS

Bailey and Telles (2006) and Mitchell-Walthour and Darity (2014) find that those with higher education or income and those who are younger tend to claim a *negro* or *preto* identification. Mitchell-Walthour and Darity (2014) also find that when skin color is darker, the likelihood of claiming a black identification increases. Scholars have examined the determinants of perceived racial discrimination (Leavitt 2015; Layton and Smith 2016). Layton and Smith find that women with dark skin are most likely to perceive gender and color discrimination. In general, those with dark skin are more likely to perceive class and color discrimination. There are fewer studies on the role that perceived discrimination has on racial identification. I tested the hypothesis that Afro-Brazilians with higher socioeconomic statuses, measured by education and income, with darker skin complexions who experience discrimination are more likely to claim a *preto* identification when compared with lighter-skinned Afro-Brazilians with lower levels of education who have not experienced discrimination. I rely on the Latin American Political Opinion Project's (LAPOP) 2010 survey because it includes a large-scale national Brazilian dataset with 2,482 respondents. My sample size is smaller because I only consider respondents who identified as *preto* or *pardo*. Statistical analysis will allow us to see general trends in identification and includes a national survey, unlike the qualitative interviews, which focused on three cities. As found in the qualitative analyses, Afro-Brazilians choose a *preto* identification because of physical features and experiencing discrimination. Skin color is a physical feature measured in the survey. The limitation of the LAPOP survey is that respondents were not asked why they identify in the category in which they identify. However, given the available survey data questions, I examine skin color by including the skin color palette included in the survey, in my analysis.

My expectation is that as skin color gets darker, the likelihood of choosing a *preto* identification increases. An 11-point skin tone indicator was used, and the interviewer matched the skin color of the respondent to one of these skin tones. While it is not true that all dark-skinned Afro-Brazilians claim a *preto* identification, neither is it true that all lighter-skinned Afro-Brazilians claim *pardo* identification. In the LAPOP survey, respondents were limited to census categories. I am interested in the sample respondents who identified as *pardo* and *preto*. There was no open-ended question regarding race or color. The question regarding discrimination was "Thinking of the past five years, did you feel like you were discriminated or treated badly or in an unjust manner because of the color of your skin? The respondent could choose a lot of times, sometimes, few times, or never. Age is a continuous variable.

I ran a logistic regression analysis. My dependent variable is the census category *preto* or *pardo*, which is a dichotomous variable. My independent variables are experiencing discrimination over the past five years, years of education, age, monthly family income, gender, and skin color.

I find that experiencing discrimination over the past five years is statistically significant at the $p<0.001$ level; monthly family income is statistically significant at the $p<0.001$ level; and skin color is statistically significant at the $p<0.001$ level (Table 2.22). The likelihood of someone on the darkest end of the spectrum claiming a *preto* identification is 85 percent; it is only 15 percent for claiming a *pardo* identification (Figure 2.1).

While income is statistically significant, education is not when claiming *preto* status. As income increases, the likelihood of claiming a *preto* identification increases (Figure 2.2). It is likely that Afro-Brazilians with higher incomes have experienced racial discrimination and understand it as such. Thus, they are more likely to claim a *preto* identification despite the stigma. Telles (2004) claims that "money darkens" rather than lightens based on his similar analyses. The long-standing belief was that Afro-Brazilians with higher incomes avoided claiming a black identification, but in contemporary Brazil, this is not the case. There is mixed evidence regarding

Table 2.22 *Logistic Regression of Choosing* Preto *or* Pardo *Identification*

Experiencing discrimination over past 5 years	2.17***	0.31
Years of education	−0.00	0.03
Age	0.00	0.01
Monthly family Income	2.44***	0.60
Gender	−0.04	0.19
Skin Color	7.29***	0.54
Constant	−6.40***	0.55

N=1336
*** $p<0.001$

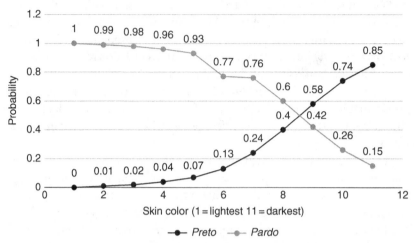

Figure 2.1 Probability of Claiming a *Preto* or *Pardo* Identification Based on Skin Color
(1–11)
Source: LAPOP 2010, version 4

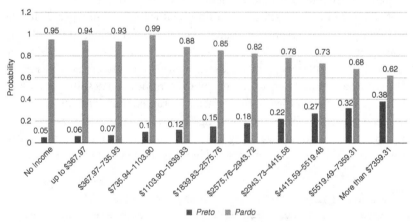

Figure 2.2 Probability of Claiming a *Preto* or *Pardo* Identification Based on Income
(USD)
Source: LAPOP 2010, version 4

education. It is not statistically significant in my analysis. In one dataset, Mitchell-Walthour and Darity (2014) find that as education increases, the likelihood of claiming a black identification increases; however, in the other dataset, only income is statistically significant. The qualitative analysis reveals that Afro-Brazilians claim a *negro* identification for a number of reasons. However, the most popular reason was skin color or other physical features. Both men and women who based identification on skin color were highly educated and tended to be dark-skinned. Because many were college students, their incomes were low.

Experiencing discrimination increases the likelihood of claiming a *preto* identification and decreases the likelihood of claiming a *pardo* identification (see Figure 2.3). The survey includes a question on whether the respondent had experienced discrimination over the past five years. Interestingly, for respondents who experienced much discrimination, the likelihood of claiming *pardo* identification is 60 percent, but only 40 percent for claiming *preto* identification. This is likely the result of the Afro-Brazilian sample having an overwhelming number of respondents claiming *pardo* identification. This is also likely the result of only offering the categories *preto* and *pardo* rather than *negro*. Yet the findings are quite revealing. Respondents who claim they have never experienced discrimination are 93 percent more likely to claim *pardo* identification, but only 7 percent more likely to claim a *preto* identification. Respondents who only experienced discrimination a few times are 86 percent more likely to claim *pardo* identification, whereas a similar respondent is only 14 percent more likely to claim *preto* identification. Thus the trend is that as the number of times one has experienced

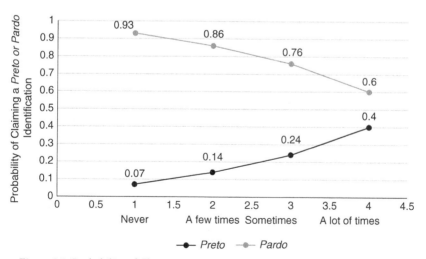

Figure 2.3 Probability of Claiming a *Preto* or *Pardo* Identification Based on color discrimination
Source: LAPOP 2010, version 4

discrimination increases, there is a corresponding increase among those claiming *preto* identification and a decrease among those claiming *pardo* identification. The qualitative results show that only 8 percent of those interviewed identified as *negro* based on the *negro* struggle. Although they were all light-skinned, men that identified as *negro* based on the *negro* struggle, mentioned discrimination. They all also wore black culturally marked hair, which could be one reason they were more likely to recall discrimination. Women who cited an example of the *negro* struggle did not discuss personal experiences of discrimination but mentioned examples of difficulties *negros* face in general. Although gender is not statistically significant in the quantitative analysis, the qualitative analysis reveal some differences in motivations for identifying as *negro*.

CHAPTER SUMMARY

In sum, high-status Afro-Brazilians are also more likely to choose *negro* or *preto* identifications. Quantitative analysis reveals that Afro-Brazilians with higher incomes, those who have experienced discrimination based on color, and those with darker skin are more like to choose a *preto* identification over a *pardo* identification. Qualitative data confirm results that identifying as *preto* or *negro* is based on skin color. Most Afro-Brazilians who identify as *negro* do so based on skin color or other physical features such as nose shape or lip size. The next most popular response was that Afro-Brazilians identify as *negro* based on ancestry or parentage. Interview results show that of those identifying as *negro* based on skin color, they tend to be highly educated but have low family incomes. This is due to the fact that many of these respondents are college students. What is telling about these interviews is that these respondents do not believe that identification is fluid, which goes against the myth that "money whitens" or that those of higher socioeconomic status become white or claim lighter identifications. In fact, some respondents say they will be the color they are until they die. Like the statistical results, there were no gender differences in terms of identifying as *negro* based on skin color. However, there are differences when examining identifying as *negro* because of family or community, and identifying as *negro* based on difficulties *negros* face. Women were more likely to identify as *negro* based on family or community composition, whereas men were more likely to identify based on discrimination or difficulties *negros* faced despite that all of the men are light-skinned. In fact, one male respondent says that *negros* are seen as dirty but that he demonstrates that he is *negro* in his posture. In this way, having the experience of discrimination does not turn some Afro-Brazilians away from claiming blackness; they embrace blackness despite stigmatization. In the interviews, this is demonstrated via people discussing their own form of consciousness or the fact that some wear their hair in black culturally marked hairstyles such as Afros and braided styles despite stigmatization.

3

Negro Group Attachment in Brazil

. . .. I am influenced by everything that happens to the *negro* population. A lot of times I do not like to be in certain places. I feel bad [when] certain exquisite places don't have *negros*. They look at you and stare at you. This is bad
(25-year-old light-skinned male college student
who is a hip-hop DJ in São Paulo).

This quote responds to a question about *negro* group attachment, which I refer to as "*negro* linked fate." The college student is recalling the experience of feeling uncomfortable in elite, presumably white, spaces, and he believes *negros* are excluded from white spaces. As an individual, he displays linked fate by identifying with *negros* as a group, saying what happens to *negros* has an impact on him. Among Afro-Brazilians, is there a shared sense of group identity because of experiences based on color? Does a shared experience of discrimination lead to *negro* linked fate? In this chapter, I examine black linked fate, the idea that blacks feel linked to other blacks because of their shared history of discrimination (Dawson 1994). Keeping in line with the common expression *negro* to denote Afro-Brazilians I employ the term *negro* linked fate throughout the text. I study *negro* linked fate through reliance on in-depth interviews conducted in Rio de Janeiro, Salvador, and São Paulo in 2012. I also rely on a 2006 original survey conducted in Salvador and São Paulo. I analyze in-depth interviews and statistical analyses to examine the Afro-Brazilian conceptualization of *negro* linked fate. I examine whether *negro* linked fate exists and its determinants. These determinants are perceived discrimination against *negros*, their socioeconomic status as measured by education and income, and their gender, age, racial or color identification, and city.

My hypothesis is that highly educated Afro-Brazilians with higher incomes who acknowledge discrimination against *negros* are more likely to display a sense of *negro* linked fate than those with lower incomes and education who do not acknowledge such discrimination. The young college student's reflection, quoted above, is one example of how higher educated Afro-Brazilians find themselves in exclusively elite white spaces. These experiences, such as being stared at by white customers or clientele, make them keenly aware of racial dynamics in Brazil. The constant reminder of one's outsider status, despite actual class, may make such individuals keenly aware of their color. These racialized experiences may lead higher-income and more highly educated Afro-Brazilians to feel attached to their racial group. Social identity theory, discussed later in this chapter, explains why those in stigmatized groups identify with the in-group. My statistical analyses reveal that where *negro* linked fate is the dependent variable, education is not statistically significant in my results. Even so, there is a positive relationship: as education increases, the likelihood of an individual demonstrating *negro* linked fate also increases. Age, city, and racial or color identification are statistically significant. Younger respondents, residents of Salvador, and *pretos* and *negros* have the highest probabilities of demonstrating *negro* linked fate. My qualitative results revealed that most Afro-Brazilians who demonstrate *negro* linked fate do so because of discrimination or *negro* suffering. Those that do not demonstrate linked fate tend to identify in non-*negro* and non-*preto* categories.

NEGRO LINKED FATE

Negro linked fate is concerned with whether one feels he/she shares common experiences with other *negros* or that what happens to other *negros* in some way has an impact on the individual. This is different from viewing oneself as racially *negro*. The previous chapter shows that Afro-Brazilians who identify as *negro* tend to do so based on physical characteristics, family or community, political consciousness, and ancestry. This is an individual understanding of identity. *Negro* linked fate is concerned with group identity or how one identifies with a group. I rely on Michael Dawson's (1994) notion of black linked fate. Dawson is concerned with whether economic differences among African Americans lead to differing political behavior. He concurs that "... the historical experiences of African Americans have resulted in a situation in which group interests have served as a useful proxy for self-interest" (77). Furthermore, he believes that linked fate can "measure the degree to which African Americans believe that their own self-interests are linked to the interests of the race" (Dawson 1994: 77). Dawson also posits that understanding one's own individual status depends on how one evaluates the status of the group.

Michael Dawson's (1994) concept of the black utility heuristic is used to understand black racial group identity and policy preferences in the U.S. He also emphasizes that the concept of black linked fate relies on historical experiences as a group which are accompanied by reinforced notions of groupness based on discrimination (Dawson 1994: xii). African Americans share a sense of linked fate because of their shared history of discrimination. Even though Dawson is careful to situate this concept within the American context, is it possible that, as race-targeted policies emerge, black linked fate is forming in other countries where racism exists?

Negro linked fate in the Brazilian context refers to an attachment to the *negro* racial group. Rather than assert that all Afro-Brazilians have faced discrimination, as Dawson assumes in the case of African-Americans, I propose that only Afro-Brazilians who acknowledge racial discrimination will display a sense of *negro* linked fate. This concept of linked fate regarding Afro-Brazilians is especially important to black politics, as it does not presume that racial discrimination is experienced by *all* African descendants. In fact, Goldsmith et al.'s (2007) work show differences in incomes among African American men based on skin color. Incomes of lighter-skinned black men are closer to parity with white men's salaries than those of darker-skinned black men. Similarly, Telles (2004) finds the same trend in income differences between African Americans. Of course, this does not mean that African Americans do not experience discrimination in other aspects of their lives, nor does it mean that lighter-skinned African Americans do not experience racial discrimination. However, it does highlight that discrimination may differ according to skin color. Furthermore, Hamilton et al. (2009) find that darker-skinned African American women are less likely to marry than lighter complexioned women. Not only are African Americans differentially subjected to discrimination, but also they do not experience it in the same way. In addition, black linked fate is not a consistent predictor of support for policies that have an impact on African Americans. Cathy Cohen (1999) demonstrates that black group interests do not always hold for issues, such as support for AIDS policies, and that homophobia within the black community can lead to less linked fate. Reuel Rogers's (2006) work on Afro-Caribbean immigrants and their political incorporation gives a more nuanced examination of differing experiences among people of African-descent in the United States. Similarly, Candis Watts Smith's (2013) work on black immigrants shows that social justice is less important an issue for black immigrants than it is for African Americans.

African descendants in the United States do not experience discrimination in the same way nor do they have uniform policy preferences. In a similar vein, Afro-Brazilians may also experience discrimination in differing ways. What is true about both societies is that they have a history of slavery and discrimination and that these shared experiences may lead to feelings of attachment to the larger, overarching, racial group. Since slavery, Afro-Brazilians have formed communities and organizations exclusively for blacks (Butler 1998). Although, retrospectively one might say Afro-Brazilians were historically discriminated against because of slavery and social exclusion, it would be difficult to argue that, in general, Afro-Brazilians *believed* they were discriminated against as a group. Brazil's racial history is such that state political actors promoted the idea of miscegenation. Moreover, the ideology of racial democracy inhibited Afro-Brazilian racial group identity and mobilization (Hanchard 1994).

However, with the implementation of racial policies, traditional and non-traditional black movement activism, and grassroots black activism, often led by black women, there may be more group consciousness. Afro-Brazilian activism, in its various forms, may lead to or reinforce feelings of a linked fate among Afro-Brazilians who acknowledge racial discrimination. If people see themselves as part of a group that is collectively discriminated against, they have increased levels of group identification with the in-group (Tajfel and Turner 1986). Branscombe et al.'s (1999) study on African Americans finds that higher levels of group identification mediate the effects of prejudice on well-being.

Considering changing racial dynamics in Brazil, perhaps there is a similar effect at play. Andrew Francis and Maria Tannuri-Pianto (2012) find that at the University of Brasília, after the implementation of affirmative action, more applicants began identifying as black. Some of this was due to changes in racial identification, although some were cases of misrepresentation. This is an example of a racial policy influencing racial identification. Racial policies and racial discourse can also have an impact on *negro* linked fate. Despite the "elite profile" of discrimination in employment, Afro-Brazilians of all classes may experience racial discrimination. Afro-Brazilians in low-income neighborhoods have experienced discrimination (Perry 2013; Smith 2016), and police brutality against Afro-Brazilian men and women is an issue that can be understood in racial terms (Mitchell and Wood 1998; Alves 2014; C. Smith 2014).

Social media plays a role in disseminating experiences of racism suffered by *negros*. This forum has also made it possible for news to travel more quickly than previously. A recent example can be found in the death of Claudia Silva Ferreira. She was an Afro-Brazilian woman who was killed by police on March 16, 2014. Police entered her neighborhood, Morro da Congonha, in

Madureira, in the North Zone in the state of Rio de Janeiro and began shooting, making the claim that they were looking for drug dealers. She was innocent and had just come from the grocery store. The police claimed they thought she was carrying coffee to drug dealers. After shooting her, they put her body in the trunk of a police car, claiming they were taking her to the hospital. After falling out of the trunk, her body was dragged 350 meters. Someone filmed the incident on a cell phone. Community members stopped traffic in the neighborhood in protest. In addition, people discussed the case on social network sites (e.g. Facebook) and blogs (e.g. *Blogueiras Negras*). These discussions centered on the fact that she was killed because she was a poor black woman. In a picture taken at a protest, an Afro-Brazilian man wore a T-shirt that read "I am black, in case of emergency do not let the police 'help' me."[1] Thus social media also plays a role in disseminating the idea that *negros*, not simply poor people, experience discrimination, which may lead to more people accepting that discrimination can also be race-based, not only class-based. This could lead to *negro* linked fate.

NEGRO GROUP IDENTITY

Negro linked fate is different from identifying as *negro*. Ethnographic and sociological scholarship differ in findings concerning *negro* group identity. Robin Sheriff (2001), in her ethnographic work on a slum community in Rio de Janeiro, finds that Afro-Brazilians essentially have a bipolar view of race as white and black but use various color degradations to soften the effect of color. In an effort to be polite, color gradations are used to describe a person. However racially, Afro-Brazilians in her study believe they are all *negros*. In this sense, Afro-Brazilians may describe themselves as a number of skin colors but believe they all belong to the racial category *negro*. Given this finding, it is plausible that Afro-Brazilians who identify as *negro* may be more likely to demonstrate *negro* linked fate. Further, Bailey (2009c) believes group identity is increasing.

PART 1: QUALITATIVE ANALYSIS OF *NEGRO* LINKED FATE IN SALVADOR, RIO DE JANEIRO, AND SÃO PAULO

Mitchell-Walthour (2011) finds that Afro-Brazilians in Salvador and São Paulo display high rates of *negro* linked fate. These findings are based on qualitative and quantitative data. Her qualitative data is based on preliminary

---

[1] Sou Negra. Em caso de emergência não deixe a polícia me "socorrer."

interviews where she finds differences in notions of *negro* linked fate. In Salvador, *negro* linked fate is transnational. People feel linked to *negros* in Brazil and throughout the African Diaspora. In São Paulo, Afro-Brazilians feel linked to *negros* in Brazil because of experiences of discrimination. This is closer to Dawson's notion of black linked fate, which is restricted to the history of discrimination that African Americans faced.

My 2012 study includes Salvador, São Paulo, and Rio de Janeiro. Along with research assistants in these cities, I conducted 76 in-depth interviews. Research assistants in each city were told to choose respondents that self-identified as Afro-descendants and were of varying socioeconomic levels and ages. The interview question, "Do you think what happens to *negros* affects you? Why or why not?"[2] was the same question used to measure Dawson's concept of black linked fate. In all three cities, more respondents displayed linked fate than did not. Of the 76 in-depth interviews conducted, only 52 respondents answered this question. Twenty-four did not respond or said, "I do not know."[3] A total of 32 respondents out of those 52 demonstrated *negro* linked fate; 11 did not demonstrate linked fate; 1 answered "sometimes"; and 1 answered "yes and no." Seven gave answers not relevant to the question. In essence, 62 percent of the sample demonstrated *negro* linked fate. Twenty-one percent did not demonstrate linked fate.

Responses were grouped into three categories: racial discrimination or *negros* are excluded or suffer, suffering in general, and serving as a role model. In all three cities, respondents that demonstrated *negro* linked fate were likely to say they felt linked to *negros* because of racial discrimination or *negro* exclusion in society. Seventy-eight percent of respondents fall into this category. Fourteen of these respondents have some college education. In all of these cities, Afro-Brazilians that mentioned racial discrimination identify as *negro* or *preto*. Twelve-and-a-half percent of respondents felt linked to *negros*, saying they themselves suffer, but did not say their suffering was based on race. Only 9.5 percent of Afro-Brazilians feel linked to *negros* because they think they serve as role models to *negros*. Afro-Brazilian women were most concerned with employment and hiring

---

[2] Você acha que o que acontece com os negros afetam você? Porque ou porque não?

[3] Some respondents were mistakenly not asked the *negro* linked question in Salvador. In Salvador, 10 people had no response to this question. The São Paulo sample included an overwhelming number of low-income and less-educated individuals compared to Salvador and Rio de Janeiro. In some cases, these respondents said "I don't know." When the interviewer encouraged them to share their opinions, they said they were embarrassed to speak. Two respondents answered in this manner, and four answered the question with an answer that was irrelevant to the question.

discrimination. Afro-Brazilian men are concerned with media underrepresentation of *negros*. Both Afro-Brazilian men and women discuss how multiple identities lead to discrimination. Women focus on race and gender, and men focus on race and class.

What is telling is the perception that there are fewer opportunities for *negros* and that *negros* are excluded, and both beliefs lead these respondents to demonstrate *negro* linked fate. It appears that *negro* linked fate in Brazil is somewhat similar to Dawson's (1994) notion of linked fate in terms of focusing on the experience of discrimination. It is significant that Afro-Brazilians notions of *negro* linked fate are mainly rooted in experiences of racial discrimination. Brazil's black movements in their various manifestations have played an important role in changing perceptions from simply believing exclusion was due to class, to Afro-Brazilians perceiving discrimination and exclusion based on race or race and class. These findings contribute to the literature on racial politics offering a comparative lens.

NEGRO LINKED FATE AS A RESULT OF RACIAL DISCRIMINATION, NEGRO EXCLUSION, AND NEGRO SUFFERING

First I give general findings of respondents that demonstrate *negro* linked fate due to racial discrimination, *negro* exclusion, and suffering.[4] Seventy-eight percent of respondents that demonstrated *negro* linked fate were likely to say they felt linked to *negros* because of racial discrimination or because *negros* suffer or are excluded in society. Twenty percent of respondents are from Salvador, 56 percent are from Rio de Janeiro, and 24 percent are from São Paulo. All but one of these respondents self-identify as *negro* or *preto*. Of those for whom information was available, 45 percent are dark-skinned, and 55 percent are light-skinned. Of those with available education data, 59 percent have some college education, 32 percent have finished high school, and 9 percent have less than a high school education. Of those for whom information is available, sixty-seven percent have a low income, 29 percent have a middle income, and 4 percent have a high income. Twenty-eight percent of sample respondents wear their hair in a black culturally marked hairstyle. The average age is 33.2.

---

[4] In addition, an Afro-Brazilian woman demonstrated *negro* linked fate because she feels linked to *negros* as a racial group. This response did not fit into the three categories. She stated, "It affects me because when a person says *negra* they are talking about the race." (18-year-old dark-skinned woman with curly hair who has not completed high school and resides in Salvador).

Women and *Negro* linked Fate Due to Racial Discrimination, *Negro* Exclusion, and *Negro* Suffering

Sixty-nine percent of Afro-Brazilian women who feel linked to *negros* due to racial discrimination or *negro* exclusion and suffering come from Rio de Janeiro, 15 percent come from São Paulo, and 16 percent are from Salvador (Table 3.1). In this sub-sample, the average age is 36.2. Thirty-eight percent are dark-skinned, and 62 percent are light-skinned. Of those for whom information is available, 75 percent have some college education, 17 percent have completed high school, and 8 percent have less than a high school level of education.

Many Afro-Brazilian women that demonstrate *negro* linked fate mention discrimination in employment or discrimination as an impediment to employment. Witnessing this discrimination, they feel linked to *negros*. One respondent, who did not complete middle school, does not use racial terms such as white and *negro* when discussing that an employer would not call back, but she uses terms such as "lighter," "prettier," and "straight hair." Oftentimes in Brazil, whiteness is coterminous with pretty, and straight hair is viewed as a characteristic of whites. Her implication is that whites are preferred over *negros* in employment. She states the following:

[What happens to *negros*] affects me because sometimes when you go to get a job, there is someone prettier with straight hair. Instead of calling you, they [the employer] call the straight haired person with lighter skin, understand? They tell you to wait, and when they do not call you this is very difficult. (35-year-old dark-skinned woman with relaxed hair who has an incomplete middle school education and resides in Rio de Janeiro)

Additional examples of discrimination when applying for employment are as follows:

Yes [I believe what happens to *negros* affects me because of] discrimination. I don't know. It is discrimination. This is in the workplace. You can have a good application but the white will get the job. The *negro* will not [get the job] because of their color. (21-year-old light-skinned *negra* college student in Rio de Janeiro)

I think it affects me. What happens with others affects me. No one is exempt from this. In employment there is preference for whites, but they know they need a *negro*. However, if a *negro* enters a store, they will see that if there is a *negro* [working in the store], they do not have *negro* characteristics. They might be *negro* but have white characteristics. They will not hire someone with African features. In class, I always tell my students that in terms of visibility, those who are marked from Africa (where these people suffer from poverty even more than in Brazil), the most poor are those with dark

Table 3.1 *Afro-Brazilian Women and Negro Linked Fate Due to Racial Discrimination, Negro Exclusion, and Negro Suffering*

City	Gender	Education	Family Salary (USD)	Age	Skin Color	Racial Identification	Hairstyle
Salvador	Female	In college	$813.08–$2,032.68	27	6	*Negra*	Straight
Salvador	Female	Completed high school	$813.08–$2,032.68	27	2	*Parda*	Curly
São Paulo	Female	In college	$2,032.68–$4,065.36	30	4.5/5	*Negra*	*Crespo*
São Paulo	Female	In college	$813.08–$2,032.68	23	3.5	*Negra*	Wavy hair
Rio de Janeiro	Female	Master's degree	$4,065–$8,130.72	31	3	*Negra*	Relaxed
Rio de Janeiro	Female	Completed high school	$813.08–$2,032.68	46	1	*Negra*	Afro
Rio de Janeiro	Female	In college	$2,032.68–$4,065.36	27	3	*Negra*	Relaxed
Rio de Janeiro	Female	In college	$813.08–$2,032.68	21	2	*Negra*	Relaxed
Rio de Janeiro	Female	Master's degree	$2,032.68–$4,065.36	28	2	*Negra*	Curly
Rio de Janeiro	Female	PhD	$4,065–$8,130.72	45	5	*Preta*	Curly
Rio de Janeiro	Female	Completed college	$2,032.68–$4,065.36	67	4	*Negra*	Relaxed
Rio de Janeiro	Female	NI	$2,032.68–$4,065.36	64	3	*Negra*	Braids
Rio de Janeiro	Female	Incomplete middle school	Up to $813.08	35	4	*Negra*	Relaxed

skin; with lighter skin you ascend more. (45-year-old dark-skinned woman with curly hair who has a PhD and resides in Rio de Janeiro).

In the above examples, both respondents believe employers prefer whites. Both of these respondents reside in Rio de Janeiro, where, like many places in Brazil, lighter-skinned people are preferred in employment, especially in places such as stores where individuals will interact with customers. One respondent believes that employers prefer whites but feel a need to have at least one *negro* person, so they hire a *negro* person who does not have "*negro*" features. The "need" she refers to is likely due to Brazil's change in racial politics where having no Afro-Brazilians in employment is problematic given the country's demographics. Some employers are aware that Afro-Brazilians are underrepresented, so according to this respondent, they may hire an Afro-Brazilian who does not have typical *negro* features.

All three of these respondents acknowledge discrimination in the hiring process and believe they are linked to *negros* because they are affected by discrimination in hiring. Afro-Brazilian women also focus on employment discrimination. They believe that discrimination, including employment discrimination, links them to *negros* because *negros* are limited in employment opportunities and are underrepresented. In addition, some believe that discrimination is hurtful, and even *negros* with high education or those that have employment feel they are disrespected These responses are below:

Yes. It principally affects me emotionally. I see discrimination in the workplace, housing, and with salaries. Discrimination hurts me. It affects me a lot. It worries me. (27-year-old dark-skinned, self-identified *negra* college student who has straightened hair and resides in Salvador).

I think I am affected because in the same way that what happens with others, also it can happen with me, understand? It is still very restricted for *negros* in employment, the media, education, or the area of health. Sometimes it is very difficult for you to see a nurse that is *negra* or a teacher that is *negro*. It is difficult (31-year-old self-identified *negra* with relaxed hair who has a medium skin tone, holds a master degree, and resides in Rio de Janeiro).

There are still limitations such as in education. It is still difficult to see a *negro* nurse or a teacher that is *negro*. When they see *negros* [in these positions] they think they are arrogant. You can have more access, but they disrespect you. (27-year-old light-skinned woman who is in college, has relaxed hair, and resides in Rio de Janeiro).

The respondents above acknowledge that there are disparities in employment and that it is difficult to see *negros* in certain occupations. One respondent indicates that when they, presumably non-Afro-Brazilians see *negros* in certain professions such as a nurse or teacher they disrespect them. In this sense, one's professional status does not protect them from discrimination. Interestingly two of the respondents discussing discrimination against *negro* professionals are light-skinned. These respondents feel linked to *negros* because of the discrimination *negros* face, and they are all concerned with workplace discrimination. These women's responses are demonstrative of the social identity theory that Tajfel and Turner (1986) discuss because their awareness of discrimination leads to embracing *negros* as a group.

Another way of discussing discrimination is based on intersectional identities. Two Afro-Brazilian women assert themselves as *negro* women acknowledging race and gender identities. Moreover, one of these women compares racism to homophobia when considering the issue of marriage. Their responses are below:

I think what affects me as a *negra* woman is the issue of prejudice and I am very violated in Brazil and treated very badly. Racism is not explicit. People say "I am not *negro*," "I am not racist," but [they say] "I do not want my son to marry with a *negro*" . . . like [what] happens a lot of time with homosexuals. I think that affects me. What affects me is the representation of *negros*." [*Negros* are] still very stereotyped and marginalized very badly. (23-year-old college student with wavy hair and light skin who self-identifies as *negra* and resides in São Paulo)

Not everything [affects me], but the issue of prejudice is always increasing and [there is] even more [prejudice] if you are a *negra* woman. [Being] a *negra* woman makes it quadruple. So what happens with others always affects me. (31-year-old light-skinned self-identified *negra* with a master's degree who has relaxed hair and resides in Rio de Janeiro)

These women believe that *negros* face prejudice and that the discrimination they face is even greater because they are *negra* women. One respondent is adamant that her gender and race lead to greater discrimination and believes that being a *negra* and being a woman quadruples the amount of prejudice one will face. Both of these women have a high level of education and are light-skinned, yet both articulate discrimination based on race and gender.

Their findings are important, because the two Afro-Brazilian women who demonstrate linked fate based on discrimination and who assert their identities as *negra* women are highly educated, and one has a high income, yet they both are aware of the difficulties *negra* women face.

Another respondent did not separate race and class and believes that her experience as a poor *preta* woman leads to an attachment to *negros*. She limits her movements by not going to certain places because of the stereotype that if one is *negro*, one is poor. This respondent resides in São Paulo, where *negros* are a minority of the population. Although the city has a history of black movement activism, in her personal life she has experienced the designation that *preta* equals poor.

Sometimes I feel affected because I am of the thought that I don't go [certain places] because I'm *preta* and *poor* because here [the assumption is that] if you are *preta*, you are poor. (30-year-old dark-skinned self-identified *negra* female college student who resides in São Paulo)

Other respondents also mention experiences of discrimination as a reason they feel what happens to *negros* affects them. One respondent mentions strangers in the street saying *neguinha* ("little black woman"), which is the diminutive of *negra*. The other respondent mentions that she had to use the service elevator, which is usually reserved for domestic workers and building maintenance workers. Both of these respondents are older and reside in Rio de Janeiro.

I think it affects me. For example, in the street many people say *neguinha*. No one likes to be called this. (46-year-old light-skinned self-identified *negra* woman who has a high school level of education, wears an Afro hairstyle and lives in Rio de Janeiro)

It determines how you are treated. I have been discriminated against such as when I had to enter the service elevator. This affects me. (67-year-old dark-skinned *negra* woman with relaxed hair who has a college degree and resides in Rio de Janeiro)

Other responses that demonstrate linked fate are below and indicate how these women as individuals, feel linked to *negos* as a group. One respondent notes that the police treat *negros* differently. Another says that Brazilian society does not acknowledge *negros'* capacity and views them as inferior.

[What happens to *negros*] affects me because I hurt. It hurts when I see people who have the capacity but society says *negros* do not have the capacity and that they are inferior. (64-year-old light-skinned *negra* woman who has less than a middle school education and resides in Rio de Janeiro)

Yes completely. Everything that happens with the group affects me individually, such as when the police treat us differently. (28-year-old *negra* light-skinned woman who holds a master's degree and resides in Rio de Janeiro)

Like I said, it affects me because it is part of my culture, understand? It is part of my blood, understand? It affects me not emotionally, but on account of prejudice. (27-year-old light-skinned *parda* woman who has completed high school, has curly hair and resides in Salvador)

In sum, Afro-Brazilian women who cite discrimination or suffering as a reason for feeling linked to *negros* often mention employment discrimination or discrimination as a barrier to employment. All of the women who mentioned discrimination in employment or as a barrier to employment have some college education. The most educated Afro-Brazilian women are acutely aware of discrimination in employment and feel linked to *negros* based on discrimination. In this way, this aligns with Silva and Reis's (2011) notion of an elite profile of discrimination, which posits that those with more education may be more aware of discrimination in employment. Afro-Brazilian women who acknowledge the intersection of prejudice based on gender and race were both light-skinned. This means that even skin color does not shield *negra* women from the effects of discrimination. We also see that a high level of education does not shield Afro-Brazilians from being racialized, such as in the case of the female college student who mentioned discrimination based on *negros* being classed as poor. However, what we see is that discrimination leads Afro-Brazilians to feel linked to *negros*. Although most Afro-Brazilian women who demonstrated linked fate based on racial discrimination tend to be highly educated, women with less education articulated they also felt linked to *negros* because of discrimination. Two Afro-Brazilian women who were not highly educated discussed experiences of racial discrimination. Another telling example of the racial environment in Brazil is that a woman responded to this question with the assertion that police treat *negros* differently. This differential treatment leads to *negro* linked fate.

Afro-Brazilian Men and *Negro* Linked Fate Due to Racial Discrimination, *Negro* Exclusion, and *Negro* Suffering

Twelve Afro-Brazilian men feel linked to *negros* due to racial discrimination or *negro* exclusion (Table 3.2). Available data demonstrated that 55 percent of the sample are dark-skinned and 45 percent are light-skinned. Twenty-five percent of these respondents live in Salvador, 33 percent reside in São Paulo, and 42 percent reside in Rio de Janeiro. Eighty-two percent come from low-income households, and 18 percent come from middle-income households, based on available data. Thirty-three percent have black culturally marked hairstyles. Forty-two percent have some college education, 50 percent have a high school education, and 8 percent have less than a high school education. In this sub-sample, the average age is 27.6, making this sample younger than Afro-Brazilian women with *negro* linked fate based on racial discrimination.

Table 3.2 *Afro-Brazilian Men Who Demonstrate Negro Linked Fate Based on Racial Discrimination or Exclusion*

City	Gender	Education	Family Salary (USD)	Age	Skin Color	Racial Identification	Hairstyle
Salvador	Male	Completed high school	$813.08–$2,032.68	31	6	*Negro*	Low cut
Salvador	Male	Completed high school	$813.08–$2,032.68	20	5	*Preto*	Curly
Salvador	Male	Completed high school	$813.08–$2,032.68	30	5	*Negro*	Low cut
São Paulo	Male	In college	$813.08–$2,032.68	26	2.5	*Preto*	Afro
São Paulo	Male	In college	Up to $813.08	25	2	*Negro*	Low cut
São Paulo	Male	Incomplete middle school	Up to $813.08	51	6	*Negro*	Low cut
São Paulo	Male	In college	Up to $813.08	29	NI	*Negro*	NI
Rio de Janeiro	Male	Completed high school	$813.08–$2,032.68	29	4	*Negro*	Low cut
Rio de Janeiro	Male	Completed high school	NI	34	1.5/2	*Negro*	Low cut
Rio de Janeiro	Male	In college	$2,032.68–$4,065.36	30	1	*Negro*	Afro
Rio de Janeiro	Male	Completed college	$2,032.68–$4,065.36	28	4	*Preto*	Dreads
Rio de Janeiro	Male	Completed high school	$813.08–$2,032.68	26	3	*Negro*	Dreads

Three respondents mention multiple identities when discussing discrimination or exclusion. In all three responses, they mention race and class. Two of these respondents specifically mention the negative impact of being poor and *negro*. Similar to Afro-Brazilian women who mentioned that life is more difficult being a *negra* woman, these respondents believe life is more difficult being poor and *negro*. Their responses are below:

[I am affected] in all ways. Brazil is a racist country . . . there is racial discrimination and social discrimination. In our country, this affects me directly. To be *negro* is [something] negative. If you are *negro* and poor, that is a double negative. If you are rich and *negro*, this is not a problem. (29-year-old self-identified *negro* male who is a college student and resides in São Paulo)

I think so. I think that when a *negro* is humiliated, when a *negro* is beaten down . . . I feel like, in a certain way offended in the same way as a "*Paraiba*" or a *nordestino*, a minority [is excluded]. I think that the minority is in some way violated or excluded from society. I feel for the minority. I am poor. I am *negro*. I am not as educated. I am not illiterate, but also I am not so educated. So when a minority is in some way violated or excluded from society, I feel in a certain way excluded as well. (29-year-old dark-skinned self-identified *negro* male with low-cut hair who has an incomplete high school education and resides in Rio de Janeiro)

It affects me every day because I am part of this class. I experience difficulties such as discrimination. (26-year-old light-skinned man with dreads who has a high school level of education and resides in Rio de Janeiro)

These men believe that the intersection of race and class has a profound effect on one's life, and they feel linked to *negros* based on these intersections. The 26-year-old man's response may refer to *negros* as simply a class or group of people, or his use of the word class can be understood in the same way as others – that *negros* are poor. This respondent lives in Rio de Janeiro, where there is a stark contrast between well-to-do neighborhoods and low-income neighborhoods, which are racialized as *negro*. The other respondent residing in Rio compares racial exclusion to exclusion that Brazilians from other regions of the country face, such as Brazilians from the northeast. The northeast is predominantly Afro-Brazilian. Although the notion of a *nordestino* is not a racial term, the term is racialized in many ways given the demographics. Oliveira (2007) shows that a political candidates background as a *nordestino* has a negative effect on voter support. The respondent who discusses exclusion based on region is articulating that exclusion is based on one's place of origin within Brazil, class, and race. Although this respondent separates the identities of poor and *negro*, he acknowledges multiple identities.

Two respondents mention exclusion in the media as areas where *negros* face exclusion. One respondent discusses a feeling of exclusion at his place of employment as well as in shopping areas. He also mentioned that *negros* are not in soap operas. Gillam (2016) discusses an increase in *negro* representation in the media. However, there is still no representation that mirrors the demographic representation of Afro-Brazilians. The other respondent mentions the media as a source that dispenses negative stereotypes of *negros*. Their responses are below:

Yes it affects me in diverse levels of society as a student, when we are discussing the issue of quotas [it], affects me in various ways because racist people still exists. What *negros* go through every day, I also go through. I still see a racist population like when I go to a place of commerce and there are not many *negros*; this affects me. In my profession it affects me because I feel excluded. I am excluded in my work [and there is also exclusion] in the soap operas. Today I saw a soap opera that had no *negros*. (30-year-old light-skinned male who wears an Afro and is in college in Rio de Janeiro)

[This] affects me because all the media reflects how the *negro* is not capable, and this affects us all. (26-year-old light-skinned male college student who wears an Afro and resides in São Paulo)

Totally! I think it's like *negro* children wake up in the morning only seeing television programs with white hosts, understand? They are not going to like their own hair, understand? They will think their skin tone, their nose, and their lips are bad. A lot of times when you are [out in] places you will think it is because of your skin color and a lot of times it might not be but you think this. I am influenced by everything that happens to the *negro* population. A lot of times I do not like to be in certain places. I feel bad [when] certain exquisite places don't have *negros*. They look at you and stare at you. This is bad. (25-year-old light-skinned *negro* male college student who wears a low-cut hairstyle and resides in São Paulo)

Incarceration is another topic Afro-Brazilian men are concerned with and that links them to *negros*. Two respondents feel linked to *negros* because *negros* have a lack of opportunity and are marginalized from society as they are incarcerated. Michelle Alexander's *The New Jim Crow* (2012) examines mass incarceration of African Americans and how those who are incarcerated are excluded from certain aspects of society such as voting and serving jury duty and also experience discrimination in employment, and housing. In Brazil, incarceration disproportionally affects Afro-Brazilians. Although these Brazilian respondents are not explicitly discussing the ramification of incarceration, one respondent views incarceration similar to Alexander in that she says incarceration serves as a physical site where people are excluded from society and cannot access certain opportunities. This respondent explains that there are fewer opportunities for *negros* and that they are the majority in places such as prisons, *favelas*, and the periphery. As Ribeiro et al. (2010) find, there is a much lower chance of access to employment for those living in certain areas of the city in Rio de Janeiro. In this context, not only does where one lives have an impact on employment opportunities, but limiting *negros* to prisons rather than workplaces can multiply the impact of non-working people in local communities and families. Time spent incarcerated is time that an individual is not gainfully employed. Despite that the respondent in Salvador says that few people assume they are *negro* in Salvador, he acknowledges that if a *negro* person suffers due to imprisonment, this has an impact on him. Responses are below:

It is difficult to respond to this question because few people assume they are *negro* . . . I don't know. [When] a *negro* is imprisoned, this affects me. (31-year-old dark-skinned man with a low-cut hairstyle who is studying for the college entrance exam and resides in Salvador)

Yes it affects me because people of this ethnicity always have a lack of access and unfortunately a lack of opportunity. We *negros* are the majority in the prisons, favelas, and the periphery.

[Interviewer: How does it affect you specifically?]

. . . People suffer from discrimination including myself. This entirely affects me. (28-year-old dark-skinned man who has completed college, wears his hair in dreads, and resides in Rio de Janeiro)

Unlike most respondents who discuss the marginalization, exclusion, and difficulties *negros* face, two respondents mention that Brazilian society is racist. One respondent is light-skinned and resides in Rio de Janeiro, and despite his light skin color, he believes Brazil is a racist country. He is linked to *negros* because what happens to *negros* has an impact on his life.

It affects me because of color. In an extremely racist country, it is clear that what happens with *negros* happens with me. It is a collective. (34-year-old light-skinned *negro* male with a college education who resides in Rio de Janeiro)

Other respondents mention that *negros* are marginalized or that life is difficult for them. One respondent in Salvador mentions that whites are also marginalized. In contrast, another respondent in Salvador mentions that he suffers in his everyday life and another mentions that *negros* suffer a lot of oppression. Responses are below:

Yes. Because I suffer this daily in work, in general, in my financial life; in everything. (31-year-old dark-skinned *negro* male with a low-cut hairstyle who has completed high school and lives in Salvador)

[It] affects me. The *negro* population is marginalized. I am *negro* but a white person is marginalized also. (30-year-old dark-skinned male with a low-cut hairstyle who has completed high school and lives in Salvador)

I am affected a lot because we *negros* suffer a lot of oppression; we suffer a lot of neglect. The rulers, the people in power, they focus on destroying our population. (20-year-old dark-skinned self-identified *preto* man with curly hair who has completed high school and resides in Salvador)

I think it affects me. To be *negro* is more difficult in Brazil. (51-year-old dark-skinned man with a low-cut hairstyle who did not complete middle school and lives in São Paulo)

In sum, Afro-Brazilian men feel linked to *negros* because of exclusion and discrimination. Men had lower levels of education than Afro-Brazilian women who demonstrate *negro* linked fate based on racial discrimination or exclusion. Male respondents who mention multiple identities mention race and class such that being *negro* and poor makes life difficult. Women assert their identities as *negra* women and acknowledge the impact of *negros* being racialized as poor but were more likely to mention race and gender as causes for a greater degree of discrimination. Both Afro-Brazilian men and women are aware of negative stereotypes of *negros*. However, men were more likely than Afro-Brazilian women to mention the lack of *negro* representation in the media or that when *negros* are represented they are represented negatively. Unlike Afro-Brazilian women, Afro-Brazilian men mentioned incarceration as demonstrative of exclusion and where Afro-Brazilians are in the majority. Unlike women, some Afro-Brazilian men explicitly stated that Brazilian society or that the country is racist. This is a strong statement given Brazil's history as a "racial paradise" and given state efforts to address racial discrimination and underrepresentation in the media. These interviews reveal that Afro-Brazilian men and women demonstrate *negro* linked fate due to different forms and experiences of discrimination and *negro* exclusion.

SUFFERING OR EXCLUSION IN GENERAL

Four respondents believe they are linked to *negros* because of general suffering. They did not mention suffering based on race. Twenty-five percent of respondents are from Salvador, 25 percent from São Paulo and 50 percent from Rio de Janeiro. Fifty percent of the sample are men, and 50 percent are women. Of those with racial information available, all identify as *negro*. The average age is 44. Of those with available data, 66 percent come from low-income households, 34 percent come from high-income households. Sixty-six percent completed high school and 33 percent attend college.

Afro-Brazilian Women Who Feel Linked to *Negros* Due to Social Exclusion

Afro-Brazilian women who feel linked to *negros* because of social exclusion reside in Rio de Janeiro and São Paulo. Both respondents are concerned with employment opportunities and believe that what happens to *negros* affects them because of employment opportunities or one's position in her place of employment. One is a college student, and there is no information for the other respondent (Table 3.3). They state the following:

It affects me. In terms of opportunities such as opportunities for employment and educational opportunities. (39-year-old dark-skinned *negra* woman in college with relaxed hair who resides in Rio de Janeiro)

I am affected in a number of ways, such as my position at work. (an Afro-Brazilian woman in São Paulo)

Similar to women who mention racial discrimination, these women are also largely concerned with employment. The difference is that they do not explicitly mention employment discrimination based on race, nor do they mention how *negros* are racialized.

Afro-Brazilian Men Who Feel Linked to *Negros* Because of Social Exclusion

The two Afro-Brazilian men who believe they are attached to *negros* due to social exclusion have high and medium levels of education (Table 3.4). They are both dark-skinned and from Salvador and the other from Rio de Janeiro. These respondents say they suffer due to class, such as disadvantages in one's financial life or a lack of resources. Feeling attached to *negros* because of class suffering is in line with the common notion that *negros* suffer because of class inequality rather than racial inequality. These respondents come from cities where Afro-Brazilians are at least half the population.

For these respondents, social inequality leads to *negro* linked fate. Responses are below:

Table 3.3 *Afro-Brazilian Women and* Negro *Linked Fate due to Suffering or Exclusion in General*

	Gender	Education	Family Salary (USD)	Age	Skin Color	Racial Identification	Hairstyle
São Paulo	Female	NI	NI	NI	NI	NI	NI
Rio de Janeiro	Female	In college	$813.08–$2,032.68	39	4	*Negra*	Relaxed

Table 3.4 *Afro-Brazilian Men and* Negro *Linked Fate due to Suffering or Exclusion in General*

City	Gender	Education	Family Salary	Age	Skin Color	Racial Identification	Hairstyle
Salvador	Male	Completed high school	Up to $813.08	31	4	*Negro*	Low cut
Rio de Janeiro	Male	Completed college	$4,065.36–$8,130.72	63	5	*Negro*	Low cut

Yes. Because I suffer daily in everything such as at work and in my financial [life]. (31-year-old self-identified *negro* male with a low-cut hairstyle and a dark skin tone who has completed high school and resides in Salvador)

It affects me because of a lack of resources. [I am affected because of] a lack of opportunity. (63-year-old dark-skinned self-identified *negro* man with a college education who wears a low-cut hairstyle and resides in Rio de Janeiro)

In sum, a less popular answer for feeling linked to *negros* is because of social exclusion. Afro-Brazilian women solely focused on employment opportunities, and men focused on difficulties in employment and a lack of resources. In general, they both had medium and high educational levels. Additionally, among those with available skin color information, they are all dark-skinned.

ROLE MODEL

Three respondents believe they were linked to *negros* because they serve as role models (Table 3.5). They all have very high levels of education; all have completed university, and one of them is pursuing a doctoral degree.

Table 3.5 *Afro-Brazilian Men and Women Who Are Linked to* Negros *Because They Serve as a Role Model*

	Gender	Education	Family Salary (USD)	Age	Skin Color	Racial Identification	Hairstyle
Salvador	Female	Completed College	NI	32	4	*Negra*	Cornrows
Salvador	Male	Completed college	$813.08–$2,032.68	30	5.5/6	Black	Low cut
Rio de Janeiro	Male	PhD student	$813.08–$2,032.68	32	4.5	*Negro*	Twist-out

In Salvador, one respondent is a male and the other a female. In Rio de Janeiro, the respondent is an Afro-Brazilian man. Two of these respondents' wear black culturally marked hairstyles (cornrows and a twist-out). These respondents feel a responsibility to serve as role models, and they think this status as a role model links them to *negros*. An example is the quote below of an Afro-Brazilian woman discussing that she serves as a role model to *negro* youth. Afro-Brazilian men also believe they are linked to *negros* because they serve as role models.

I think so, and in the classroom with black youth, I want to help them. They are my brothers and sisters. (32-year-old dark-skinned *negra* woman who has completed college and resides in Salvador)

Yes I have a connection. I have contact [with students at the Steve Biko Cultural Institute]. I come here and I converse with students preparing for the *vestibular*. I am the mirror for them. I can see how I was before and how I am today. (30-year-old dark-skinned black male with a low-cut hairstyle who has completed college and resides in Salvador)

I feel a little sad in the sense of having a responsibility that what happens with the *negro* population and the general Brazilian population. We are at a place together to develop an attitude of defining who we are and the *negro* population needs [that] more than others. (32-year-old *negro* dark-skinned male doctoral student with a twist-out hair-style who resides in Rio de Janeiro)

The finding that *negro* linked fate is based on feeling responsible to the population and serving as a role model is an unexpected finding. This was not the most popular response, yet it is noteworthy that all these respondents live in cities where Afro-Brazilians are a significant portion of the population. The doctoral student also believes that *negros* can define themselves, and he believes self-definition is most needed for this population.

In summary, most Afro-Brazilians feel linked to *negros* because of racial discrimination and exclusion. Afro-Brazilian women discuss discrimination in employment, and when mentioning intersectional identities they mention racial and gender discrimination. Afro-Brazilian men discuss exclusion at the intersection of class and race. They are less concerned with racial discrimination in employment than women are.

NOT DEMONSTRATING *NEGRO* LINKED FATE

In the general sample, 11 respondents did not demonstrate *negro* linked fate. Fifty-five percent of those not demonstrating *negro* linked fate have lower education (less than a high school education). Afro-Brazilian men (73 percent) overwhelmingly make up those with no sense of linked fate. The average age is 35.2. Those that fall in this category tend to choose non-*negro* and non-*preto* identifications. Thirty-six percent of these respondents are from Salvador, 55 percent are from São Paulo, and 9 percent are from Rio de Janeiro. Given the racial demographics of São Paulo, it is surprising that most of the Afro-Brazilians who say they do not feel linked to *negros* reside in São Paulo. One reason for this discrepancy is that the São Paulo survey sample includes a large number of low-income respondents who may not want to be associated with *negros*, as expressed through their non-*negro* identifications. Bailey and Telles (2006) find that those who identify as *moreno* tend to have lower educational levels.

Afro-Brazilian Women Who Did Not Demonstrate *Negro* linked Fate

Afro-Brazilian women who do not feel linked to *negros* tend to identify as *negra*. Sixty-six percent of them identify as *negra* and 34 percent identify as *morena* (Table 3.6). Thirty-three percent wear their hair in black culturally marked hairstyles. These women have a medium level of education; two completed high school, and one still attends high school. Sixty-six percent are dark-skinned, and 34 percent are light-skinned. In this sub-sample, they are all young, with the average age being 19.7. Those with available income data come from low-income households. All respondents had short answers, simply stating "no" or "no, it does not affect me."

Table 3.6 *Afro-Brazilian Women Who Do Not Demonstrate* Negro *Linked Fate*

City	Gender	Education	Family Salary (USD)	Age	Skin Color	Racial Identification	Hairstyle
Salvador	Female	Incomplete high school	Up to $813.08	15	5	*Negra*	Relaxed
São Paulo	Female	Finished high school	NI	20	4	*Negra*	Braids
São Paulo	Female	Finished high school	$813.08–$2,032.68	24	1	*Morena*	Relaxed

Afro-Brazilian Men Who Did Not Demonstrate *Negro* linked Fate

Afro-Brazilian men who did not demonstrate *negro* linked fate have lower educational levels (Table 3.7). In this sub-sample, the average age is 46 years old. Sixty-three percent have less than a high school level of education. Of those for whom skin color information is available, they are all dark-skinned. Eighty-eight percent identify in non-*preto* or non-*negro* categories such as *pardo, cafuso, moreno,* and *mulato*. Despite their dark skin tones, generally they do not identify as *negro*, nor do they feel linked to *negros* as a whole. Many of their responses were terse. However, some of these responses reveal deeply held beliefs, not only in Brazil but throughout Latin America, that if one mentions "race" or color, they are racist (Sue 2013). One example is a 74-year-old self-identified *moreno* man with tightly curled hair who resides in São Paulo. He responds to the question "Do you think what happens to *negros* affects you," saying "No we are all equal." Because he is older, he grew up during a time when simply mentioning "race" was viewed as racist, and the myth of racial democracy was more prevalent in society than today. Another respondent believes that since he is financially secure, he does not feel linked to *negros* and that inequality is class-based.

I don't believe that it affects me a lot today because our salary is guaranteed. The government sends retirement money. The difference is social. (59-year-old dark-skinned self-identified *pardo* man with a low-cut hairstyle who has an incomplete high school education and resides in Salvador)

Two other men also responded in individualistic ways, asserting their personal livelihood and that they are not affected by what happens to *negros*. They stated the following:

Table 3.7 *Afro-Brazilian Men Who Do Not Demonstrate* Negro *Linked Fate*

City	Gender	Education	Family Salary (USD)	Age	Skin Color	Racial Identification	Hairstyle
Salvador	Male	Completed high school	$813.08–$2,032.68	25	5.5	*Preto*	Short curly hair
Salvador	Male	Incomplete high school	Up to $813.08	59	5	*Pardo*	Low cut
Salvador	Male	Incomplete middle school	$813.08–$2,032.68	46	5	*Cafuso*	Low cut
São Paulo	Male	Incomplete middle school	Up to $813.08	74	6	*Moreno*	Crespo
São Paulo	Male	Completed High School	$813.08–$2,032.68	18	4	*Mulato*	Low cut
São Paulo	Male	Completed High School	$813.08–$2,032.68	49	NI	*Pardo*	NI
São Paulo	Male	Incomplete Middle School	NI	28	NI	*Moreno*	NI
Rio de Janeiro	Male	Incomplete middle school	Up to $813.08	69	5	*Pardo*	Low cut

No! Each one lives [their life]. I live in my world. Each one lives in their world. I am not bothered by anyone. (25-year-old dark-skinned *preto* man with short curly hair who has a high school level of education and resides in Salvador)

No, I have freedom to enjoy everything in life. (69-year-old dark-skinned self-identified *pardo* male with a low-cut hairstyle who has an incomplete middle school level of education and resides in Rio de Janeiro)

For these men, they have freedom and live in their "own world" where they are not bothered by others. The 69-year-old Afro-Brazilian man in Rio de Janeiro believes he is not connected to *negros* because he has freedom and can do anything he wants in life. This respondent has a very low level of education, and his family income is in the lowest income bracket. Despite racial inequality in both cities, these respondents do not mention social or racial inequality and do not demonstrate *negro* linked fate.

In sum, most Afro-Brazilians who do not feel attached to *negros* are men. Women had very short answers, making it difficult to fully access why they do not demonstrate *negro* linked fate. An overwhelming number of men identify in non-*negro* and non-*preto* identifications. Many black activists believe that choosing non-*negro* categories is a strategy to deny blackness. If this is the case, it is logical that these men would not feel attached to *negros*. These men believe their individual needs are met, therefore they do not have an attachment to *negros*. In addition, older men dismiss any discussion based on race as racially divisive, so they reaffirm that everyone is equal.

SUMMARY OF IN-DEPTH INTERVIEWS

These in-depth interviews show that most Afro-Brazilian participants demonstrate *negro* linked fate in Salvador, Rio de Janeiro, and São Paulo. *Negro* linked fate is largely due to the experience of racism and *negro* exclusion. Exclusion occurs in the workplace, the media, and leisure spaces. Exclusion and marginalization of the *negro* population, guides whether one feels attached to *negros* as a group. These interviews confirm that, in contemporary Brazil, Afro-Brazilians believe their life chances are profoundly shaped by race and this has a positive impact on *negro* linked fate.

In sum, Afro-Brazilian women who cite discrimination or suffering as a reason for feeling linked to *negros* often mention employment discrimination or discrimination as a barrier to employment. All of these women have some college education. Afro-Brazilian men who feel linked to *negros* because of the experience of exclusion and discrimination had lower levels of education than Afro-Brazilian women. Men were more likely than Afro-Brazilian women to mention the lack of *negro* representation in the media or that when *negros* are represented, it is in a negative light. Unlike Afro-Brazilian women, Afro-Brazilian men mentioned incarceration as demonstrative of *negro* exclusion. Some respondents mentioned multiple identities as magnifying discrimination. Women tended to assert their identities based on race and gender, and men mentioned race and class.

Not all Afro-Brazilians feel linked to *negros*. Most of these respondents self-identify as non-*negro* and non-*preto*. They tend to be less educated. Of those that did not demonstrate *negro* linked fate, they tend to be men. They were also more likely to reside in São Paulo, followed by Rio de Janeiro. Despite living in different cities, men in all three cities had an individualistic way of thinking about their position in life and were personally satisfied. I now turn to quantitative analysis of the determinants of *negro* linked fate based on data collected in Salvador and São Paulo.

PART 2: QUANTITATIVE ANALYSIS OF *NEGRO* LINKED FATE

I rely on original survey data of 674 respondents collected in 2006 in Salvador and São Paulo to examine the determinants of *negro* linked fate. In this section, I test the hypothesis that highly educated and higher income Afro-Brazilians who acknowledge discrimination against *negros* are more likely to display *negro* linked fate than those who have less education, have lower incomes, and do not acknowledge discrimination against *negros*. Descriptive statistics show that 82 percent of Afro-Brazilian respondents in the sample have a sense of *negro* linked fate. Statistical analyses reveal that younger respondents are also more likely to demonstrate *negro* linked fate. I find that respondents in Salvador are more likely to demonstrate *negro* linked fate than respondents in São Paulo. In addition, *negro* linked fate is higher for respondents who self-identify as *negro* or *preto* than other categories.

Descriptive Results of 2006 Survey: Gender, Education, and Age

Fifty-two percent of the respondents are women, and 48 percent are men. The sample's average age is 33, and ages range from 16 to 83. Forty-five percent of the sample in Salvador and 36 percent of the sample in São Paulo had completed some high school education or had finished high school. In Salvador, 15 percent did not complete middle school, and in São Paulo, 24 percent did not do so. Nineteen percent of respondents in Salvador and 14 percent in São Paulo were studying for college entrance exams. In 2006, the minimum monthly salary was 350 Brazilian *reais*. I convert this to the USD based on the OECD's purchasing power parity rate of 1.096. Twenty-six percent of the sample in São Paulo belong to the up to US$638.69 (two minimum salaries) bracket, and 40 percent were in this category in Salvador. Forty-four percent of the Salvador respondents belong to the more than US $638.69–$1596.72 bracket (more than two to five minimum salaries), and 46 percent belong to this category in São Paulo. Twenty-two percent in São Paulo are part of the US$1596.72 to $3193.43 bracket (five to ten minimum monthly salaries), while 12 percent belong to this bracket in Salvador. Although the sample in São Paulo is less educated than the Salvador sample, they earn more money. This is likely due to it being a more developed city.

The color question is an open-ended question. To answer, respondents told the interviewer their color without a list of racial or color categories. Racial or color identifications respondents mentioned are *branco, mulato, moreno claro, pardo, moreno, marrom, moreno jambo, negro,* and *preto.* Education is measured as years of study and includes 1–3 years, 4–7 years, 8–10 years, 11–14 years, and 15 or more years. In general, 1–8 years includes middle school, 9–11 years includes high school, and 12–17 years includes college.

Essential to Dawson's theory of black linked fate is that group attachment exists because of the history of discrimination in the US. Qualitative results reveal that Afro-Brazilians who demonstrate *negro* linked fate overwhelmingly do so because of racial discrimination or exclusion of *negros.* For this reason, I am especially interested in the relationship between *negro* linked fate and acknowledgment of discrimination against *negros.* I expect that respondents with higher incomes and education who believe whites discriminate against *negros* are more likely to demonstrate *negro* linked fate than those with lower incomes and education levels who do not believe that whites discriminate against *negros.* My dependent variable is *negro* linked fate, and my independent variables are discrimination against *negros,* racial identification, gender, age, city, income, and education. This survey did not have a question examining whether the individual respondent has experienced racial discrimination. Therefore, discrimination against *negros* is made operational through a question about white prejudice against *negros.* The survey question is "In your opinion, do whites have prejudice against *negros?* If so, how much?" The options are "yes, there is a lot of prejudice"; "yes, there is a little prejudice;" "yes, there is prejudice but I don't know how much"; and "no, there is no prejudice."

Only 13 percent of respondents said there is no prejudice against *negros*. Twenty percent believe there is prejudice, but they do not know how much. Nineteen percent believe there is a little prejudice against *negros* and 48 percent believe there is a lot of prejudice against *negros*. Throughout this analysis, I refer to this variable as discrimination.

SURVEY RESULTS AND ANALYSIS

In the survey, respondents were asked the question "Do you believe what happens to *negros* affects you?" This question activates the concept of *negro* linked fate, and respondents could answer "yes" or "no." Eighty-two percent of respondents answered yes, thus indicating a high amount of racial solidarity among Afro-Brazilians.

In the logistic regression analysis, *negro* linked fate is the dependent variable and the independent variables are age, gender, racial identification, city, education, income, and discrimination. Age, city, and racial identification are all statistically significant (Table 3.8). In contrast to my expectation, income, education and discrimination are not statistically significant, although discrimination approaches significance.

Racial Identification and *Negro* Linked fate

I ran a simulation to find predicted probabilities of *negro* linked fate varying color/race (Table 3.9). Holding the variables age, gender, city, income, discrimination, and education constant, Afro-Brazilian respondents who identify as *negro* are 1.31 times more likely to demonstrate *negro*

Table 3.8 *Logistic Regression of* Negro *Linked Fate*

	Coefficient	Standard Error
Discrimination	0.46	(0.29)
Age	−0.02*	(0.01)
Gender	−0.11	(0.22)
Racial Identification	1.35***	(0.37)
City	0.62*	(0.23)
Income	−0.16	(0.57)
Education	0.59	(0.46)
Constant	0.54	(0.61)

N 602
*p<0.05 *** p<0.001

Table 3.9 *Predicted Probability of Demonstrating*
Negro *Linked Fate Based on Color*

Branco	0.68
Mulato	0.71
Moreno Claro	0.75
Pardo	0.78
Moreno	0.81
Marrom	0.86
Moreno Jambo	0.88
Negro*	0.89
Preto	0.93

* Two respondents identified as *negão*. These respondents
were added to the *negro* category.

linked fate than Afro-Brazilian respondents who identify as *branco*.
Holding the variables age, gender, city, income, discrimination, and education at their means, Afro-Brazilian respondents who identify as *preto* are
93 percent likely to demonstrate *negro* linked fate. In contrast, holding
these variables at their means, Afro-Brazilians who identify as *mulato* are
71 percent likely to demonstrate linked fate.

City and *Negro* Linked Fate

I ran a simulation holding the independent variables of discrimination, age,
gender, income, and education constant at their means. Afro-Brazilians in São
Paulo are 79 percent likely to demonstrate *negro* linked fate compared to Afro-
Brazilians in Salvador, who are 88 percent likely to demonstrate *negro* linked
fate. This is an unexpected finding. I would expect respondents in Salvador to
demonstrate less *negro* linked fate because of the racial dynamics found in this
predominantly Afro-Brazilian city. I expected Afro-Brazilians to be less unified
in a city where they are the majority and where the common thought is that
there is less discrimination because of their dominant status. In São Paulo, a
city where Afro-Brazilians are a minority, I would expect more racial solidarity.

Age and *Negro* Linked Fate

As age increases, there is less support for *negro* linked fate (Table 3.10). A 33-
year-old, the average age of the sample, is 84 percent likely to demonstrate
negro linked fate. A 50-year-old is 80 percent likely to demonstrate *negro*
linked fate. Compare this to a 67-year-old, who is only 74 percent likely to

Table 3.10 *Likelihood of* Negro *Linked Fate*
by Age (%)

Age	*Negro* linked fate
33	84
50	80
67	74
83	67

demonstrate *negro* linked fate. An 83-year-old respondent is 67 percent likely to demonstrate *negro* linked fate.

It is likely the changing dynamics of racial discourse has an impact on group attachment. Younger Afro-Brazilians are more likely to feel attached to the group. The Brazilian nationalist identity (that everyone is Brazilian and that citizens are not differentiated according to race and ethnicity) continues to exist. However, such discourse is likely much stronger for older generations than younger people. Today's racial discourse acknowledges differences and seeks to include people based on race and class, as is expressed through the state's support of affirmative action and social policies. Interestingly, along with black movement activism, the state's commitment to equality and its recognition of racism may aid Afro-Brazilians perceptions' that discrimination is not only class-based but is also race-based. Younger people are exposed to this racial discourse, which may lead to younger respondents feeling more attached to *negros* than older respondents.

Age, Color, City, and *Negro* Linked Fate

I ran a logistic regression to examine predicted probabilities of respondents demonstrating *negro* linked fate varying racial identification, city, and age but holding education, gender, and income constant at their means. This shows how these variables interact and how demonstrated *negro* linked fate dramatically changes with the interaction of these variables. A 20-year-old respondent living in Salvador who identifies as *negro* is 93 percent likely to demonstrate *negro* linked fate. A 74-year-old respondent residing in São Paulo who identifies as *negro* is 72 percent likely to demonstrate *negro* linked fate. However, a 74-year old respondent residing in São Paulo who identifies as *moreno* is only 59 percent likely to demonstrate *negro* linked fate. The 20-year-old *negro* respondent residing in Salvador is 1.58 times more likely to demonstrate *negro* linked fate than the 74-year-old *moreno* respondent residing in São Paulo.

In sum, an overwhelming percentage of Afro-Brazilian respondents in Salvador and São Paulo display a sense of *negro* linked fate. Age, city, and racial identification all play a role on one's attachment to *negros*. Older respondents are less likely to display *negro* linked fate than younger respondents. Respondents in Salvador are more likely to feel attached to *negros* than respondents in São Paulo. These findings confirm the qualitative data acknowledging that racial identification plays a role on demonstrating *negro* linked fate. Although discrimination is not statistically significant, the variable comes close to reaching significance. The in-depth interviews reveal that respondents that demonstrate *negro* linked fate tend to focus on discrimination and exclusion against *negros*. As long as Afro-Brazilians perceive that their lives are shaped by racial discrimination, I expect them to demonstrate *negro* linked fate.

CONCLUSION

Qualitative and quantitative results reveal that most Afro-Brazilians in Salvador, São Paulo, and Rio de Janeiro, three major cities in Brazil, demonstrate *negro* linked fate. The in-depth interviews reveal those who acknowledge race-based discrimination are more likely to demonstrate *negro* linked fate. Interview responses were grouped into three categories: racial discrimination or *negros* are excluded or suffer, suffering in general, and serving as a role model. In all three cities, respondents that demonstrated *negro* linked fate were likely to say they felt linked to *negros* because of racial discrimination or because *negros* suffer or are excluded in society. Afro-Brazilian women who mentioned the impact of discrimination as a result of multiple identities tended to mention race and gender, while men mentioned race and class. Afro-Brazilian women were more likely to mention discrimination in employment or in hiring. Afro-Brazilian men also mentioned employment discrimination, but it was more common for men than women to mention discrimination in media. Afro-Brazilians who do not demonstrate *negro* linked fate tend to be men, to be less educated, and to identify in non-*negro* and non-*preto* categories. These interview results are rich because they demonstrate how intersectional identities and experiences have an impact on *negro* linked fate.

Survey results are useful at showing general trends in expressing linked fate. The limitation of the survey data is that the survey question asks if respondents think whites are prejudiced against *negros*. Unfortunately, it did not include a survey question about their personal experiences of color discrimination. Nonetheless, the statistical analyses demonstrate that Afro-Brazilians who identify as *negro* or *preto* have a higher probability of demonstrating *negro* linked fate than those identifying as non-*negro* and non-*preto*. This is consistent with interview results. Older respondents are less likely to demonstrate linked fate than younger respondents, and respondents residing in Salvador are more likely to demonstrate linked fate than respondents in São Paulo. Interview results were largely led by respondents in Rio de Janeiro, making it difficult to compare interview results and survey results in terms of cities. The consistent finding is that in the cities with high proportions of Afro-Brazilians, such as Salvador and Rio de Janeiro, there were higher numbers of respondents with *negro* linked fate than in São Paulo. This result is surprising given city demographics where Afro-Brazilians are a majority, thus I expected less group cohesion.

Telles and Bailey (2013) find that a large majority of white Brazilians and Afro-Brazilians (referred to as "dominants" versus "minorities" in their article) attributed poverty of blacks to structural racism, and most did not blame individuals. In Brazil, however, Afro-descendants were 1.5 times more likely to acknowledge the unequal treatment of Afro-descendants than whites. They believe this divergence is due to racial policies such as affirmative action, in which there may be an emergence of conflicting racial interests between dominants and minorities. My study of Afro-Brazilians reveals nuances in how Afro-descendants believe they are treated differently and how differential treatment results in a sense of group identity.

Afro-Brazilians acknowledge that racism and exclusion is race-based, not simply class-based. As citizens continue to believe exclusion is based on race, mobilizing around racial identification will become easier. Past work noted the difficulty of mobilizing when the predominant societal belief held that discrimination was based on class and that racism was not a serious issue in Brazil (Hanchard 1994; Twine 1998). Today, Brazil is a different country: race-based policies have been enacted and people more openly discuss race. Yet race plays an ever-present role in shaping the economic, political, and social circumstances of Afro-Brazilians, thus giving potential rise to *negro* linked fate.

4

Negro Linked Fate and Racial Policies

In this chapter I examine the impact of *negro* linked fate on political behavior and opinion. I use the original 2006 survey to analyze the impact of *negro* linked fate on support for affirmative action and support for teaching black culture in schools. Implemented in 2003, Law 10.639/03 requires that schools teach African and Afro-Brazilian history. I focus on political opinions about three issues: affirmative action in universities and employment, the teaching of Afro-Brazilian history, and whether the president should nominate *negros* for political positions. Nominating Afro-Brazilians is not a federal policy; however, I asked the survey question to gauge if respondents believe this is important. As mentioned earlier in the book, former President Lula appointed four Afro-Brazilians to national positions. However, after President Dilma Rousseff was removed from office and Michel Temer took over the presidency, his initial appointees were all white males. There was public outcry at his blatant dismissal of the importance of diversity. Examining the relationship between *negro* linked fate and policies that have an impact on Afro-Brazilians is important so that policy studies are understood not only in an individual sense where individual demographic information is taken into consideration, but also variables that take into account whether one's interest considers group interests. The concept of *negro* linked fate is a variable that considers group attachment.

My three hypotheses concern the role of *negro* linked fate in supporting racial policies. I expect Afro-Brazilians with a sense of *negro* linked fate to be more likely to support racial policies than those without a sense of *negro* linked fate. More specifically, the first hypothesis is that Afro-Brazilians with a sense of *negro* linked fate will be more likely to support affirmative action than those with no linked fate. The second hypothesis is that Afro-Brazilians with a sense of *negro* linked fate and higher socioeconomic status (as measured by education and income) will be more likely to support the teaching of Afro-Brazilian history in schools. The third hypothesis is that Afro-Brazilians with a sense of *negro* linked fate and higher socioeconomic status as measured by education and income will be more likely to support the idea that the president should nominate *negros* to positions within the government. In 2013, the Constitution and Justice Commission of the House of Deputies approved quotas for Afro-Brazilian parliamentarians in the house and legislative assemblies (Neri 2013). To date, Brazil does not have political quotas for Afro-Brazilians.

A BRIEF HISTORY OF QUOTAS IN UNIVERSITIES

Affirmative action policies in the form of quotas in universities were first implemented at the State University of Rio de Janeiro in 2003. These policies were for Afro-Brazilian and Indigenous students who attended public high schools. While there has been continued debate, affirmative action policies have been successful at democratizing elite public universities in that they provide an opportunity for low-income Afro-Brazilian students to earn college degrees. Penha-Lopes (2013) notes that quota students entering the State University of Rio de Janeiro faced challenges, such as transportation costs not sufficiently covered by short-term scholarships, a steep learning curve because of the courses' heavy reading loads, and, in some cases, racism from other students and professors. However, some professors and administrators support the presence of quota students and admit that these students are more engaged and motivated in the classroom. Quota students in Penha-Lopes's study, and in general, have been quite academically successful. Even considering admission criteria such as the *vestibular*, these students actually outperformed non-quota students in some areas of study. Valente and Berry (2017) rely on college exit exams and find that in public and private universities, quota students outperform non-quota students in a number of areas of study. They attribute the ProUni scholarship to quota students outperforming non-quota students at private universities because these students have to maintain certain grades to maintain the scholarship. The ProUni program, or University for All program, was established in 2005 and provides scholarships to low-income students attending private universities. I mention these results because opponents believe that having quotas lowers the quality of the university, but this is not the case.

In 2012 President Dilma Rousseff passed legislation specifying that all federal public universities would have four years to enact quotas for black and indigenous students: in 2022 the program will be re-evaluated. Before passing this legislation, the Supreme Court unanimously voted on the constitutionality of quotas in universities. Penha-Lopes (2013) notes that this decision came after multiple events organized by quota advocates.

It is important to note Dietrich's (2015) findings that in 2013 only 26 percent of students in higher education studied at public universities and 74 percent studied at private universities. Of those at public universities, only 15.5 percent of all students studied at public federal universities (Dietrich 2015: 155). In other words, most students studying at public universities are enrolled at public state universities. In 2009, only 11 percent of non-white students 18–24 years old, compared to 28 percent of white students in the same age bracket, entered university (Dietrich 2015: 161).

Penha-Lopes (2013) details the context leading up to Rousseff's 2012 legislation. In 2011, the Secretariat of Policies for the Promotion of Racial Equality (SEPPIR) announced the creation of a course considering race and gender to train managers. The course was to be made available in eighteen federal public universities, and it was expected that 6,700 people would graduate. The Public Ministry of the Union (*Ministério Público da União*) announced ethnic-racial quotas for internships. They had already reserved spots for people with disabilities. To be considered for a quota spot, candidates needed to prove they attended public schools. In the same year the Federal Supreme Court (*Supremo Tribunal Federal*) announced it would release a judgment about the legitimacy of racial quotas in universities the following month. On June 1, Luiza Bairros, the minister of SEPPIR, presented an amendment to the National Plan of Education that included fifty items concerning access to education. In June 2011, Sérgio Cabral, the governor of Rio de Janeiro, signed a decree that reserved 20 percent of public state courses for black and indigenous people. These quotas were meant to allow quota students who graduated from universities the opportunity to gain state government jobs. Penha-Lopes notes that Mato Grosso do Sul and Paraná have had quotas for public courses since 2003. In July 2011, quota students who received scholarships from ProUni would only have to pay half of bus fares in Rio de Janeiro. It was in this climate that the Supreme Court made their ruling verifying the constitutionality of quotas, and then President Rousseff passed legislation regarding quotas for all federal public universities.

According to the Brazilian Institute of Political Opinion and Statistics (Instituto Brasileiro de Opinião Pública e Estatística; IBOPE) survey by the *Data Folha de São Paulo* newspaper, in the year 2013, 62 percent of Brazilians supported quotas. There was more support for student quotas based on income or origin of school, and less support based on color. Of the respondents, 77 percent supported quotas based on income, 77 percent supported quotas based on origin of school, and only 64 percent supported quotas based on color. The opposition to quotas for poor students, black students, and students from public schools tended to come from whites, Brazilians in Classes A and B (wealthy and upper classes), those with university degrees, and those in capitals in the North and Central-West regions. The most support for quotas came from those who had five to eight years of study (the equivalent of elementary to middle school), those in the emerging Class C (the lower middle class), and those living in the Northeast and cities in the interior areas of the country (Toledo 2013).

It appears that today most Brazilians support quota programs. However, as previously mentioned there are differences in support depending on the beneficiaries. These findings are based on a general examination of the Brazilian population. I am interested in Afro-Brazilian support for quotas. I expect a large percentage of Afro-Brazilians to support the program, given the general findings that those in the newly emerging Class C (of which Afro-Brazilians make up a significant proportion) are most likely to support affirmative action. I will consider whether Afro-Brazilians with *negro* linked fate are more supportive of affirmative action programs. In my survey I use the term affirmative action to refer to quota programs. Considering the high level of *negro* linked fate in the 2006 survey findings and the in-depth interview findings that linked fate stems from racial discrimination and *negro* suffering, it is likely that *negro* linked fate will serve as a strong predictor of affirmative action, a program aimed at addressing racial discrimination. Thus my hypothesis is that Afro-Brazilians who demonstrate *negro* linked fate are more likely to support affirmative action policies than those with no sense of *negro* linked fate.

SURVEY STATISTICS

I use the same 2006 original survey as used in the previous chapter. In this case, experience of race is made operational with the concept of *negro* linked fate. The survey question regarding affirmative action is "Affirmative action is a program that focuses on discrimination against *negros* and *pardos*. It tries to encourage universities and workplaces to have a higher percentage of *negros* and *pardos*. Do you believe affirmative action programs are important?"[1] My dependent variable is support for affirmative action, and my independent

---

[1] Ação afirmativa é um programa que enfoca o problema da discriminação contra negros e pardos. Ela tenta incentivar que nas universidades e no trabalho tenha uma porcentagem maior de negros e pardos. Você acredita que programas de ação afirmativa são importantes?

variables are gender, income, racial identification, age, *negro* linked fate, education, and city. Before analyzing *negro* linked fate and support of racial policies, I describe how my variables are measured. Education is measured as years of education. Education is coded as 0 (one to three years), 0.25 (four to seven years), 0.5 (eight to ten years), 0.75 (eleven to fourteen years), and 1 (more than fifteen years). Income is coded as no income (0), up to two minimum monthly salaries (0.25), two to five monthly minimum salaries (0.50), five to ten minimum monthly salaries (0.75), and ten to twenty monthly minimum salaries (1).[2] An open-ended question asked regarding color, elicited the following categories: white (*branco*), mixed-race (*mulato*), *moreno claro, moreno, moreno jambo, marrom*, the census category for mixed-race (*pardo*), *negro*, and the census category *preto*. They are coded as *branco* (0), *mulato* (0.13), *moreno claro* (0.26), *pardo* (0.39), *moreno* (0.52), *marrom* (0.65), *moreno jambo* (0.78), *negro* (0.91), and *preto* (1).

COLOR AND RACE

Respondents were asked to identify their color in an open-ended question. In the open-ended question they could identify a color category with words of their own choosing. Considering the open-ended color categories of the entire sample, 1 percent identify as *moreno claro*, 2 percent identify as *mulato*, 4 percent identify as *branco*, 15 percent identify as *preto*, 18 percent identify as *pardo*, 19 percent identify as *moreno*, and 41 percent identify as *negro* (Table 4.1). Identifying in a non-*negro* or non-*preto* category allows one to acknowledge racial mixture, which is part of Brazil's national identity. *Moreno* is an ambiguous category with which nearly any Brazilian can self-identify, including a range that includes those with dark skin to those with very light skin. *Pardo* is a census category acknowledging racial mixture. *Moreno claro* translates as light brown. The English translation of *moreno escuro* is dark brown. *Mulato* is mixed-race. Table 4.1 gives the percentage results of respondents identifying in the open-ended question.

Overall, *negro* is the most claimed category (Table 4.2). Considering open-ended color categories, in Salvador, the most popular category is *negro*, followed by *pardo* and *moreno*. In São Paulo, *negro* is the most popular category, followed by *moreno*, and *pardo*.

---

[2] In 2006 the minimum monthly salary was 350 Brazilian reais. I convert this to USD based on the OECD's purchasing power parity rate of 1.096. Two monthly minimum salaries equates to US$638.69.

Table 4.1 *Color/Race of Respondents in 2006 Original Survey*

Color/Racial Category	Percentage of 2006 Survey
Branco	4
Mulato	2
Moreno Claro	1
Pardo	18
Moreno	19
Marrom	0
Moreno Jambo	0
Negro	41
Preto	15
Total	100

Table 4.2 *Number of Afro-Brazilian respondents in Salvador and São Paulo by Color/Race*

Salvador		São Paulo	
Color and Racial Categories		Color and Racial Categories	
Branco	8	Branco	20
Mulato	8	Mulato	4
Moreno Claro	3	Moreno Claro	6
Pardo	64	Pardo	52
Moreno	45	Moreno	79
Marrom	1	Marrom	1
Moreno Jambo	0	Moreno Jambo	1
Negro*	154	Negro*	111
Preto	55	Preto	40
Total	338	Total	314

* Two respondents identified as *negão*. These respondents were added to the *negro* category.

Logistic Regression of *Negro* Linked Fate and Affirmative Action

My expectation is that Afro-Brazilian respondents with a sense of *negro* linked fate are more likely to support affirmative action than those without a sense of *negro* linked fate. A cross tabulation of the sample reveals that 70 percent of the sample support affirmative action and 30 percent of respondents do not.

In the logistic regression analysis, affirmative action is the dependent variable; the independent variables are city, income, education, *negro* linked fate, racial identification, gender, and age. *Negro* linked fate, city, and age are all statistically significant variables (Table 4.3). Younger people are more likely to support affirmative action than older people. Results also show that

Table 4.3 *Logistic Regression Analysis:* Negro *Linked Fate and Support for Affirmative Action*

	Logistic regression of support for affirmative action	
	Coefficient	Standard Error
Negro linked fate	1.08***	(0.24)
Gender	-0.17	(0.19)
Income	0.76	(0.48)
Color	-0.15	(0.34)
Age	-0.02**	(0.01)
Education	0.43	(0.40)
City	-0.66***	(0.20)
Constant	0.58	(0.53)

** P <0.01 *** p<0.001
N 600

respondents in São Paulo are more likely to support affirmative action than those in Salvador.

Negro Linked Fate and Support for Affirmative Action

To provide a sense of the impact *negro* linked fate has on support for affirmative action, I report the predicted probability of support depending on whether one demonstrates *negro* linked fate. Holding all independent variables constant at their means, a respondent with a sense of *negro* linked fate is 76 percent likely to support affirmative action, while respondents with no sense of *negro* linked fate are only 52 percent likely to do so. As noted earlier, and as evidenced in the regression analysis, *negro* linked fate is a better predictor of support for affirmative action than racial identification, which is not statistically significant. In short, a respondent with a sense of *negro* linked fate is 1.46 times more likely to support affirmative action than a respondent without a sense of *negro* linked fate. In-depth interviews confirm the idea that *negro* linked fate is largely due to racial discrimination and *negro* exclusion. For this reason, it is possible that these respondents are more supportive of the policy.

Age and Support for Affirmative Action

As age increases, there is less support for affirmative action. Perhaps this is due to the fact that younger people are more exposed to the discourse of quotas in contemporary society. Younger people may be more willing to

Table 4.4 *Age Predicted Probability of Support for Affirmative Action*

Age	% Likelihood of Support for Affirmative Action
16	78
33	73
50	67
67	60
83	54

realize that such measures are necessary, whereas older respondents may believe the problem of inequality is due to class and are thus less willing to support affirmative action programs based on race.

I created simulations of predicted probabilities of support for affirmative action based on age. As can be seen in Table 4.4, in general, support is relatively high, but a 16-year-old is 78 percent likely to support affirmative action compared to an 83-year-old who is only 54 percent likely to support affirmative action. In other words, a 16-year-old is roughly 1.4 times more likely than an 83-year-old to support affirmative action.

City and Support for Affirmative Action

A respondent in São Paulo is 79 percent likely to support affirmative action, while a respondent residing in Salvador is only 66 percent likely to support affirmative action. Although, support in Salvador is still quite high, I believe support in São Paulo is higher because Afro-Brazilians are a minority in the city and are aware of the difficulties of access to higher education and employment because this is clearly visible in a city where they are the minority.

Support for Affirmative Action Based on *Negro* Linked Fate, City, and Age

I now consider how the variables *negro* linked fate, city, and age interact to demonstrate differences in support for affirmative action. Rather than simply report probabilities of support based on respondents of the same age in both cities, I analyze the results by varying age and city to demonstrate differences in support of affirmative action. Considering all statistically significant variables, a 23-year-old Afro-Brazilian respondent residing in São Paulo who demonstrates *negro* linked fate is 84 percent likely to support

Table 4.5 *Likelihood of Support for Affirmative Action Considering City, Age, and Negro Linked Fate*

City	Age	Demonstrated *Negro* Linked Fate	% Likelihood of Support for Affirmative Action
Salvador	55	No	36
São Paulo	55	No	52
Salvador	23	Yes	74
São Paulo	23	Yes	84

affirmative action (Table 4.5). However, an Afro-Brazilian respondent in Salvador who is 55 years of age and does not share a sense of *negro* linked fate is only 36 percent likely to support affirmative action. This is a difference of 48 percentage points!

Results confirm the idea that *negro* linked fate is an important pre-dictor of support for affirmative action. This is a significant finding because as Afro-Brazilians become more cognizant of exclusion against *negros* and identify as a group based on this exclusion, they may push for policies that seek redress as a racially excluded group. As more Afro-Brazilians are educated and acknowledge racial discrimination as such, there is a greater possibility of feeling linked to others because of similar experiences.

A BRIEF CONTEXT OF LAW 10.639/03

Law 10.639/03 was passed in 2003. This law makes teaching about African and Afro-Brazilian history and culture mandatory in primary and high schools. The law was passed in an earlier climate of re-democratization in which social movements increasingly put demands on the state. Other important educational reforms accompanied it, such as the Law of Guidelines and Bases no 9.394 (*Lei de Diretrizes e Bases no 9.394*) of 1996, which addressed the flexibility of curriculum, valued inclusion and diversity in education, and reaffirmed the instructor's autonomy (Pereira 2008). Henriques (2005) notes that racism takes place in schools because of the way blacks are naturalized as inferior and whites are naturalized as superior. Educational material mostly discusses blacks during the period of slavery and illustrates that they are subservient and not in socially privileged positions. The pedagogy in schools is Eurocentric and involves racist socialization (Henriques 2005: 13).

Black movement activists challenged these prevalent stereotypes by advocating for the teaching of African and Afro-Brazilian history in schools. The law was the result of black movement activism that sought to challenge negative stereotypes of blacks in schools (Santos 2014). Amilcar Pereira (2015) also places black movement activists at the center of advocacy for the Law of Teaching African and Afro-Brazilian History and Culture. He cites Abdias do Nascimento's (1989) book, Brazil, Mixture or Massacre? Essays in the Genocide of a Black People, in which it is shown that the education system contributed to cultural discrimination because African culture and the development of Africa were not taught in schools. As part of the National Convention of the Black by the Constituent Assembly (*Convenção Nacional do Negro pela Constituinte*) in Brasilia in 1986, black movement organizations specifically demanded that schools be obligated to teach African and Afro-Brazilian History (Santos 2014: 24). Throughout Brazil, states and municipalities introduced and passed laws forbidding the use of racist texts in schools and sought the inclusion of African and Afro-Brazilian history in schools. These concerns were addressed in the State Constitution of Bahia in 1989, in Belo Horizonte in 1990, and in the municipality of Porto Alegre in Rio Grande do Sul in 1991. Thus, these states and municipalities set a precedent for such federal legislation because of the pressure black movement activists put on state and city governments. The expectation is that by valorizing Afro-Brazilians in school curriculum, attitudes about Afro-Brazilians in society will change since schools are major forces in the socialization of children. In my analysis, I consider two questions dealing with teaching Afro-Brazilian history in schools, and I run two different logistic regression analyses.

Logistic Regression of Teaching Afro-Brazilian History in Schools

Law 10.639/03 is an example of another racial policy enacted in Brazil. Many teachers were, and many still are, ill-prepared to teach it because they lack resources such as texts dealing with Afro-Brazilian and African history, or they have not received training on how to discuss sensitive topics such as race and discrimination. However, some teachers have participated in training programs in order to learn how to incorporate such teachings into their curricula. Some teachers are open to embracing blackness, while others are resistant and do not believe they should have to integrate African and Afro-Brazilian history into their courses. This is the current context of the policy. The 2006 survey question asked "Do you

Table 4.6 *Logistic Regression of Support for Teaching Black History in Schools*

	Coefficient	Standard Error
Negro linked fate	2.20***	(0.43)
Gender	-0.25	(0.41)
Income	1.40	(0.99)
Color	0.91	(0.70)
Age	0.02	(0.02)
Education	-1.05	(0.83)
City	1.07**	(0.47)
Constant	0.21	(1.12)

N 593
**p<0.05 ***p<0.001

think children should go to schools that teach Afro-Brazilian history?" My hypothesis is that respondents who demonstrate *negro* linked fate and those with higher education are more likely to support teaching Afro-Brazilian history in schools than those with no sense of linked fate and lower levels of education. Although they are not statistically significant, interestingly, income and education work in opposite directions among respondents. The more education a person has, the less likely he or she is to agree that Afro-Brazilian history should be taught in schools. In contrast, the more income a person has the more likely he or she is to believe Afro-Brazilian history should be taught in schools. Respondents in Salvador are more likely to support this policy than respondents in São Paulo. Given that Salvador is known as the cradle of Afro-Brazilian culture, this is no surprise. Ninety-five percent of the sample agrees that Afro-Brazilian history should be taught in schools, thus there is little difference in the sample. The regression analysis shows that *negro* linked fate is a predictor of support for teaching Afro-Brazilian history in schools (Table 4.6). Respondents who demonstrate affinity with *negro* linked fate are more likely to support the policy than those with none. City is also statistically significant. Respondents in Salvador are more likely to support the policy than those in São Paulo.

Negro Linked Fate and Teaching Afro-Brazilian History in Schools

A respondent who demonstrates *negro* linked fate is 98 percent likely to support Afro-Brazilian history in schools when holding all other independent variables constant at their means. A respondent with no sense of *negro* linked fate is 86 percent likely to support the policy. While this percentage is high, this is a difference of 12 percentage points.

City and Teaching Afro-Brazilian History in Schools

A simulation of predicted probabilities shows support for teaching Afro-Brazilian history in public schools is nearly the same in São Paulo (96 percent) and in Salvador (98 percent).

Negro Linked Fate, City, and Support for Teaching Afro-Brazilian History in Schools

A respondent residing in Salvador with a sense of *negro* linked fate is 99 percent likely to support the policy, holding all other independent variables constant at their means (Table 4.7). Support decreases to 79 percent for a respondent residing in São Paulo with no sense of *negro* linked fate, holding all other independent variables constant at their means. While support is still high, these simulations demonstrate important intersections of demographic variables and highlight the role of *negro* linked fate.

While it is puzzling that the combined factors of income and education did not have an impact on support for teaching Afro-Brazilian history in schools, this is likely the result of the overwhelming percentage of the sample that supports the policy. I did not expect one's city to have an impact on support for the policy. However because of Salvador's historic and contemporary role as the source of Afro-Brazilian culture, it is no wonder that Afro-Brazilians in Salvador are more likely to support the policy than those in São Paulo. My expectation was partially correct about

Table 4.7 *City,* Negro *Linked Fate, and Support for Teaching Afro-Brazilian History in Schools*

City	Demonstrated *Negro* Linked Fate	Likelihood of Support for Teaching Afro-Brazilian History in Schools
Salvador	No	91
São Paulo	No	79
Salvador	Yes	99
São Paulo	Yes	97

the role of *negro* linked fate's predictive power on support for the racial
policy of teaching Afro-Brazilian history in schools.

The Importance of Political Candidates Discussing Preservation of *Negro* History in Schools

I consider another survey question from the 2006 original survey to
examine teaching *negro* history in schools. The survey question states,
"In the 2004 municipal elections did you think it was important that
candidates running for city council discuss the preservation of *negro*
history in schools?" Survey options were very important, important, a little
important, and not important.[3] I ran an ordered logistic regression where
preserving *negro* history was the dependent variable. Independent variables are *negro* linked fate, racial/color identification, income, education,
gender, and age.

My hypothesis is that respondents demonstrating *negro* linked fate and
highly educated respondents will believe it is important that political
candidates discuss preserving *negro* history in schools. The ordered logistic regression reveals that *negro* linked fate, racial identification, income,
education, age, and gender are all statistically significant. Unlike the
logistic regression where only *negro* linked fate and city are statistically
significant, in the ordered logistic regression analysis, income and education are statistically significant (Table 4.8). Respondents with a sense of
negro linked fate are 53 percent more likely to believe preserving *negro*
history in schools is important than those with no sense of linked fate.
Respondents with higher incomes are 17 percent less likely to support
preserving *negro* history in schools than respondents with lower incomes.
As education increases, respondents are 326 percent more likely to agree
that political candidates should discuss preserving *negro* history than
those with lower educational levels. Older respondents compared to
younger respondents are 2 percent more likely to support *negro* history
in schools. Respondents in Salvador are 142 percent more likely to support preserving *negro* history than respondents in São Paulo.

Education and income go in different directions, which is puzzling. It is
understandable that respondents with more education would support

---

[3] Nas eleições municipais de 2004, você achou que foi importante que os candidatos que
concorreram para vereador discutissem: A preservação da historia negra nas escolas.
Muito importante, Importante, Um pouco importante, Não importante.

Table 4.8 *Odds Ratio from Ordered Logistic of Importance of Preserving* Negro *History in Schools*

Independent Variables	
Negro Linked Fate	1.53*
	(0.32)
Racial/Color Identification	0.98
	(0.28)
Income	0.17***
	(0.07)
Education	4.26***
	(1.49)
Gender	1.25
	(0.20)
Age	1.02*
	(0.01)
City	2.42***
	0.41

Pseud R2 0.0562
N 601
*P<0.05 **P<0.01 ***P<0.001
Note: Numbers in parenthesis are standard errors

preserving *negro* history in schools as they may be more familiar with black movement racial discourse. It is also possible that they are more likely to acknowledge the absence of Afro-Brazilian history in higher education as opposed to respondents who do not have higher levels of education and are unexposed to the educational underrepresentation of Afro-Brazilians. Because there is usually a positive correlation of income and education, it is not clear why these results are in the opposite direction.

While I would expect younger respondents to be more concerned with *negro* history in schools than older respondents, it is possible that younger people are less confident that a political candidate will keep their promises to discuss certain issues.

NOMINATING *NEGROS* IN NATIONAL POLITICS

Former President Luis Inácio Lula da Silva made unprecedented strides as he nominated Afro-Brazilians to federal political office. In 2003, SEPPIR was created and President Lula appointed Matilde Ribeiro to

Table 4.9 *Logistic Regression of Support for the Presidential Nomination of* Negros
to Important Positions

	Coefficient	Standard Error
Negro linked fate	1.52***	(0.32)
Gender	-0.13	(0.30)
Income	2.05***	(0.76)
Color	0.76	(0.52)
Age	-0.00	(0.01)
Education	-1.06*	(0.61)
City	0.66**	(0.32)
Constant	0.38	(0.83)

*p<0.10 **p<0.05 ***p<0.001
N 581

preside. This was unprecedented because no other president had nominated so many Afro-Brazilians to such high positions. Former President
Dilma Rousseff, Lula's handpicked successor, was elected from the Worker's
Party but did not appoint such a large number of Afro-Brazilians. In fact, she
only nominated Luiza Bairros (as minister of SEPPIR). Since blacks are
underrepresented in politics, President Lula's nominations helped increase
black representation at the national level. I am interested to see whether
Afro-Brazilians think nominating *negros* is important and whether *negro*
linked fate has an impact on the support of the nomination of *negros*. In
general, my survey demonstrates that 90 percent of respondents believe it is
important for the president to nominate blacks; 10 percent do not agree.

Those with a sense of *negro* linked fate are more likely to believe
it is important for the president to nominate *negros* to positions in the
government[4] (Table 4.9). As income increases, so does support for the president to nominate *negros*. In contrast, as education increases, support for the
president to make black nominations decreases. Respondents residing in
Salvador are more likely to support the nomination of *negros* than respondents
in São Paulo.

Negro Linked Fate and Support for Nominating *Negros*

Respondents with a sense of *negro* linked fate are 95 percent likely to
support Afro-Brazilian nominations from the president, while those

---

[4] Você acredita que é importante que o presidente nomeie negros para posições no governo?

without a sense of *negro* linked fate are 79 percent more likely to share that feeling. Here again, *negro* linked fate is a better predictor of support than racial identification. Moreover, it is likely that those who feel attached to *negros* as a racial group are more likely to support such a policy because the assumption is that Afro-Brazilians holding prestigious political positions can have a greater impact on Afro-Brazilian communities. Even those without a sense of *negro* linked fate overwhelmingly support such a proposition, quite telling of the Afro-Brazilian sample in Salvador and São Paulo.

Income and Support for Nominating *Negros*

Support that the president should nominate *negros* increases as income increases. A respondent with no family income is 84 percent likely to think it is important that the president nominate *negros* to important positions. A respondent with a family income of up to two monthly minimum salaries is 90 percent likely to support the president nominating *negros*, while a respondent in the family income bracket of two to five times the minimum salary is 94 percent likely to demonstrate support. Finally, respondents in the five to ten times minimum salary income bracket are 96 percent likely to support the policy, while a respondent in the ten to twenty minimum salaries income bracket is 97 percent likely to support such a policy.

Education and Support for Nominating *Negros*

Even though there is less support for the idea that the president should nominate *negros* as education increases, support is still very high (Table 4.10). A respondent with one to three years of schooling is 96 percent likely to support this policy, while this drops to 89 percent for respondents with 15 or more years of schooling, the equivalent of graduate level or post-baccalaureate education.

Afro-Brazilians across all educational levels overwhelmingly support this policy; however, the decrease in support based on the educational attainment of the respondent is notable. It is possible that Afro-Brazilians with higher levels of education believe politicians should be selected solely based on merit. In fact, Mitchell-Walthour (2015) finds that Afro-Brazilian support for affirmative action decreases with more education, which gives credence to this idea.

Table 4.10 *Education and Support for the President
Nominating* Negros *to Political Positions*

Years of Education	Support for the President Nominating *Negros* (%)
1–3	96
4–7	95
8–10	94
11–14	92
15 or more	89

Table 4.11 *Interaction of City,* Negro *Linked Fate, Income, and Education*

City	Income Level	Education Level	Demonstrated *Negro* Linked Fate	Likelihood of Support of President Nominating *Negros*
Salvador	Lowest	Lowest (1–3 years)	No	90
Salvador	Highest (10–20 times minimum salary)	Highest (15 or more years)	Yes	98
São Paulo	Lowest (no family salary)	Lowest (1-3 years)	No	65
São Paulo	Lowest	Lowest (1-3 years)	Yes	96

City and Support for Nominating *Negros*

Respondents in São Paulo are 90 percent likely to support the policy, while respondents in Salvador are 95 percent likely to do so. The difference is only 5 percent, but is unexpected.

Interaction of City, *Negro* Linked Fate, Income, and Education

To provide a sense of the impact that statistically significant variables such as city, *negro* linked fate, income, and education have on support for presidential nominations of *negros*, I created a simulation of predicted probabilities of support for nominating *negros*. Age, racial identification, and gender are held constant at their means. A respondent in Salvador with a sense of *negro* linked fate, with the highest income level (10 to 20 times the minimum salary) and with the highest level of education (15 or more years of education) is 98 percent likely to support the idea that the president should nominate *negros* to important positions (Table 4.11). A respondent in Salvador not demonstrating *negro* linked fate in the lowest income bracket with the lowest level of education (one to three years) is 90 percent likely to support the policy. However, this drops significantly, to 65 percent, for a respondent in São Paulo with no sense of *negro* linked fate, with the lowest income (no family salary) and with an education level of one to three years. Support rises to 96 percent for a similar respondent who resides in São Paulo who demonstrates *negro* linked fate in the lowest income bracket and has the lowest level of education. These simulations show that *negro* linked fate is a strong predictor of support that the president nominate *negros*.

SUMMARY

Negro linked fate is a powerful predictor of support for racial policies such as affirmative action and teaching Afro-Brazilian culture in schools. It is also a powerful predictor of support that political candidates should discuss preserving *negro* history in schools and that the president should nominate *negros* to political office. Respondents that demonstrate *negro* linked fate are more likely to support these policies and ideas than those with no sense of *negro* linked fate. There are two findings that are contradictory. Respondents with higher income are less supportive of political candidates discussing the preservation of *negro* history in school, and those with higher levels of education are more likely to support preserving *negro* history in schools. Similarly, as education increases, there is less support for the president nominating Afro-Brazilians to political office, while as income increases, there is a greater chance that respondents support the president nominating Afro-Brazilians.

While there is no such policy for the president to nominate *negros* to important positions, it is useful to examine whether this is important to Afro-Brazilians, especially considering the significant underrepresentation of Afro-Brazilians in politics. As Afro-Brazilians make more demands on government and politicians, is it possible they will expect more Afro-Brazilian representation and hold the president accountable? As Brazil continues its anti-corruption campaign, it is not clear if diversity is at the forefront of politics. If Michel Temer's initial choice of only white males as cabinet appointees is any indication, there is need to worry that diversity and commitment to racial policies will wane as important issues. Yet as racial discourse among everyday people and activists point out glaring omissions of segments of the population, this may lead to more *negro* linked fate and, in turn, more advocacy of racial policies.

Afro-Descendants Perceptions of Discrimination
and Support for Affirmative Action

In this chapter I examine Latin American Afro-descendants' support of affirmative action policy based on racial identification, perception of discrimination, and skin color. Ideally I would examine support of affirmative action based on *negro* linked fate. However, the 2012 LAPOP survey does not include such a question. I examine Latin American countries that have enacted some form of racial policy for Afro-descendant populations. Land entitlement for Afro-descendants and university affirmative action are examples of racial policies. Examples of affirmative action are affirmative action in university admissions and scholarships for Afro-Honduran students to attend university established in 2007. In 2006, the Ministry of Education and Culture in Uruguay instituted a scholarship for Afro-descendants to continue postgraduate study (Hernandez 2013). In addition, some Latin American countries such as Ecuador, Guatemala, Honduras, Nicaragua, Bolivia, Brazil, and Colombia instituted legislation to assist Afro-descendant rural populations (Paschel 2016). Tianna Paschel (2016) finds that Colombia is at the forefront of land entitlement when compared to Brazil and Honduras.

Afro-descendants are 30 percent of the population in Latin America but are over half the poor (Morrison 2007). Eighty percent of Afro-Colombians live below the poverty line (Hernandez 2013: 75). More than 60 percent of Indigenous and Afro-descendant people are poor in Bolivia, Honduras, and Nicaragua (Morrison 2012). Brazil's Afro-descendant population is 53 percent. The Afro-descendant population is 4 percent in Nicaragua, 1 percent in Honduras, 2 percent in Bolivia, and 10.5 percent in Colombia (Santana 2013). There are discrepancies between official statistics of Afro-descendant populations and estimates of activists. Minority Rights Group International (2014) estimates that the Afro-descendant population in Colombia ranges from 10.6 percent to 26 percent. Some states in Colombia are heavily Afro-descendant. The Choco state is over 80 percent Afro-descendant, and its capital, Quibdo, is 95 percent Afro-Colombian. As the case of Colombia demonstrates, there is inconsistency in official numbers of Afro-descendants. Census statistics may not mirror actual populations because some people are reticent to claim an identity that acknowledges African ancestry.

I selected countries that have enacted policies beneficial to Afro-descendants because it is possible that the implementation of such policies led to increased awareness of racial discrimination against Afro-descendants. While it would be an overstatement to claim that racial discourse in these countries are comparable to Brazil, these countries have had more open dialogue about Afro-descendant communities and racism than in the past. In the 1980s and 1990s, there was a proliferation of social movements in Latin America focusing on Afro-descendants.

My hypothesis is that Afro-descendants who identify as *negro* and that respondents who perceive discrimination are more likely to support affirmative action. In Salvador and São Paulo, I find that Afro-Brazilian respondents who perceive discrimination are more likely to support affirmative action policy than those who do not perceive discrimination (Mitchell-Walthour 2012). To examine support for affirmative action, I rely on the 2012 LAPOP survey. Unfortunately, the Ecuador sample does not include a question on discrimination, so it is not included in my analysis. Guatemala did not have a *negro* category, so it was not included. I include Bolivia, Brazil, Colombia, Honduras, and Nicaragua. I run regression analyses to examine support of affirmative action based on location of residence (urban versus rural), age, gender, income, education, and perception of discrimination. I examine three forms of discrimination in three separate multinomial logistic regression analyses. These are perceptions of discrimination in public places, in school or employment, and in government offices.

PERCEIVED DISCRIMINATION

Before I discuss findings from the multinomial logistic regression analyses, I report descriptive statistics of these data. Throughout Latin America, Afro-descendants are less likely to say they have experienced discrimination even though they admit discrimination exist. This is largely due to the Latin American discourse and belief that class trumps race or that discrimination is class-based rather than race-based. Latin American Afro-descendant activists have tried to change this discourse by emphasizing

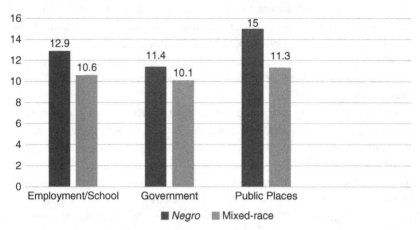

Figure 5.1 Afro-Descendants in Latin America who have experienced discrimination in employment, government, or public places (%). Countries included Bolivia, Brazil, Colombia, Honduras, and Nicaragua.

that racial discrimination plays a prominent role in the economic, political, and social lives of Afro-descendants. Brazil, Colombia, and even Mexico have run public campaigns to increase awareness about racial discrimination (Nobles 2001; Paschel 2016; Sue 2013).

The LAPOP survey's term for "black" in Colombia, Bolivia, Nicaragua, and Ecuador is *negro*. However, in Brazil, the LAPOP survey employs the census term *preto*. Brazilian mainstream media and black movement activists use the term *negro* to refer to *pretos* and mixed-race people. In the LAPOP survey, *negro* was not a category respondents could choose in the Brazilian sample. In this section, I refer to self-identifying blacks as *negro*, and this includes those identifying as *preto* in the Brazilian sample. Similarly, the Brazilian census category and the LAPOP category *pardo* denotes racial mixture, while *mulato* is on the LAPOP survey for Bolivia, Colombia, Honduras, and Nicaragua. In this section, I refer to this population as mixed race. Considering the countries in this sample, 15 percent of Afro-descendants who identify as *negro* say they have experienced discrimination in public places, while 11.3 percent of mixed-race Afro-descendants say they have experienced discrimination in public places (Figure 5.1). Regarding perceptions of discrimination in work or school, 12.9 percent of Afro-descendants identifying as *negro* say they have experienced discrimination in work or school, and 10.6 percent of mixed-race Afro-descendants say they have experienced discrimination in work or school. Finally, 11.4 percent of *negros* say they have experienced discrimination in government offices, and 10.1 percent of mixed-race people say they have experienced discrimination in government offices.

Considering all three forms of discrimination, the highest percentage of all three categories is discrimination in public places. Given that throughout Latin America, Afro-descendants occupy some of the lowest-paid positions in society, it is possible they are less likely to perceive discrimination in low-skilled employment where there is less wage difference between Afro-descendants and whites. Arias et al. (2004) find that the largest discriminatory wage penalties for Afro-Brazilians exist in the highest-paid occupations. This is an example of wage penalties in high skilled occupations. Conversely, there may be greater wage parity in low-skilled jobs.

Both *negros* and mixed-race people have the highest percentage of perceiving discrimination in public places rather than in employment and government. As seen previously in this book, when Afro-descendants in Brazil discuss discrimination, although they mention public places, they most often refer to discrimination in hiring or in the workplace. Unlike my qualitative results solely focusing on three Brazilian cities, it is possible that more Afro-descendants in Latin America admitted to discrimination in public places because these are places where people are openly stereotyped as poor and criminal. It is in the public sphere where one's dignity may be challenged, as Afro-descendants are not treated with the same respect as lighter-skinned people. As noted in Chapter 1, which focuses on racial spatiality, Afro-descendants are made to feel as though they do not belong in certain places. Jaime Alves (2014) articulates the maintenance of social exclusion in Brazil, and in particular in the city of São Paulo, through assaults on the black body. The state's intentional targeting of Afro-descendants relies on negative stereotypes of Afro-descendants as valueless and criminal, which are the same stereotypes that Afro-descendants may encounter in public. In fact, when I was conducting interviews in São Paulo, I witnessed the power of stereotypes as a white man dressed in a suit was running holding a briefcase. An Afro-Brazilian man was chasing after him, and the police showed up and pointed a gun at the Afro-Brazilian man. However, others who were also chasing the white man screamed, "No, it was the other guy who is the thief." This demonstrates how entrenched stereotypes of dark-skinned people are, and it also exemplifies how Afro-descendants are readily stereotyped as thieves in public settings.

Examining perceptions of discrimination and political behavior are important because perceiving discrimination can have an impact on political behavior, such as support for policies and political trust. Relying on

the 2008 AmericasBarometer, Levitt (2015) examines the impact of perceived discrimination on political trust. He focuses on Mexico, Guatemala,
Colombia, Bolivia, Peru, and Brazil. His sample includes whites, *mestizos*,
indigenous people, and the combined category of *negro, mulato*, and other.
He finds that most respondents felt the most discrimination in government
offices (11.83 percent). Public spaces were the second most frequent site of
discrimination, where 10.62 percent of respondents perceived discrimination, and lastly 9.02 percent of respondents cited social gatherings as a site
of discrimination (Levitt 2015: 421–422). He finds that *mestizos* have the
highest percentage (62 percent) of believing they have been treated unfairly
based on appearance or the way they speak. Nineteen percent of indigenous people believed so, followed by 13 percent of whites and 6 percent of
negros, mulatos or others. In Latin America, generally *mestizo* refers to
those of indigenous and European ancestry. This is true in Mexico, Bolivia,
Colombia, Guatemala, and Peru (all countries in his survey). In Brazil,
mestizo is not a census term. It can indicate indigenous and European
ancestry but can also indicate racial mixture between someone of African
ancestry and European ancestry, or a combination of indigenous, African,
and European ancestry. Levitt's main finding is that those who perceive
discrimination are more likely to demonstrate less political trust.
Nevertheless, it is important to note that he combines the categories of
mixed-race, *negro*, and other in his analysis. Combining these categories
hides differences in perception of discrimination among *negros* and mixed-
race people (*mulatos*).

Descriptive Statistics of Education and Income

In the sample, years of education of *negros* and mixed-race respondents
range from 0 to 18 years or more, and the average years of education is 8.3
years. Bolivia has the highest years of education of all five countries, with an
average of 9.9 years. Colombia has the next highest, with an average of 9.2
years. Brazil has an average of 8.4 years of education. Honduras has an
average of 7 years, and Nicaragua has the lowest average with an average of
5.8 years.

In terms of monthly family income, there are 17 income categories for
monthly family income that range from no income to US$1215.69
(Table 5.1). I converted income based on the Brazilian *real* to the USD
relying on the OECD's 2012 purchasing power parity rate. LAPOP's 17
categories across countries ensures that monthly salaries are comparable.
Monthly incomes are ordered from 0 to 16, with 0 representing no salary

Table 5.1 *Average Family Income Rankings of Afro-Descendants*

	Average Family Income Category by Country		
Ranking	Salary Converted to PPP USD in 2012	Country	Average Salary Ranking
0	$0		
1	$65.36		
2	$65.36–$137.25		
3	$137.91–$202.61		
4	$203.27–$267.97		
5	$268.63–$339.87	Honduras	4.5
6	$340.52–$405.23	Bolivia	5.9
7	$405.88–$477.12	Colombia	7.2
8	$477.78–$535.95	Nicaragua	7.7
9	$536.60–$607.84		
10	$608.50–$679.74		
11	$680.39–$738.56	Brazil	11.3
12	$739.22–$810.46		
13	$811.11–$915.03		
14	$915.69–$1,013.07		
15	$1,013.73–$,1215.69		
16	$1,21 5.69+		
N	1115		

and 16 representing an income of US$1,215.69 or more. On average, Afro-descendants in Brazil are doing much better economically than their Afro-descendant counterparts in Bolivia, Honduras, Nicaragua, and Colombia. Afro-descendants in Brazil have an average salary ranking of 11.3, which is approximately a family income of US$680.39–$738.56. Afro-descendants in Nicaragua have the next highest average family income at a rank of 7.7, which is approximately US$477.78–$535.95 per month. Considering that Honduras is the poorest country in Latin America, it is no surprise that it has the lowest monthly family income of all countries. The average Afro-descendant family in Honduras makes a monthly family salary of US$268.63–$339.87.

Descriptive Statistics of Age and Gender

The average age of the overall sample is 37.8. In the Brazilian sample, the average age is 37.9, and in Colombia, the average age is 36.2 (Table 5.2). In Bolivia, the average age is 28.4, while it is 40.5 in Honduras. In Nicaragua,

Table 5.2 *Average Age by Country*

Bolivia	28.4
Brazil	37.9
Colombia	36.2
Honduras	40.5
Nicaragua	40.2
N=1171	

the average age is 40.2. In the general sample, 51 percent are men and 49 percent are women. Examining gender by country, there are more men in the sample than women, the exception being Honduras, where 51 percent of the *negra* sample is women and 58 percent of the mixed-race sample is women.

Country and Skin Tone of Afro-Descendants

Considering skin tone is important, as it greatly shapes one's life chances in Latin America (Telles 2014). I now examine the average skin tone of Afro-descendants by country. The LAPOP color palette rates skin tone of respondents from 1 to 11, where 1 is the lightest and 11 is the darkest skin tone. Across these countries, on average, *negros* are darker than mixed-race people. In the Nicaragua and Bolivia sample, skin tone number 11 was not included in the survey. On average, *negros* in Honduras have a darker skin tone than *negros* in Bolivia, Brazil, Colombia, and Nicaragua. The lightest *negros* are located in Nicaragua, with an average skin color of 5.7 (Figure 5.2). Mixed-race people in Honduras have the darkest skin tone of Latin Americans with an average of 7.3. Mixed-race Bolivians have the lightest skin tone of mixed-race people, with an average of 4.3.

Descriptive Statistics of Support for Affirmative Action

Respondents were asked the question, "Universities ought to set aside openings for students with darker skin, even if that means excluding other students. How much do you agree or disagree?" Respondents could choose 1 to 7, with 1 denoting strongly disagree and 7 denoting strongly agree. For the sake of analysis, I consider 4 a middle or neutral category. Considering support by country, mixed-race people in Bolivia, Colombia, Honduras, and Nicaragua are more likely than *negros* to

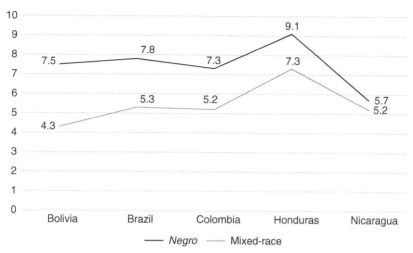

Figure 5.2 Average skin tone of *Negros* and Mixed-Race People in Select Latin American Countries (2012 LAPOP Survey)

support affirmative action (Table 5.3). However, in the Brazilian sample, *negros* are more likely to support the program. These results demonstrate that mixed-race people believe there is a need for redress for those of darker skin. It is not clear why *negros* are less supportive of the program. It is possible that they believe affirmative action would further stigmatize darker-skinned people. It is also important to note that the sample size is extremely small for some countries given that this is a sub-sample.

The survey framing of affirmative action is framed as zero sum in that exclusion is a requirement of supporting a racialized policy. Such discourse is not in line with black activists who fight for racial policies as a form of redress for past and present inequality and exclusion. They argue that darker-skinned people have been excluded from education and, therefore, should now be included – not that others should be excluded. Inclusion does not mean excluding others. The framing of this question is especially problematic as Kay et al. (2015) find that the framing of racial policies has an impact on support for the policy. Nonetheless, I rely on this survey, as it is the most recent LAPOP survey that includes a question on affirmative action. However, I am cautious of results given the framing of the affirmative action question.

Table 5.3 *Support for Affirmative Action by Racial Identification and Country (%)*

	Disagree(1–3)	4	Agree (5–7)	Total	N
Bolivia					
Negro	33.3	33.3	33.3	99.9	3
Mulato	0	50	50	100	2
Brazil					
Preto	42	10	48	100	207
Pardo	50	7	43	100	638
Colombia					
Negro	37	10	64	100	60
Mulato	12.5	12.5	75	100	24
Honduras					
Negro	40	14	46	100	28
Mulato	33	0	66	100	3
Nicaragua					
Negro	42	5	53	100	43
Mulato	30	15	55	100	20

MULTINOMIAL LOGISTIC REGRESSION ANALYSIS 1: DISCRIMINATION IN PUBLIC PLACES

I now test my hypothesis that Afro-Latin Americans who have experienced discrimination are more likely to support affirmative action than those who have not experienced discrimination. I run three separate multinomial logistic regressions to examine three different types of discrimination. One is discrimination in public places, discrimination in work or school, and discrimination in government offices.

In my first multinomial logistic regression analysis, I examine support for affirmative action as the dependent variable and the independent variables are racial identification, discrimination in public places, urban/ rural, gender, age, income, education, and skin color. Gender, education, and income are statistically significant (Table 5.4–5.6). Women are less likely to support affirmative action than men. Respondents with higher incomes compared to those with lower incomes are less likely to disagree with affirmative action. Highly educated respondents compared to lower education respondents are less likely to agree with affirmative action. Age is not statistically significance and does not even approach statistical significance. This is in contrast to the finding that younger respondents are more supportive of affirmative action in Brazil (Mitchell-Walthour 2012). The finding regarding education may be explained with the idea of meritocracy.

Table 5.4 *Multinomial Regression Odds Ratios Predicting Support for Affirmative Action Disagree a lot (1) Agree a lot (7) (Lapop 2012 Survey)*

	Model 1						Model 2						Model 3					
	1	2	3	5	6	7	1	2	3	5	6	7	1	2	3	5	6	7
Racial Identification Negro (1) Mulato (0)	.65 (.17)	.66 (.21)	.82 (.27)	.89 (.27)	.70 (.21)	1.01 (.27)	.63 (.17)	.68 (.22)	.79 (.27)	.91 (.28)	.72 (.22)	1.01 (.27)	.64 (.17)	.69 (.22)	.78 (.26)	.93 (.29)	.70 (.21)	1.00 (.27)
Discrimination In public places No (0) Yes (1)							1.07 (.40)	.69 (.33)	.99 (.47)	.82 (.36)	.65 (.30)	1.07 (.40)	1.07 (.39)	.69 (.33)	.99 (.47)	.80 (.36)	.67 (.30)	1.07 (.41)
Urban/ Rural													.87 (.31)	.84 (.37)	1.10 (.49)	.60 (.27)	1.90 (.72)	1.11 (.40)
Gender Male (1) Female (2)																		
Age																		
Income																		
Education																		
Skin Color (Light to Dark)																		
Observations	998						992						992					

Note: Standard errors in parentheses
*p<.05 ** p<0.01 *** p< 0.001
Base outcome is 4

Table 5.5 Multinomial Regression Odds Ratios Predicting Support for Affirmative Action Disagree a lot (1) Agree a lot (7) (Lapop 2012)

	Model 4						Model 5						Model 6					
	1	2	3	5	6	7	1	2	3	5	6	7	1	2	3	5	6	7
Racial Identification Negro (1) Mulato (0)	.63 (.17)	.68 (.22)	.77 (.26)	.90 (.28)	.70 (.21)	.99 (.27)	.64 (.17)	.69 (.22)	.78 (.26)	.92 (.29)	.71 (.22)	1.01 (.27)	.76 (.22)	.82 (.28)	.75 (.27)	.96 (.31)	.69 (.22)	.99 (.29)
Discrimination In public places No (0) Yes (1)	1.04 (.39)	.67 (.32)	.98 (.46)	.80 (.36)	.66 (.30)	1.06 (.40)	1.03 (.38)	.66 (.32)	.96 (.45)	.77 (.34)	.65 (.30)	1.03 (.39)	.95 (.35)	.63 (.31)	.95 (.45)	.77 (.35)	.51 (.24)	.92 (.35)
Urban/Rural	.86 (.31)	.83 (.37)	1.08 (.48)	.60 (.27)	1.89 (.72)	1.10 (.40)	.86 (.31)	.83 (.37)	1.08 (.48)	.59 (.27)	1.89 (.72)	1.10 (.40)	1.05 (.41)	.97 (.46)	1.22 (.59)	.60 (.29)	1.48 (.60)	.92 (.36)
Gender Male (1) Female (2)	.99 (.01)	.99 (.01)	.99 (.01)	.99 (.01)	.99 (.01)	1.00 (.01)	.99 (.01)	.99 (.01)	.99 (.01)	.99 (.01)	.99 (.01)	1.00 (.01)	.99 (.01)	.99 (.01)	.99 (.01)	.99 (.01)	.99 (.01)	.99 (.01)
Age							1.30 (.33)	1.30 (.40)	1.20 (.39)	1.67 (.50)	1.25 (.36)	1.52 (.40)	1.44 (.39)	1.47 (.47)	1.40 (.47)	1.63 (.51)	1.08 (.33)	1.36 (.37)
Income													1.07 (.04)	1.08 (.04)	1.06 (.05)	1.00 (.04)	.94 (.04)	.96 (.03)
Education																		
Skin Color (Light to Dark)																		
Observations	989						989						941					

Note: Standard errors in parentheses
*P<.05 ** p<0.01 *** p< 0.001
Base outcome is 4

Table 5.6 *Multinomial Regression Odds Ratios Predicting Support for Affirmative Action Disagree a lot (1) Agree a lot (7) (2006 Survey)*

	Model 7						Model 8					
	1	2	3	5	6	7	1	2	3	5	6	7
Racial Identification Negro (1) Mulato (0)	.77 (.22)	.82 (.28)	.76 (.28)	.97 (.32)	.68 (.22)	.99 (.29)	.69 (.23)	.78 (.31)	.66 (.28)	.76 (.29)	.55 (.21)	.84 (.28)
Discrimination In public places No (0) Yes (1)	.93 (.35)	.70 (.34)	1.00 (.48)	.84 (.38)	.55 (.27)	1.09 (.43)	.93 (.35)	.70 (.34)	1.01 (.48)	.84 (.39)	.56 (.27)	1.09 (.43)
Urban Rural	.95 (.37)	.79 (.38)	1.05 (.52)	.51 (.25)	1.20 (.50)	.68 (.27)	.98 (.39)	.80 (.39)	1.09 (.54)	.53 (.26)	1.26 (.53)	.70 (.28)
Gender Male (1) Female (2)	.99 (.01)	.98 (.01)	.98 (.01)	.98 (.01)	.98 (.01)	.98* (.01)	.99 (.01)	.98 (.01)	.98 (.01)	.98 (.01)	.98 (.01)	.98* (.01)
Age	1.39 (.37)	1.46 (.46)	1.37 (.46)	1.64 (.52)	1.06 (.32)	1.36 (.38)	1.41 (.38)	1.46 (.47)	1.40 (.47)	1.69 (.53)	1.08 (.33)	1.39 (.39)
Income	1.06 (.04)	1.09* (.05)	1.07 (.05)	1.01 (.04)	.95 (.04)	1.00 (.04)	1.06 (.04)	1.09* (.05)	1.06 (.05)	1.01 (.04)	.95 (.04)	1.00 (.04)
Education	.98 (.04)	.91 (.04)	.95 (.05)	.93 (.05)	.91 (.04)	.86*** (.04)	.98 (.04)	.91 (.04)	.95 (.05)	.93 (.05)	.91 (.04)	.86** (.04)
Skin Color (Light to Dark)							1.05 (.08)	1.01 (.09)	1.04 (.10)	1.10 (.09)	1.08 (.09)	1.06 (.08)
Observations	935						935					

Note: Standard errors in parentheses
*p<.05 ** p<0.01 *** p< 0.001
Base outcome is 4

205

Highly educated people may believe they were able to achieve success because of individual efforts. For this reason, they may be less supportive of affirmative action policy. Afro-Latin Americans with more income are more supportive of affirmative action. Mitchell-Walthour (2015) finds similar results in her study of support for affirmative action in Brazil. Those with higher incomes are less likely to disagree with affirmative action. Surprisingly, perception of discrimination is not statistically significant. Racial identification was not statistically significant. It is possible that perception of discrimination is not statistically significant in this model because of the framing of the affirmative action question. People who have suffered from discrimination would not likely advocate for a policy that would exclude others.

I find that women are 98 percent less likely than men to agree a lot with affirmative action compared to having a neutral response. This finding is surprising given that women tend to suffer multiple types of discrimination. However, the framing of the affirmative action question may account for women being less likely to support a program that excludes some. Respondents with higher education versus those with lower education are 86 percent less likely to agree strongly than to have a neutral response about affirmative action. This finding is consistent with studies on support for affirmative action in Brazil, where regardless of racial identification, Brazilians with more education are less likely to agree with affirmative action (Toledo 2013). In sum, in this regression analysis, there is no evidence that Afro-descendants who identify as *negro* and respondents who perceive discrimination in public places are more likely to support affirmative action.

MULTINOMIAL LOGISTIC REGRESSION ANALYSIS 2: DISCRIMINATION IN SCHOOL OR WORK

In my second multinomial logistic regression analysis, I examine support for affirmative action as the dependent variable. The independent variables are racial identification, discrimination in work or school, location, gender, income, education, and skin color. Discrimination in school or employment, age, gender, and location are not significant. Education and income are statistically significant in Model 8 (Table 5.7–5.9).

In Model 2 discrimination in work or school approaches significance but ultimately is not statistically significant. It is statistically significant in Model 5 but in an unexpected direction. Respondents who experienced

Table 5.7 Multinomial Regression Odds Ratios Predicting Support for Affirmative Action Disagree a lot (1) Agree a lot (7) (Lapop 2012 Survey)

	Model 1						Model 2						Model 3					
	1	2	3	5	6	7	1	2	3	5	6	7	1	2	3	5	6	7
Racial Identification	.65	.66	.82	.89	.70	1.01	.69	.72	.90	.98	.74	1.06	.70	.73	.89	1.00	.71	1.05
	(.17)	(.21)	(.27)	(.27)	(.21)	(.27)	(.19)	(.24)	(.30)	(.31)	(.23)	(.29)	(.19)	(.24)	(.30)	(.31)	(.22)	(.29)
Negro (1) Mulato (0)																		
Discrimination							.59	.86	.76	.40	.86	.89	.58	.85	.76	.39	.90	.89
In work or school							(.22)	(.38)	(.36)	(.20)	(.36)	(.33)	(.22)	(.38)	(.36)	(.20)	(.37)	(.33)
No (0)																		
Yes (1)																		
Urban/													.81	.95	1.16	.57	2.07	1.21
Rural													(.31)	(.43)	(.52)	(.27)	(.80)	(.45)
Gender																		
Male (1)																		
Female (2)																		
Age																		
Income																		
Education																		
Skin Color (Light to Dark)																		
Observations	998						972						972					

Note: Standard errors in parentheses
*p<.05 ** p<0.01 *** p< 0.001
Base outcome is 4

207

Table 5.8 Multinomial Regression Odds Ratios Predicting Support for Affirmative Action Disagree a lot (1) Agree a lot (7) (Lapop 2012 Survey)

	Model 4						Model 5						Model 6					
	1	2	3	5	6	7	1	2	3	5	6	7	1	2	3	5	6	7
Racial Identification Negro (1) Mulato (0)	.69 (.18)	.72 (.24)	.89 (.30)	.96 (.30)	.71 (.22)	1.03 (.28)	.70 (.19)	.72 (.24)	.89 (.30)	.99 (.99)	.72 (.22)	1.05 (.29)	.82 (.24)	.87 (.30)	.86 (.31)	1.01 (.34)	.70 (.23)	1.03 (.30)
Discrimination In work or school No (0) Yes (1)	.56 (.21)	.82 (.36)	.73 (.35)	.38 (.19)	.87 (.36)	.87 (.33)	.55 (.21)	.81 (.36)	.72 (.34)	.37* (.19)	.86 (.36)	.85 (.32)	.56 (.21)	.80 (.35)	.72 (.34)	.37 (.19)	.81 (.34)	.76 (.29)
Urban/ Rural	.80 (.30)	.93 (.42)	1.14 (.52)	.57 (.27)	2.06* (.80)	1.19 (.45)	.80 (.30)	.93 (.42)	1.14 (.52)	.57 (.27)	2.06 (.80)	1.20 (.45)	.92 (.37)	.99 (.48)	1.22 (.60)	.54 (.27)	1.53 (.64)	.95 (.38)
Gender Male (1) Female (2)	.99 (.01)	.99 (.01)	.99 (.01)	.99 (.01)	.99 (.01)	1.00 (.01)	.99 (.01)	.99 (.01)	.99 (.01)	.99 (.01)	.99 (.01)	1.00 (.01)	.99 (.01)	.99 (.01)	.98 (.01)	.99 (.01)	.99 (.01)	.99 (.01)
Age							1.26 (.33)	1.19 (.37)	1.17 (.38)	1.63 (.49)	1.18 (.35)	1.47 (.39)	1.36 (.37)	1.31 (.42)	1.34 (.45)	1.56 (.49)	.98 (.30)	1.27 (.35)
Income													1.05 (.04)	1.06 (.04)	1.04 (.05)	.99 (.04)	.93 (.04)	.95 (.03)
Education																		
Skin Color (Light to Dark)																		
Observations	969						969						924					

Note: Standard errors in parentheses
*p<.05 ** p<0.01 *** p< 0.001
Base outcome is 4

208

Table 5.9 *Multinomial Regression Odds Ratios Predicting Support for Affirmative Action Disagree a lot (1) Agree a lot (7) (Lapop 2012 Survey)*

Model 7

	1	2	3	5	6	7
Racial Identification Negro (1) Mulato (0)	.81 (.23)	.85 (.30)	.85 (.31)	1.00 (.33)	.67 (.22)	1.02 (.30)
Discrimination In work or school No (0) Yes (1)	.54 (.21)	.85 (.41)	.75 (.36)	.39 (.20)	.87 (.37)	.83 (.32)
Urban/ Rural	.90 (.37)	.85 (.42)	1.11 (.55)	.49 (.25)	1.31 (.55)	.75 (.30)
Gender Male (1) Female (2)	.99 (.01)	.98 (.01)	.98* (.01)	.98 (.01)	.98 (.01)	.98* (.01)
Age	1.35 (.37)	1.35 (.44)	1.36 (.46)	1.59 (.50)	1.01 (.31)	1.32 (.37)
Income	1.05 (.04)	1.09 (.05)	1.06 (.05)	1.00 (.04)	.95 (.04)	.99 (.04)
Education	.98 (.04)	.91* (.04)	.94 (.05)	.94 (.05)	.91 (.04)	.91 (.04)
Skin Color (Light to Dark)						.86** (.04)
Observations	920					

Model 8

	1	2	3	5	6	7
Racial Identification Negro (1) Mulato (0)	.73 (.24)	.83 (.33)	.78 (.33)	.79 (.31)	.57 (.21)	.89 (.30)
Discrimination In work or school No (0) Yes (1)	.54 (.21)	.86 (.38)	.75 (.36)	.39 (.20)	.87 (.37)	.87 (.32)
Urban/ Rural	.92 (.37)	.86 (.42)	1.13 (.56)	.51 (.26)	1.36 (.58)	.77 (.32)
Gender Male (1) Female (2)	.99 (.01)	-.98 (.01)	.98 (.01)	.98 (.01)	.98 (.01)	.98 (.01)
Age	1.37 (.37)	1.35 (.44)	1.37 (.47)	1.63 (.52)	1.02 (.31)	1.34 (.38)
Income	1.05 (.04)	1.09 (.05)	1.06 (.05)	1.00 (.04)	.95 (.04)	.99 (.04)
Education	.98 (.04)	.91 (.04)	.94 (.05)	.91 (.05)	.91 (.04)	.87** (.04)
Skin Color (Light to Dark)	1.05 (.08)	1.01 (.09)	1.04 (.10)	1.10 (.09)	1.08 (.09)	1.06 (.08)
Observations	920					

Note: Standard errors in parentheses
*p<.05 ** p<0.01 *** p< 0.001
Base outcome is 4

discrimination are less likely to agree with affirmative action. However, it is not significant in the final model. They are In model 8 income is statistically significant. As income increases, respondents are more likely to disagree with affirmative action policy. This finding is consistent with findings about affirmative action in Brazil.

In Model 8, respondents with higher education compared to those with lower education, are 87 percent less likely to agree a lot with affirmative action over the neutral category. In addition, those with higher education compared to those with lower education are 91 percent less likely to disagree with affirmative action over the neutral category. In addition, my expectation that those who identify as *negro* rather than *mulato* would be more likely to agree with affirmative action was not met. In a sense, this may indicate that even though Afro-descendants have mobilized throughout Latin America, social movement activists have not been effective in Afro-descendant populations viewing discrimination as racialized discrimination that can be addressed through racialized policies such as affirmative action. Furthermore, the survey question does not specify Afro-descendants but rather employs the term "dark-skinned." The combination of the survey question, small sample sizes, and differences in racial discourse in these countries may be the reason for such inconsistent results. A large dataset only focusing on Afro-descendants and carefully constructed survey questions on affirmative action would be more appropriate for this study.

MULTINOMIAL LOGISTIC REGRESSION ANALYSIS 3: DISCRIMINATION IN GOVERNMENT

In my third multinomial logistic regression analysis, I examine support for affirmative action as the dependent variable; and the independent variables are racial identification, discrimination in government, location, gender, age, income, education, and skin color. Racial identification, income, and age, are not statistically significant (Table 5.10–5.12). Education and gender are statistically significant. The trend for education is similar to the previous model. The trend regarding gender is similar to the first model. I did not expect gender differences. Those with higher education versus those with lower education are 86 percent less likely to strongly agree over the neutral category. Women versus men are 97 percent less likely to agree strongly over the neutral category. In sum, my expectation that racial identification as *negro* and perception of discrimination would

Table 5.10 Multinomial Regression Odds Ratios Predicting Support for Affirmative Action Disagree a lot (1) Agree a lot (7) (Lapop 2012 Survey)

	Model 1						Model 2						Model 3					
	1	2	3	5	6	7	1	2	3	5	6	7	1	2	3	5	6	7
Racial Identification Negro (1) Mulato (0)	.65 (.17)	.66 (.21)	.82 (.27)	.89 (.27)	.70 (.21)	1.01 (.27)	.69 (.19)	.69 (.22)	.99 (.34)	.93 (.28)	.72 (.22)	.99 (.27)	.71 (.19)	.69 (.23)	.99 (.34)	.94 (.29)	.69 (.21)	.00 (.27)
Discrimination In government No (0) Yes (1)							.93 (.38)	.79 (.41)	.77 (.43)	.66 (.34)	.65 (.32)	.84 (.36)	.94 (.39)	.79 (.41)	.77 (.43)	.68 (.35)	.61 (.31)	.84 (.35)
Urban/ Rural													.74 (.31)	.92 (.37)	1.00 (.49)	.62 (.27)	1.98* (.72)	1.14 (.40)
Gender Male (1)Female (2)																		
Age																		
Income																		
Education																		
Skin Color (Light to Dark)																		
Observations	998						956						956					

Note: Standard errors in parentheses
*p<.05 ** p<0.01 *** p< 0.001
Base outcome is 4

Table 5.11 *Multinomial Regression Odds Ratios Predicting Support for Affirmative Action Disagree a lot (1) Agree a lot (7) (Lapop 2012 Survey)*

	Model 4						Model 5						Model 6					
	1	2	3	5	6	7	1	2	3	5	6	7	1	2	3	5	6	7
Identification	.70	.68	.98	.91	.69	.97	.71	.69	.98	.93	.69	.99	.83	.80	.94	.97	.67	.98
Negro (1) Mulato (0)	(.19)	(.22)	(.33)	(.28)	(.21)	(.26)	(.19)	(.23)	(.34)	(.29)	(.21)	(.27)	(.24)	(.27)	(.34)	(.31)	(.22)	(.28)
Discrimination	.92	.78	.76	.67	.61	.82	.91	.77	.76	.66	.60	.80	.91	.80	.78	.66	.57	.74
In government No (0) Yes (1)	(.38)	(.40)	(.42)	(.34)	(.30)	(.35)	(.38)	(.39)	(.42)	(.34)	(.30)	(.34)	(.38)	(.41)	(.44)	(.34)	(.28)	(.32)
Urban/	.73	.91	.99	.62	1.97	1.12	.73	.91	.99	.61	1.97	1.12	.86	1.02	1.03	.61	1.54	.94
Rural	(.27)	(.40)	(.46)	(.28)	(.75)*	(.41)	(.27)	(.40)	(.46)	(.28)	(.75)	(.41)	(.34)	(.49)	(.52)	(.30)	(.63)	(.36)
Gender	.99	.99	1.00	.99	.99	1.00	.99	.99	1.00	.99	.99	1.00	.99	.99	.99	.99	.99	.99
Male (1) Female (2)	(.01)	(.01)	(.01)	(.01)	(.01)	(.01)	(.01)	(.01)	(.01)	(.01)	(.01)	(.01)	(.01)	(.01)	(.01)	(.01)	(.01)	(.01)
Age							1.30	1.21	1.12	1.70	1.24	1.55	1.43	1.34	1.28	1.67	1.06	1.37
Income							(.34)	(.37)	(.37)	(.51)	(.36)	(.41)	(.39)	(.43)	(.44)	(.52)	(.32)	(.38)
Education													1.06	1.06	1.04	.99	.94	.96
Skin Color (Light to Dark)													(.04)	(.04)	(.05)	(.04)	(.04)	(.03)
Observations	953						953						906					

Note: Standard errors in parentheses
*p<.05 ** p<0.01 *** p<0.001
Base outcome is 4

Table 5.12 *Multinomial Regression Odds Ratios Predicting Support for Affirmative Action Disagree a lot (1) Agree a lot (7) (Lapop 2012 Survey)*

	Model 7						Model 8					
	1	2	3	5	6	7	1	2	3	5	6	7
Identification	.84	.80	.96	.97	.66	.98	.77	.74	.89	.76	.53*	.84
Negro (1) Mulato (0)	(.24)	(.28)	(.35)	(.32)	(.21)	(.28)	(.25)	(.29)	(.37)	(.29)	(.20)	(.28)
Discrimination	.88	.86	.79	.70	.60	.84	.87	.85	.79	.68	.59	.83
In government No (0) Yes (1)	(.37)	(.45)	(.45)	(.36)	(.30)	(.37)	(.37)	(.44)	(.44)	(.35)	(.30)	(.36)
Urban/ Rural	.79	.84	.93	.51	1.24	.70	.81	.86	.95	.54	1.31	.72
	(.32)	(.41)	(.48)	(.25)	(.52)	(.28)	(.33)	(.42)	(.49)	(.27)	(.55)	(.29)
Gender	.99	.99	.99	.98	.98	.98	.99	.98	.99	.98	.98	.98*
Male (1) Female (2)	(.01)	(.01)	(.01)	(.01)	(.01)	(.01)	(.01)	(.01)	(.01)	(.01)	(.01)	(.01)
Age	1.37	1.33	1.25	1.64	1.05	1.38	1.38	1.34	1.25	1.68*	1.06	1.40
	(.37)	(.43)	(.43)	(.52)	(.32)	(.38)	(.38)	(.43)	(.44)	(.53)	(.32)	(.39)
Income	1.05	1.08	1.04	1.01	.96	1.00	1.05	1.08	1.04	1.01	.95	1.00
	(.04)	(.05)	(.05)	(.04)	(.04)	(.04)	(.04)	(.05)	(.05)	(.04)	(.04)	(.04)
Education	.99	.92	.97	.93	.91	.86**	.99	.92	.97	.93	.91	.86**
	(.04)	(.05)	(.05)	(.05)	(.04)	(.04)	(.04)	(.05)	(.05)	(.05)	(.04)	(.04)
Skin Color							1.04	1.04	1.04	1.11	1.10	1.07
(Light to Dark)							(.08)	(.09)	(.10)	(.09)	(.09)	(.08)
Observations	901						901					

Note: Standard errors in parentheses
*p<.05 ** p<0.01 *** p<0.001
Base outcome is 4

increase support for affirmative action was not met, as they were not statistically significant.

CONCLUSION

In conclusion, Brazil has led the way in highlighting the pernicious effects of racial discrimination on the lives of Afro-Brazilians. Black movement activists, local grassroots organizing by women, and even hip hop groups have raised racial consciousness by discussing discrimination in terms of racial discrimination, not only class discrimination. Activists have also successfully advocated for affirmative action policies in university. While the results in this study of Latin American countries contradict evidence of studies on affirmative action support in Brazil, there are some trends that hold. One is that higher levels of education lead to a reduction in support of affirmative action. However, age is in direct opposition to the literature on Afro-Brazilian support for affirmative action, which shows that younger people are more likely to support the program. Because this sample is a subsample of the larger LAPOP study, larger N studies solely focusing on Afro-descendants might give a more accurate picture of Afro-descendant political opinion. In-depth interviews are essential to understanding how Afro-descendants understand affirmative action policies. Similar to studies that examine support for affirmative action based on race versus class status, additional studies would have to vary terminology. The 2012 LAPOP study uses the term "dark-skinned" rather than "Afro-descendant" or terms such as *negro* and *mulato*. A future study should ask questions that vary racially specific terminology, skin color, and class. Support should also be reframed in terms of inclusiveness rather than exclusion.

Conclusion

The Racialization of Political Events

Yesterday August 31, 2016 was the completion[1]
of the coup d'état- the state coup d'état against
President Dilma. . . . . Xongani [Fashion and
accessory store] started in 2010, in a moment
when there was an explosion of various
public policies from Lula's government.
People were studying more [and] people were working
more. And it was this place that I. . . was able to [take on this]
endeavor. It was in this moment
that blacks were having the possibility of
conquering more things financially,
politically, as well as educationally, [and] in work, you know?
And it was in this moment that we
negros, we could think about other things. And it is
for this reason that I am so moved, upset, and sad to
see that a group of machismo, racist, slave-o-crat, and
conservative people were able to destroy
the free will of the majority of the population.

In this final chapter, I discuss three current events that demonstrate the
saliency of race in Brazil. The first event is the 2014 presidential campaign.
The media debated the idea that the conditional cash program *Bolsa Família*

---

[1] Xongani 2016. *Ontem dia 31 de agosto de 2016 foi consumado o golpe – um golpe de estado
contra a Presidenta Dilma . . . a Xongani é de 2010, que era o momento que tava bombando
as políticas públicas do governo Lula. Várias. A galera tava estudando mais, a galera tava
trabalhando mais que, que os negros estavam tendo possibilidade. E foi nesse lugar que eu eu
pude emprender. Foi nesse momento de, de, de conquistar mais coisas. Tanto financeir-
amente quanto politicamente, quanto na educação, sabe, no trabalho. E foi nesse momento
que nós negros, a gente pode pensar em outras coisas. É é por isso que eu tou tão comovida, e
desistruturada, e triste, de perceber que um grupo de pessoas machistas, racistas, escravo-
cratas, é, conservadores conseguiram destruir a vontade da maioria da população.*

was a form of clientelism and that former President Dilma Rousseff received votes from *Bolsa* recipients simply on this basis. The second event is that some activists articulated and understood the anti-Rousseff protests and Rousseff's 2016 removal from office in racialized terms. The third event is mobilization around police brutality. These current events demonstrate that analyzing the saliency of race is essential when analyzing political events that are seen through a racial lens.

The first example of the saliency of race is the racialization of *Bolsa Família* recipients during the 2014 presidential campaign. *Bolsa Família* is a cash transfer program in which the government provides families with a monthly stipend as long as they meet certain conditions, such as children regularly attending school and getting medical check-ups. The *Bolsa Família program* helped lift millions of Afro-Brazilians into the lower middle class. Afro-Brazilians are 73 percent of the 14 million families that benefited from the *Bolsa Família* program (Arruda 2014). Seventy-eight percent of the 22 million people that escaped extreme poverty due to this program are Afro-Brazilian. Because of the large number of Afro-Brazilians benefiting from this program, many have joined the new lower middle class.

During Rousseff's 2014 election campaign, the *Bolsa Família* program was viewed by some media outlets and voters as a form of clientelism, and stereotypes of Northeasterners were prevalent in social media. In typical Brazilian fashion, without naming "race," Northeasterners were stereo-typed as lazy, uneducated, and unintelligent. In addition, memes were circulated on social media that showed Afro-Brazilian women with their children with statements that indicated they were lazy *Bolsa Família* recipients who wanted hand-outs from the government. The stereotype was very similar to the American stereotype of the welfare queen. This stereotype was strongly promoted during Ronald Reagan's presidency and the idea was that low-income black women were lazy, unwilling to work, and simply wanted to receive welfare payments while whites were hard-working people whose hard-earned money, through taxes, supported these women.

In Brazil, the media circulated the idea that Rousseff won votes based on high percentages of *Bolsa Família* recipients. Yet in municipalities that did not have a high number of recipients, she still won the majority of votes, therefore it was not entirely true that her victory was solely based on a high percentage of recipients voting (Vasconcelos 2014). In addition, in the second round, the increase in votes were in municipalities that were not highly dependent on *Bolsa Família* (Mendonça 2014). There was and continues to be a debate among academics whether *Bolsa Família* should be seen as a form of clientelism, which is the idea that votes are exchanged for goods.

Simone Bohn (2011) argues that it is not a form of clientelism. Natasha Sugiyama and Wendy Hunter (2013) do not find evidence of clientelism and argue that there is less clientelism in Brazil today than in the past. Brian Fried also finds evidence that clientelism is in decline (Fried 2012). However, Cesar Zucco and Timothy Power (2013) find a relationship between the program and support for former President "Lula".

In other words, *Bolsa Família* recipients who tend to be low income and Afro-Brazilian are not viewed as people who think carefully and rationally when casting their votes. While Afro-Brazilians do not overwhelmingly support the Workers Party, the party to which Rousseff belongs, the majority of Afro-Brazilians were affiliated with the Workers Party. It is likely that a high number of *Bolsa* recipients supported her due to her political party. This is similar to the idea that some Americans believed African Americans only voted for President Barack Obama because he is African American rather than the fact that African Americans are overwhelmingly Democrats and thus vote for politicians who are affiliated with the Democratic Party. Underlying both ways of thinking is that Afro-descendants are simple-minded people whose voting patterns can be reduced to clientelism, in the case of Brazil, or voting based on a candidate's skin color, in the case of the U.S. Lorrie Frasure (2010) shows that initially, Barack Obama did not receive support from African Americans who tended to be more supportive of Hillary Clinton. This book, *The Politics of Blackness in Contemporary Brazil*, shows that Afro-Brazilians offer nuanced explanations of their voting patterns and political behavior. A study of support for Rousseff would have to go beyond political party or simply examining *Bolsa Família* recipients versus non-recipients. Such a study would benefit from including racialized experiences such as discrimination and racial group attachment. The example of the saliency of race in the 2014 political campaign highlights the need for studies of elections considering racial group and individual behavior.

The second political event I focus on is President Dilma Rousseff's removal from office. Some Afro-Brazilian activists believe Rousseff's removal from office could have deleterious effects on Afro-Brazilians, such as a dismantling of education and social policies such as *Bolsa Família*. Ana Paula Xongani, the YouTuber mentioned at the beginning of this chapter is a black woman and owner of Xongani Art with Fabric, an online store that specializes in African-inspired clothing and accessories in São Paulo. After President Dilma Rousseff was removed from office, some of her supporters, such as Ana Paula Xongani, considered her removal a *coup d'état*.

The removal was not simply viewed as based on corruption. Rather, those leading the effort were viewed as sexist, racist, and against social policies and progress that uplifted blacks, browns, and low-income people. In 2016, Rousseff was impeached on charges of corruption because of misusing budget funds. She was not found guilty of being involved in the *Operação Lava Jato*, the Operation Carwash corruption case involving the state run PetroBras oil company. Some leftist activists, including black movement activists, are opposed to corruption but believe her removal was a *coup d'état* because of the political motivations of then Vice President Michel Temer. Temer is from the Brazilian Democratic Movement party, a centrist political party. Temer has also been accused of and found guilty of corruption, and Eduardo Cunha, who mainly led the charge of corruption against Rousseff, was convicted of corruption. A number of factors led to the persistent effort to impeach Rousseff. The coalition between a centrist and a leftist party made Rousseff vulnerable to political disagreement and tension that would naturally lead to different policy objectives. Rousseff was also a target of blame for the economic recession. Furthermore, citizens were dissatisfied because of the escalating cost of living due to the Olympics and World Cup. Citizens felt like their everyday needs were not addressed. For some, the economic and social dissatisfaction fueled political dissatisfaction.

Rousseff's removal from office must also be understood in the context of a contentious election in 2014. Rousseff's 2014 re-election was not easy, as the election was marred by the unexpected event of death of presidential candidate Eduardo Campos, of the Brazilian Socialist Party (PSB), in an airplane crash. Subsequently, his party chose Marina Silva, an Afro-Brazilian woman, who is an Evangelical Christian and environmentalist to run. In the first round, Silva received 21 percent of the vote. Rousseff won 59.6 percent of the vote, and Aécio Neves won 15.4 of the vote. After Rousseff realized Silva was gaining popularity she began to air negative advertisements, and these were quite effective in allowing her to gain a lead. In the second round of voting, Rousseff won 52 percent of the vote and Neves won 48 percent. The small percentage difference in her win highlights how competitive and contentious the election was. Rousseff's re-election was soon met with protests and later allegations of corruption.

The anti-corruption and anti-Rousseff protests revealed racial dynamics and racism in Brazil. In one of the most well-known cases, a picture circulated on social media of an Afro-Brazilian nanny dressed in her work uniform pushing a stroller while the white parents of the children walked in front of her as they attended a protest. The photo of the couple and their nanny revealed entrenched racial divisions in which the position of the black woman was naturalized as the caretaker to whites. In addition, it revealed that class divisions might make it difficult for low-income and working-class Afro-Brazilians to have leisure time to attend protest marches. There was another protest where a white man wore blackface with a rope around his neck. The protestor in blackface demonstrated racism in a supposedly "race neutral" protest concerning anti-corruption.

An example of viewing Rousseff's removal from office in racialized group terms, despite Rousseff not being black, can be found in Dennis Oliveira's writing, in which he claims that supporters of the "coup" were racist because they were against Rousseff's social policies and the impact of these policies. Citing programs such as "Water for All," "ProUni," "My House, My Life," and the National Program of Access to Technical Training and Employment, which all mainly benefit Afro-Brazilians, Oliveira says

But the coup against Dilma is racist because it is supported precisely by people who feel uncomfortable with these small advances. They [sic] are those who are uncomfortable with black people frequenting university campuses and sharing space with the children of the elite. Or that they find in lines at airports those black women who should be their servants. Or those who shout against "consumerism" mainly due to seeing the mall with many more black faces than they would like (Oliveira 2016).

Another example is Rosana Aparecida da Silva, Secretary to Combat Racism at the Central Única of Workers (Central Única dos Trabalhadores) in São Paulo. She states:

Also it is a fact that the coup will be terrible for all of Brazil, but it will be even more devastating for the black population, especially for *negra* women. We do not doubt this! In the *Bolsa Família* Program, 73 percent of the beneficiaries are *negros*, 68 percent of the households are headed by *negra* women. It is thanks to cash transfer policies such as these, that extreme poverty that afflicts *negro* folks were reduced by 72 percent from 2003 to 2014. (Silva 2016, translation my own)

Both Oliveira and Silva discuss policies that benefit Afro-Brazilians. However, Oliveira's observation also gets at one of the main findings in this book. No longer does the idea of a racial democracy inhibit Afro-Brazilians from simply thinking about their lives as only shaped by class. Intersectional identities determine some Afro-Brazilians' worldviews, and this book shows that more than a majority of Afro-Brazilians in Brazil's three largest cities (São Paulo, Rio de Janeiro, and Salvador) exhibit *negro* linked fate. Further, Oliveira highlights the idea of racial spatiality. Public spaces such as malls, airports, and universities are naturalized as white spaces. Social policies that lifted Afro-Brazilians out of poverty and racial policies such as university affirmative action democratized and integrated more public spaces. Racial dynamics changed so there was an increase in Afro-Brazilians as consumers in places where they were not often seen. According to Oliveira and Silva, Rousseff's removal from office might be detrimental to these programs and thereby Afro-Brazilians as a whole.

MOBILIZATION AGAINST POLICE BRUTALITY

The third example of the saliency of race is mobilization against police brutality. Police brutality is not a new phenomenon in Brazil. However, mobilization against police brutality demonstrates how the issue is now understood in racialized *and* class terms. Further, mega-events such as the World Cup and the Olympics increased publicity about what some organizations call black genocide. Police brutality is viewed as a threat against low-income people and Afro-Brazilians as a group, and not simply random acts of violence against individuals. Preparations for the World Cup and Olympics had devastating effects on low-income Afro-Brazilian communities. In 2008, Police Pacification Units (UPPs) were implemented to "pacify" communities by going into *favela* communities that were viewed as highly dangerous and criminal. These heavily armed units came into communities in military gear. The devastating effect was that many innocent Afro-Brazilians were killed. Some of the high profile cases were the deaths of Aramildo Dias de Souza and Douglas Pereira. Souza was a bricklayer who lived in the Rocinho community in Rio de Janeiro. He was said to have been mistaken for a drug dealer and was tortured and killed by police. His body was never recovered. Thirteen of the 25 military police officers accused were convicted. This case received international attention, which pressured local government to take the case seriously. Pereira was a dancer on the television show *Esquenta* who was beaten and shot in the back by police who had a shootout with drug dealers in the Morro Pavão-Pavãozinho neighborhood in Rio de Janeiro. His case also received international attention. Pereira's death was reported in the *Los Angeles Times* and the *Guardian*, and on the BBC, and NBC, while Amarildo's was covered on the BBC and in the *Independent* (United Kingdom), and the *Guardian*. While some of these media stories positioned Brazil as a violent country that was not prepared to host mega-events, other reports revealed deep racial, economic, and political inequalities in the country and showed how black activists mobilized to challenge these inequalities.

Reaja ou Será Morte (React or Be Killed) is a campaign against police brutality based in Salvador, Bahia, which started in 2005. The women led group *Mães de Maio* (Mothers of May) is a group that fights against police brutality and honors the victims of police brutality in São Paulo. In 2015, the (Inter)National March Against the Genocide of Black People was held throughout Brazil where approximately 51,000 people participated (Smith 2016). People marched in cities such as São Paulo, Salvador, Rio de Janeiro, Belo Horizonte, and Brasília. These marches were transnational in their scope, as Afro-Brazilians made connections to victims of police brutality in the United States. One example is a banner that was carried in São Paulo with the words "*Somos Todos Mike Brown!*" or "We are all Mike Brown!" A 26-year-old woman participated in the march in Salvador and stated, "This country loves our Black culture, our music, our bodies, but hates the fact we still exist as the majority. Salvador is [on] the front line of the war against African people in Brazil. My people built this city-this country-through slavery. We will not be silent. Black lives have value; Africans all over the diaspora want to live." These marches were concerned with African descendant men and women who suffer from police brutality throughout the African diaspora. Black women play a key role in this mobilization. Another attendee of the march in Salvador, Mirits, is a 31-year-old woman who is part of the *Colectivo Negrada* organization from Espírito Santo. She stated,

The police are murdering a lot of Black women, along with men. In my state of Espírito Santo, the police are occupying spaces of Black communities in the name of security, and they are terrorizing people. It's [sic] clearly become a matter of genocide of Black people in Brazil. Women are the soul of this movement; we must band together as sisters of color to fight their killings of our people. (quoted in Forde 2015)

These young black women activists are like their predecessors, Leila Gonzalez and Luiza Barrios and present day leaders such as Matilde Ribeiro and Deise Benedito, among others. These women acknowledge that black women face discrimination and different structures of oppression place black women in unique dominated positions when compared to white women. While race is salient, scholarship focusing on inequality in Brazil cannot view issues of race and gender secondary to class.

Current black activism focusing on police brutality has the potential to have a profound impact on racial discourse because it not only emphasizes a link with African descendants as a larger racial group but also is transnational and intersectional in its vision. Such a transformative politics allows for a different way of thinking about studies on race, politics, and inequality.

INEQUALITY AND VIOLENCE

Considering the saliency of race and other intersectional identities in current and political events, I believe that studies on marginalization in Brazil, including the impact of racial discrimination on political behavior, need to critically analyze exclusion as a form of violence. In her discussion of the ways in which race is constituted in Brazil, Christen Smith (2016) states,

> Whether it is the physically violent moment when the police decide to use force against black bodies, the structurally violent moment when employers decide to discriminate in hiring based on appearance, or even the symbolically violent moment when children's entertainment stars associate black women with ugliness and foul odors; words, gestures, actions, movements, looks, and attitudes produce racial meaning dialogically. Racial formation in Brazil, in addition to being constituted by historical context, social reality, and epistemology; is also constituted by the nonarbitrary ways that race is inscribed onto the body. (13)

Too often are studies of inequality separated from studies concerning citizens lived realities. Her claim that race is inscribed on the body and that race is performed is well taken. Her discussion about the role that violence plays in maintaining an Afro-Paradise where foreigners celebrate exotic black bodies at the same time that the state destroys these bodies through terror and killing, highlights how state actors create racial categories for economic and social gain. Exclusion and discrimination are violent. Johan Galtung (1990) argues that cultural violence legitimizes direct violence and structural violence. An example of direct violence is killing, while an example of structural violence could be exploitation. Such acts can be legitimated through culture, and Galtung considers a number of aspects of culture such as ideology, religion, art, and empirical science. Smith's (2016) example of cultural violence is children's entertainment celebrities who associate negative stereotypes with black women. Her example of direct violence is police brutality and structural violence is employer discrimination. Yet violence has not become a framework for most social science studies on structural inequality. In Brazil, one's economic, political, and social position is naturalized based on skin color, hair texture, and other physical features. The ideology of the dominant society is that Afro-Brazilians belong in lesser paid jobs, that dark skin and tight curly hair indicates that one is inferior to those of light skin and straight hair and that power should be the exclusive domain of whites. Studying political inequality requires the researcher to understand how Afro-Brazilians experience the world and in this book, many Afro-Brazilians' way of viewing and explaining the political and social world are through raced-based and class exclusion, where they are situated differently according to intersectional identities. Such exclusion is a violent process as citizens are not able to fully experience citizenship and freedom of movement without worry. Despite this reality, Black movement activism demonstrates that Afro-descendants still challenge political and social inequality.

Brazil experienced unprecedented economic growth, millions joined the lower middle class and social and racial policies were implemented that improved the life chances of Afro-descendants. The current political climate threatens social and race-based programs that have a tremendous impact on some of the most vulnerable people in society. Progressive Afro-descendants and allies must challenge policies and politicians that threaten the well-being of African descendants and must strive for a more just and equal society. As Ana Paula Xongani (2016) states on her YouTube channel, "You know we always have to resist and I believe in our strength and our resistance to organize politically. And it is important that we remember that nothing is guaranteed."

Appendix

2005–2006 Survey of Political Opinion, Racial Attitudes and Candidate Preference (in Portuguese)

PESQUISA SOBRE OPINIÃO POLÍTICA, ATITUDES RACIAIS E PREFERÊNCIAS DE CANDIDATO

Interviewer asked survey questions and filled out survey.
Data _____

1. Entrevistador: Anote *tua* cor _____
2. Entrevistador: Anote *tua* idade_____
3. Entrevistador: Anote *teu* nível de educação _____
4. Entrevistador: Anote *teu* sexo: 1 □M 2□F
5. Entrevistador: Anote a cor do entrevistado. (*Escolhe um*)
   1□Branco 2□Preto 3 □Amarelo 4□Pardo 5□Índio
   6□outro_____

Informação demográfico
6. Qual é sua cor? _____
7. Qual é sua cor da lista? (*Escolhe um*)
   1 □Branco 2□Preto 3□Amarelo 4□Pardo 5□Índio
   6□Outro_____
8. Qual é a sua idade? _____
9. Anote o sexo do entrevistado. 1□M 2□F
10. Você mora em qual cidade? 1□Salvador 2□São Paulo
11. Você mora em qual bairro? 1□Federação 2□Itapoãn 3□Periperi

Partido político, Opinião de envolvimento nos políticos e Assuntos de voto
12. Qual é o partido de sua preferência?_____
13. Qual tipo de afiliação ou preferência você tem com esse partido?
    1□Muito forte 2□ Forte 3□Media 4□Não forte

14. Há um partido político que você acredita que é seu inimigo ou adversário?
    1☐Sim 2☐Não
    Se sim, qual? _____

15. Você tem confiança nos políticos?
    1☐Sim 2☐Não
    Porque sim ou porque não?_____
    _____
    _____

16. Quando você vota, o que é mais importante o partido ou o candidato?
    1☐O partido 2☐O candidato

17. Você já trocou de partido político?
    1☐ Sim 2☐Não

18. Que é o mais importante quando você seleciona um candidato?
    _____
    _____

19. Você acredita que sua situação econômica pessoal seria a mesma independente do candidato que ganhasse ou seria diferente de acordo com o candidato?
    1☐Mesmo 2☐Diferente

20. Um político já deu algo para você em troca do seu voto?
    1 ☐Sim 2☐Não
    Si sim, o que? _____

21. Um político já prometeu melhorar os serviços públicos do seu bairro como ruas melhores ou melhora da água ou algo assim para ter o seu voto?
    1☐Sim 2☐Não

22. Quando os políticos fazem promessas durante suas campanhas você acredita neles?
    1☐Sim 2☐Não

Opinião sobre o quanto é difícil para as pessoas abaixo, que eu vou ler para você, ser eleito para um cargo político.

23. Uma pessoa que tem um nível baixo da educação.
    1☐Muito difícil 2☐Um pouco difícil 3☐Não teria problema

24. Uma pessoa que não tem recursos econômicos.
    1☐Muito difícil 2☐Um pouco difícil 3☐Não teria problema

25. Um Negro.
    1☐Muito difícil 2☐Um pouco difícil 3☐Não teria problema

26. Uma pessoa que não tem um político em sua família.
    1☐Muito difícil 2☐Um pouco difícil 3☐Não teria problema

Política e Preferências de Candidato

27. *Agora eu vou fazer para você algumas perguntas sobre a importância que os políticos deram para alguns temas específicos nas eleições municipais de 2004.*
    Nas eleições municipais de 2004, você achou que foi importante que os candidatos que concorreram para vereador discutissem os temas abaixo.

    a. Falar sobre a discriminação no trabalho
       1☐Muito importante 2☐Importante 3☐Um pouco importante 4☐Não importante
    b. Melhoria na educação
       1☐Muito importante 2☐Importante 3☐Um pouco importante 4☐Não importante
    c. O Emprego
       1☐Muito importante 2☐Importante 3☐Um pouco importante 4☐Não importante
    d. A preservação da historia negra nas escolas
       1☐Muito importante 2☐Importante 3☐Um pouco importante 4☐Não importante
    e. O direito da mulher
       1☐Muito importante 2☐Importante 3☐Um pouco importante 4☐Não importante
    f. Os direitos dos homossexuais
       1☐Muito importante 2☐Importante 3☐Um pouco importante 4☐Não importante
    g. Programas para as pessoas que tem AIDS
       1☐Muito importante 2☐Importante 3☐Um pouco importante 4☐Não importante
    h. reparações raciais
       1☐Muito importante 2☐Importante 3☐Um pouco importante 4☐Não importante
    i. Habitação
       1☐Muito importante 2☐Importante 3☐Um pouco importante 4☐Não importante
    j. Transporte coletivo
       1☐Muito importante 2 ☐Importante 3☐Um pouco importante 4☐Não importante

k. Combate a corrupção

 1☐Muito importante 2☐Importante 3☐Um pouco importante 4☐Não importante

28. Você acredita que é importante que o político é evangélico?

 1☐Sim 2☐Não

29. Nas eleições municipais de 2004, onde você teve informação sobre as pessoas que concorreram para vereador?

 1☐Jornal 2☐Radio 3☐Televisão 4☐Outro_____

30. Se um candidato para vereador tiver a plataforma abaixo qual candidato você escolheria?

 ☐a. O candidato quer melhorar educação, transporte, trabalhar nos projetos para melhorar os bairros, e quer combate a corrupção no governo.

 ☐b. O candidato que melhorar educação e transporte, combate a corrupção e desigualdades raciais e sócio ambientais, e quer trabalhar nos projetos para melhorar os bairros.

31. Se um candidato para vereador tiver a plataforma abaixo qual candidato você escolheria?

 ☐a. O candidato quer trabalhar para os direitos dos trabalhadores, combate a corrupção, projetos para aumentar emprego, educação, saúde publica.

 ☐b. O candidato quer trabalhar para os direitos dos trabalhadores, combate a corrupção, diretos da mulher, projetos para aumentar emprego, educação, saúde publica.

32. Se um candidato para vereador tiver a plataforma abaixo qual candidato você escolheria?

 ☐a. O candidato quer trabalhar para os direitos dos trabalhadores, combate a corrupção, projetos para aumentar emprego, educação, promover atividades culturais, promover direitos para os idosos.

 ☐b. O candidato quer trabalhar para os direitos dos trabalhadores, combate a corrupção, diretos da mulher, projetos para aumentar emprego, educação, promover direitos para os idosos.

Opinião do Governo

33. Você concorda ou discorda que pessoas como você não tenham nenhuma influencia nas decisões do governo?

 1☐Concordo fortemente

 2☐Concordo

3☐Nem concordo ou discordo
4☐Discordo
5☐Discordo fortemente
34. Você acredita que tem corrupção no governo?

a) 1 ☐Sim 2☐Não
b) Si sim, porque? _____

_____

Política de Raça
35. Você conhece algumas organizações negras?
1☐Sim 1☐Não
36. Você conhece o movimento negro?
1☐Sim 2☐Não
37. Você acredita que o movimento negro é correto em relação ao preconceito no Brasil?
1☐Sim 2☐Não
38. Você acredita que o movimento negro só defende os direitos dos seus membros?
1☐Sim 2☐Não
39. Você é membro de alguma organização para melhorar as condições dos negros?
1☐Sim 2☐Não
40. Você gostaria de ser membro de alguma organização contra racismo?
1☐Sim 2☐Não
41. Porque há um número pequeno de negros entre os políticos?

_____

_____

42. Você acredita que os políticos dão importância às necessidades dos negros em suas campanhas?
1☐Sim 2☐Não
43. É importante que os políticos se preocupem com relações raciais?
1☐Sim 2☐Não
44. É importante que os políticos se preocupem com pobreza?
1☐Sim 2☐Não
45. Você acredita que o que acontece com os negros afeta você?
1☐Sim 2☐Não
46. Você acredita que os negros devem formar um partido político próprio?
1☐Sim 2☐Não

47. Ação afirmativa é um programa que enfoca o problema da discriminação contra negros e pardos. Ela tenta incentivar que nas universidades e no trabalho tenha uma porcentagem maior de negros e pardos. Você acredita que programas de ação afirmativa são importantes?
    1☐Sim 2☐Não
48. Você acredita que o fato de ser negro determina como você é tratado?
    1☐Sim 2☐Não
49. Você acredita que você é julgado mais pelo seu caráter do que pela sua cor?
    1☐Sim 2☐Não
50. Você acredita que você é julgado mais pela sua classe social que pela sua cor?
    1☐Sim 2☐Não
51. Você acredita que as crianças devem freqüentar escolas que ensinam a história dos afro-brasileiros?
    1☐Sim 2☐Não
52. Você acredita que negros devem votar em candidatos negros?
    1☐Sim 2☐Não
53. Na sua opinião, qual é o maior problema dos negros?

    _____

    _____

54. Você acredita que é importante que o presidente nomeie negros para posições no governo?
    1☐Sim 2☐Não
55. Você acredita que todos os Afro-descendentes de diferentes cores de pele são negros?
    1☐Sim 2☐Não

Cultura
56. Você conhece essas pessoas ou organizações?

    a. Benedita da Silva 1☐Sim 2☐Não
    b. Pelé   1☐Sim 2☐Não
    c. Ilê Aiyê

        a) 1☐Sim 2☐Não
        b) O que você acha sobre Ilé Aiye?

        _____

        _____

d. Gilberto Gil   1☐Sim 2☐Não
e. Marina da Silva   1☐Sim 2☐Não
f. Zumbi dos Palmares   1☐Sim 2☐Não
g. Joaquim Benedito Barbosa Gomes   1☐Sim 2☐Não
h. Matilde Ribeiro   1☐Sim 2☐Não
i. Fala Preta   1☐Sim 2☐Não
j. Criola   1☐Sim 2☐Não
k. Abayomi   1☐Sim 2☐Não
l. DJ Malboro   1☐Sim 2☐Não
m. Carlinhos Brown   1☐Sim 2☐Não
n. Santa Anastácia   1☐Sim 2☐Não
o Simples Rapórtagem   1☐Sim 2☐Não

57. a. Você assiste ou brinca o Carnaval?   1☐Sim 2☐Não
    b. Você escuta Axé?   1☐Sim 2☐Não
    c. Você escuta Samba?   1☐Sim 2☐Não
    d. Você escuta pagode?   1☐Sim 2☐Não
    e. Você joga ou assiste capoeira?   1☐Sim 2☐Não
    f. Você escuta Funk?   1☐Sim 2☐Não
    g. Você escuta Rap?   1☐Sim 2☐Não
    h. Você escuta Hip Hop?   1☐Sim 2☐Não
    i. Você escuta a Arrocha?   1☐Sim 2☐Não

58. Quando você pensa na África, o que você acredita?

_____

_____

Preconceito de Raça

59. Você acredita que a posição econômica dos negros é melhor, a mesma ou pior que os brancos?
    1☐Melhor
    2☐A mesma
    3☐Pior

60. Quando você pensa em homens negros, qual é a primeira coisa que lhe vem a cabeça?

    a) _____

    O que mais a imagem de um homem negro faz você pensar?

    b) _____

61. Quando você pensa em mulheres negras, qual é a primeira coisa que lhe vem a cabeça?

    a) _____

    O que mais a imagem de uma mulher negra faz você pensar?

    b) _____

62. Quando você pensa em homens brancos, qual é a primeira coisa que lhe vem a cabeça?

    a) _____

    O que mais a imagem de um homem branco faz você pensar?

    b) _____

63. Quando você pensa em mulheres brancas, qual é a primeira coisa que lhe vem a cabeça?

    a. _____

    b. O que mais a imagem de uma mulher branca faz você
    _____

64. Quem são mais inteligentes, os brancos ou os negros?
    1☐Brancos
    2☐Negros
    3☐Não há diferença.

65. Você acredita que os negros são preguiçosos?
    1☐Sim 2☐Não

66. Você acredita que negros podem ter sucesso?
    1☐Sim 2☐Não

67. Você acredita que negros com dinheiro e educação não são negros?
    1☐Sim 2☐Não

68. Você acredita que negros não gostam quando outros negros têm sucesso?
    1☐Sim, sempre 2☐Sim, as vezes 3☐Não

69. Quais os grupos que são mais afetados pelo preconceito? (escolhe um)
    1☐Os negros importantes e com educação
    3☐Mulheres negras
    2☐Trabalhadores negros
    4☐Todos os negros

70. Você votaria ou já votou alguma vez em um político negro?
    a. 1☐Já votou em político negro
    b) Para quem você votou?_____

2□Não votou, mas votaria
3□Não votou e não votaria

b. Si já votou em político negro você votaria de novo? 1□Sim 2□Não

71. Se você tivesse um chefe negro, você
1□Não ligaria
2□Se incomodaria mas o aceitaria
3□Não aceitaria e procuria por um outro trabalho

72. Em sua opinião os brasileiros brancos têm preconceito contra os negros? Se sim, quantos?
1□Não têm preconceito
2□Sim têm muito preconceito
3□Sim um pouco de preconceito
4□Sim tem preconceito, mas eu não sei quanto ou como

73. Sobre os brasileiros negros, eles têm preconceito contras os brancos? Se sim, quantos?
1□Não têm preconceito
2□Sim têm muito preconceito
3□Sim têm um pouco preconceito
4□Sim tem preconceito mas eu não sei como

74. Você tem preconceito contra os negros? Se sim, quantos?
1□Não, eu não tenho preconceito
2□Sim, eu tenho muito preconceito
3□Sim, eu tenho um pouco preconceito
4□Sim, eu tenho preconceito mas eu não sei como
5□Eu não sei se eu tenho preconceito

75. Você tem preconceito contra os brancos? Se sim, quantos?
1□Não, eu não tenho preconceito
2□Sim, eu tenho muito preconceito
3□Sim, eu tenho um pouco preconceito
4□Sim, eu tenho preconceito mas eu não sei como
5□Eu não sei se eu tenho preconceito

76. Você alguma vez teve relação ou casou com alguém de outra raça?
1□Nunca teve relação ou casou
2□Teve relação mas não casou
3□Casou com uma pessoa de outra raça Se sim, que cor?
_____

□Branco negro pardo/moreno amarelo Índio outro

77. Se seu filho quisesse casar com uma pessoa negra você
1□Não ligaria

2☐Se incomodaria mas aceitaria

3☐Não permitiria o casamento

78. Em sua opinião quais são alguns problemas importantes dos negros hoje no Brasil?

_____

_____

Informação sócio-demográfico

79. Qual é o seu estado conjugal? 1☐Casado 2☐Solteiro

80. a. Quantos anos você estudou?

1☐1 a 3 anos de estudo

2☐4 a 7 anos de estudo

3☐ 8 a 10 anos de estudo

4☐11 a 14 anos de estudo

5☐15 anos ou mais de estudo

b. Qual é seu nível de ensino?

1☐Não completo fundamental

2☐Fundamental

3☐ Médio

4☐Pré-vestibular

5☐Superior

6☐ Mestrado

7☐Doutorado

81. a Freqüenta algum lugar religião?

1☐Sim 2☐Não

b.(Que tipo)_____

82. O culto ou a missa dessa igreja tem um componente Afro-brasileira?

1☐Sim 2☐Não

83. Você esta trabalhando atualmente? a. 1☐ Sim 2☐Não 3☐No answer

a. Se sim, responda se você é:

1☐Funcionário público

2☐Assalariado com carteira assinada

3☐Conta própria regular (paga INSS)

4☐Autônomo universitário (profissional liberal)

5☐Empregador mais de dois empregados

6☐Assalariado sem carteira assinada

7☐Conta própria temporário (bico/freelancer)
8☐Auxiliar de família sem remuneração fixa

b. Se não que é sua ocupação?

9☐Estudante
10☐Aposentado
11☐Dona de casa
12☐Desemprego
13☐No answer

Renda

84. Somando o seu trabalho principal com outros trabalhos pagos e rendas, ao todo quanto você ganhou no mês passado?
1☐Até 1 salário mínimo (300 reais)
2☐Mais de 1 a 2 salários mínimos
3☐Mais de 2 a 4 salários mínimos
4☐Mais de 4 salários mínimos
5☐Não teve renda

85. Somando a sua renda das pessoas que moram com você, de quanto foi aproximadamente a renda familiar em sua casa no mês passado?
1☐Até 2 salários mínimos
2☐Mais de 2 a 5 salários mínimos
3☐Mais de 5 a 10 salários mínimos
4☐Mais de 10 a 20 salários mínimos
5☐Não teve renda

POLITICAL CANDIDATE PREFERENCE SURVEY IN 2008
(IN PORTUGUESE)

Bom dia eu sou _____. Estamos realizando uma pesquisa para uma pesquisadora dos Estados Unidos da Universidade de Duke. Eu gostaria de fazer uma entrevista com você, que vai durar de 15 a 20 minutos. O seu nome ou qualquer informação que possa identificar quem é você não será gravado. A pesquisa é sobre um candidato político imaginário e queria sua opinião política e sua preferência de um candidato. Você permite que eu posso lhe entrevista? Se você tiver qualquer dúvida, é só me falar.

Data _____

1. Entrevistador: Anote *sua* cor _____
2. Entrevistador: Anote *tua* idade_____

3. Entrevistador: Anote *seu* nível de educação _____
4. Entrevistador: Anote *seu* sexo: ☐M ☐F
5. Entrevistador: Anote a cor do entrevistado. (*Escolhe um*)
   ☐ Branco ☐Preto ☐Amarelo ☐Pardo ☐Índio ☐Outro_____
6. Entrevistador: Anote a cor de pele do entrevistado. (*Escolhe um*) [*0-sem cor*]
   ☐ 0 ☐ 1 ☐2 ☐3 ☐4 ☐5 ☐6 ☐7 ☐8 ☐9 ☐ 10

Informação demográfico
7. Qual é sua cor? _____
8. Dentro das categorias utilizadas pelo IBGE você se considera? (*Escolhe um*) ☐Branco ☐Preto ☐Amarelo ☐Pardo ☐Indígena ☐Outro_____
9. Qual é a sua idade? _____
10. Anote o sexo do entrevistado. _____
11. Você mora em qual cidade? _____
12. Você mora em qual bairro? _____

Entrevistador: Leia a propaganda e mostre a propaganda ao entrevistado

Opinião Política preferências de candidato
13. Qual é a cor do candidato político nessa propaganda? _____
14. Porque você acha que o candidato é desta cor?
    _____

15. a. Você votaria esse candidato para deputado federal?
       ☐Sim ☐Não ☐Talvez
    b. Porque sim ou porque não?_____
    _____

16. Dos temas que ele discutiu, qual é mais importante para você?
    _____

17. Você acha que o candidato tem experiência suficiente para ser deputado federal?
    ☐Sim ☐ Não
18. A experiência do candidate e importante quando voce vota?
    ☐Muito importante ☐Importante ☐Um pouco importante ☐Não importante
19. a. Qual é o partido de sua preferência?_____
    b. Qual tipo de ligação ou preferência você tem com esse partido?
       ☐Muito forte ☐ Forte ☐Media ☐Fraco

20. a. Você já votou alguma vez em um político negro? □Sim □Não
    b. (Se o entrevistado já votou em político negro) Para quem você votou?_____
21. O que você acha sobre a qualidade da democracía brasileira? [Pode escolher 1 a 10. Um é muito mal e dez é muito bom]
Muito mal   Muito bom
  1   2   3   4   5   6   7   8   9   10
22. Você concorda que o governo deve gastar dinheiro para programas sociais como programas de saúde, programas para crianças, e programas para famílias carentes?
□Concordo muito □Concordo □Concordo um pouco □Não concordo
23. Quando você vota, o que é mais importante o partido ou o candidato?
□O partido □O candidato
24. Qual tema é mais importante a você?
□Saúde □Segurança □Combate Racismo □Transporte
25. Qual programa é mais importante a você?
□Os programas para melhorar a habitação□Entretenimento para emprego
□ações afirmativas
26. Você acha que é importante que os politicos discutirem emprego?
□Não importante □Um pouco importante □Muito importante

Atitudes Raciais
27. Você concorda que o racismo é um problema no Brasil?
□Concordo muito □Concordo □Concordo um pouco □Não concordo
28. Em sua opinião os brasileiros brancos têm preconceito contra os pretos? Se sim, qual o grau de preconceito?
□Não têm preconceito
□Sim têm muito preconceito
□Sim um pouco de preconceito
□Sim tem preconceito, mas eu não sei quanto ou como
29. Em sua opinião os brasileiros brancos têm preconceito contra os pardos? Se sim, quantos?
□Não têm preconceito
□Sim têm muito preconceito
□Sim um pouco de preconceito
□Sim tem preconceito, mas eu não sei quanto ou como

30. Jà teve alguma expêrencia com o racismo? ☐Sim ☐Não

31. Ação afirmativa é um programa de medidas que foca o problema da discriminação contra pretos e pardos. Ela tenta incentivar que nas universidades e no mercado de trabalho exista uma porcentagem maior de pretos e pardos. Você acha que programas de ação afirmativa são importantes?
    ☐Muito importante ☐Importante ☐Pouco importante ☐Não são importantes

32. Você acha que você é julgado mais pela sua classe social que pela sua cor?
    ☐Classe ☐Cor

33. Você acha que os pardos e pretos tem a mesma chance que os brancos ganhar emprego?
    ☐Sim ☐Não

34. Você conhece o movimento negro?
    ☐Sim ☐Não

35. Você acredita que o movimento negro é correto em relação ao pre-conceito no Brasil?
    ☐Sim ☐Não

36. O Lei Federal 10.693/03 requere o ensino da história Africana e Afro-Brasilera mas escolas em todos os níveis. Você acha que esse lei é importante?
    ☐Muito importante ☐Importante ☐Pouco importante ☐Não importante

37. Você é membro de alguma organização para melhorar as condições dos negros?
    ☐Sim ☐Não

38. Em geral, você acha o que acontece aos negros no Brasil vai afeta o que acontecem em sua vida?
    ☐Não ☐Não muito ☐Algum ☐Muito

39. Você acha que a situação econômico dos negros é melhour, o mesmo, ou pior que os brancos?
    ☐Muito pior ☐Pouco pior ☐Mesmo ☐Pouco melhor ☐Muito melhor

Informação Socio-demografíco

40. Somando o seu trabalho principal com outros tipos de renda, quanto você ganhou ao todo no mês passado?
    ☐Até 1 salário mínimo (R$415)
    ☐Mais de 1 a 2 salários mínimos (mais de R$415 a 830)
    ☐Mais de 2 a 4 salários mínimos (mais de R$830 a 1660)

□Mais de 4 salários mínimos (mais de R$1660)
□Não teve renda

41. Somando a sua renda e a das pessoas que moram com você, de quanto foi aproximadamente a renda familiar em sua casa no mês passado?
□Até 2 salários mínimos (R$830)
□Mais de 2 a 5 salários mínimos (mais de R$830 a 2075)
□Mais de 5 a 10 salários mínimos (mais de R$2075 a 4150)
□Mais de 10 a 20 salários mínimos (mais de R$4150 a 8300)
□Não teve renda

42. Qual é o seu estado conjugal civil?
□Casado □Solteiro □Divorciado □ Viúvo

43. Quantos anos você estudou?

a. □1 a 3 anos de estudo

□4 a 7 anos de estudo
□ 8 a 10 anos de estudo
□11 a 14 anos de estudo
□15 anos ou mais de estudo

b. Qual é seu nível de ensino?

□Fundamental incompleto
□Fundamental completo
□Médio incompleto
□Médio complete
□Pré-vestibular
□Superior incompleto
□Superior completo
□Mestrado
□Doutorado

POLITICAL CANDIDATE PREFERENCE SURVEY 2008
(IN ENGLISH)

Good day! _____. I am a member of a team of researchers from the United States at Duke University. I would like to do an interview with you that should last from 15 to 20 minutes. Your name and other information that could identify you will not be recorded. The interview is about a fictitious political candidate and I would like to know your political opinions and candidate preference. Do you permit me to do the interview? If you have any questions let me know.

    Date _____

1. Interviewer: Note your color _____
2. Interviewer: Note your age_____
3. Interviewer: Note your level of education _____
4. Interviewer: Note your sex: □M □F
5. Interviewer: Note the respondents color (Choose one) □ white □black □yellow □brown □indigenous □other_____
6. Interviewer: Note the skin color of the respondent. (Choose one) □0 □1 □2 □3 □4 □ 5 □ 6 □7 □ 8 □9 □ 10

Demographic Information
[The interview begins here] Before I read the advertisement of the imaginary candidate I will ask some demographic questions

7. What is your color? _____
8. Among the groups used by the IBGE which one do you consider yourself? (Choose one) □White □Black □Yellow □Brown □Indigenous □Other_____
9. What is your age? _____
10. Note the sex of the respondent. _____
11. Which city do you live in? _____
12. Which neighborhood do you live in ? _____

Interviewer: Read the advertisement and show it to the respondent.

Political Opinion and Candidate Preference
13. What is the color of the political candidate in this advertisement?
_____
14. Why do you think the candidate is this color?
15. a. Would you vote for this candidate for federal deputy?
    □Yes □No □Maybe
   b. Why or why not?_____

16. Out of the issues he addresses, what is the most important?
_____

17. Do you think the candidate has enough experience to be a federal deputy?
    □Yes □ No
18. How important is experience when you vote?
    □Very Important □important □A little important □Not important
19. a. What political party do you prefer? _____
    b. How strong is your affiliation?
       □Very strong □Strong □Medium □Weak

20. a. Have you already voted for a black politician?
       □Yes □No
    b. If you have already voted for a black politician who did you vote for?

    _____

21. What do you think about the quality of Brazilian democracy? [One is very bad and ten is very good.]
    Very bad Very good
    1 2 3 4 5 6 7 8 9 10
22. How much do you agree with government spending on social programs such as healthcare, programs for children, or programs for needy families?
    □Agree a lot □ Agree somewhat □Agree a little □ Do not agree
23. When you vote for a candidate do you vote on the basis of the candidate or the political party?
    □Candidate □Political party
24. Which one of these issues is the most important?
    □Health □Safety □Combat Racism □ Transportation
25. Which program is most important to you?
    □Programs to improve housing □Job training □Affirmative action
26. How important is it that politicians address unemployment?
    □Not important at all □A little important □Very important
27. Do you agree that racism is a problem in Brazil?
    □Agree a lot □Agree □Agree a little □Do not agree
28. In your opinion do white Brazilians have prejudice against blacks (*pretos*)?
    □There is no prejudice
    □Yes a lot of prejudice
    □ Yes a little prejudice
    □Yes a little prejudice but I don't know how much

29. In your opinion do white Brazilians have prejudice against browns (*pardos*)?
    ☐There is no prejudice ☐Yes a lot of prejudice ☐ Yes a little prejudice
    ☐Yes a little prejudice but I don't know how much
30. Have you ever had an experience of racism? ☐Yes ☐No
31. Affirmative action is a program that focuses on discrimination against blacks (*pretos*) and browns (*pardos*). It tries to increase the number of blacks and browns in universities and in the labor market. Do you think affirmative action programs are important?
    ☐Very important
    ☐Somewhat important
    ☐A little important
    ☐Not very important
    ☐Not important
32. Are you judged more by your class or color?
    ☐Class ☐Color
33. Do you think browns and black have the same chance as whites to get jobs?
    ☐Yes ☐No
34. Do you know the black movement?
    ☐Yes ☐No
35. Do you think the black movement is correct in relation to prejudice in Brazil?
    ☐Yes ☐No
36. Federal Law 10.693/03 requires the teaching of African and Afro-Brazilian history in primary schools, middle and kindergarten. Do you think this law is important?
    ☐Very important ☐ Important ☐A little important ☐Not important
37. Are you a member of an organization to better the condition of blacks?
    ☐Yes ☐No
38. In general, do you think what happens to blacks in brazil will affect what happens in your life?
    ☐No
    ☐Not a lot
    ☐Some
    ☐A lot

39. Do you think the economic situation of blacks is better, the same, or worse than whites?

☐Much worse ☐A little worse ☐ Same ☐A little better ☐A lot better

Socio-demographic information

Monthly Family Income

38. Summing your main work with other types of income, how much did you make in the past month?
    - ☐ Up to 1 minimum salary (415 reais)
    - ☐ More than 1 to 2 minimum salaries
    - ☐ More than 2 to 4 minimum salaries
    - ☐ More than 4 minimum salaries
    - ☐ No salary

39. Summing your income with people who live with you, how much family income did your family make last month?
    - ☐ Up to 2 minimum salaries
    - ☐ More than 2 to 5 minimum salaries
    - ☐ More than 5 to 10 minimum salaries
    - ☐ More than 10 to 20 minimum salaries
    - ☐ No salary

40. What is you marital status? ☐Married ☐Single ☐Divorced ☐Widow

41. a. How many years have you studied?

    - ☐1 to 3 years of study
    - ☐4 to 7 years of study
    - ☐ 8 to 10 years of study
    - ☐11 to 14 years of study
    - ☐15 years or more

    b. What is your level of school?

    - ☐Fundamental incomplete
    - ☐Fundamental complete
    - ☐ Incomplete high school
    - ☐Completed high school
    - ☐Pre-college
    - ☐Incomplete college
    - ☐Complete high school
    - ☐ Master degree
    - ☐Doctorate degree

2012 COLOR, REPRESENTATION, AND AFFIRMATIVE ACTION IN BRAZIL: IN-DEPTH INTERVIEW SURVEY (IN ENGLISH)

Note skin color (Interviewers noted skin color from 1 (light) to 5 (dark) and photos denoting colors were provided to interviewer.)

Note hair type (wavy, curly, relaxed/megahair, braids and photos denoting hair types were provided to interviewer)

Politics

1. Afro-Brazilians are more than half the population of Brazil but there are not many black politicians at the federal, state, or local level? In your opinion why is this so or in other words why is there a low number of black politicians?
2. Do you think it is important to vote for black political candidates?
3. Do you vote for black politicians? If so, why and which ones have you voted for?
4. What are some major issues specific to blacks?
5. Should politicians address specific to blacks?
6. Why does the United States, a country where blacks are only 12% of the population, have a black president?
7. Why is it difficult for Blacks in Brazil to elect black mayors and governors?
8. Do you think Brazil will ever elect a black president?

Race/Color

9. What is the difference between *negro* and *preto* and why do some people self-identify as *preto* and others as *negro*?
10. Why do some Afro-Brazilians not identify as *negro* or *preto*?
11. Do you identify as black, why or why not?
12. What is blackness in Brazil?
13. Do you think what happens to blacks affects you?

Affirmative Action

14. What are quotas? What is affirmative action?
15. What do you think about them?
16. The Supreme court unanimously supported quotas. What do you think about this?

The Economy and Politics

17. What do you think about Brazilian democracy?
18. What do you think about the current growth of the Brazilian economy?

19. How will this growth impact Blacks in Brazil?
20. What is your political party affiliation and why?

Demographic Information
1. What is your color?
2. Considering the categories of the Brazilian Institute of Geography and Statistics, what is your color? Choose one.
   ☐White ☐Black ☐Brown ☐Yellow ☐Indigenous
3. How old are you? _____
4. Note respondent's gender. ☐Male ☐Female
5. Which city do you live in? _____
6. Which neighborhood do you live in? _____
7. What is your marital status?_____
8. How many years have you studied?
   ☐1–3 ☐4–7 ☐8–10 ☐11–14 ☐15 or more
9. What is your level of education?
   ☐fundamental incomplete
   ☐fundamental complete
   ☐ incomplete high school
   ☐completed high school
   ☐pre-college
   ☐incomplete college
   ☐complete high school
   ☐ master degree
   ☐doctorate degree
10. What is your profession? _____
11. What is your individual income level?
    ☐ Up to 1 minimum salary
    ☐ More than 1 to 2 minimum salaries
    ☐ More than 2 to 4 minimum salaries
    ☐ More than 4 minimum salaries
    ☐ No income
12. What is your Family's income level?
    ☐ Up to 2 minimum salaries
    ☐ More than 2 to 5 minimum salaries
    ☐ More than 5 to 10 minimum salaries
    ☐ More than 10 to 20 minimum salaries
    ☐ No income

2012 RAÇA E REPRESENTAÇÃO E AÇOES AFIRMATIVAS NO
BRASIL: IN-DEPTH INTERVIEW SURVEY (IN PORTUGUESE)

Anote a cor de pele.

Anote o tipo de cabelo.

1. Os negros são mais de metade da população brasileira mas ha poucos
   politícos negros nos niveis federal, estadual e local. Na sua opinião,
   porque isso ocorre, em outras palavras, por que há um número pequeno
   de políticos negros?
2. O Sr./Sra acha que e importante votar em candidatos políticos negros?
3. O(a) senhor/senhora vota em politícos negros? Si sim, porque e votou
   em
   quais candidatos?
4. Quais sao as temas ou necesidades especificas aos negros no Brasil?
5. O Sr./Sra. acha que os políticos (em geral) dão importância as necessidades dos negros nas suas campanhas?
6. Porque os Estados Unidos, um pais onde os negros só são 12 porcentagem da população tem um presidente negro?
7. Porque e difícil aos negros no Brasil se elegem prefeitos ou governadores?
8. O Sr./Sra. Acha que Brasil elegira um presidente negro?

Raça ou Cor

9. Qual e a diferença entre preto ou negro e porque algumas pessoas se
   identificam como pretos e outros como negros?
10. Porque alguns afro-brasileiros não se identficam com pretos ou
    negros?
11. Você se identifca como negro? Porque ou porque não?
12. O que significa negritude no Brasil?
13. Você acha que o que acontece com os negros afetam voce? Porque ou
    porque não?

Ações Afirmativas

14. O que sao cotas? O que sao açoes afirmativas?
15. O que o Sr./Sra. Acha sobre cotas e açoes afirmativas?
16. O Supremo Tribunal Federal votam unanimo em favor de cotas. O que o
    Sr./Sra. Acha sobre a decisão dos cotas do Supremo Tribunal Federal?

A Economia e Políticos

17. O que voce acha sobre democracía brasileira?
18. O que o Sr./a Sra acha sobre o cresimento da economia Brasileira?

19. Como seria o impacto do crescimento da economia Brasileira nos negros?
20. Qual é o partido de sua preferência e porque?

Informação Demográfico

1. Qual é sua cor? _____
2. Dentro das categorias utilizadas pelo IBGE você se considera? (Escolhe um)

   ☐Branco ☐ Preto ☐Amarelo ☐Pardo ☐Índio ☐Outro_____
3. Qual é a sua idade? _____
4. Anote sua sexo. _____
5. Você mora em qual cidade? _____
6. Você mora em qual bairro? _____
7. Qual é o seu estado conjugal? ☐Casado ☐Solteiro ☐Viuvo
8. a.Quantos anos você estudou?

   ☐1 a 3 anos de estudo

   ☐4 a 7 anos de estudo

   ☐ 8 a 10 anos de estudo

   ☐11 a 14 anos de estudo

   ☐15 anos ou mais de estudo
9. Qual é seu nível de ensino?

   ☐fundamental incompleto

   ☐fundamental completo

   ☐ médio incompleto

   ☐médio completo

   ☐pré-vestibular

   ☐superior incompleto

   ☐superior completo

   ☐ mestrado

   ☐doutorado
10. Você está trabalhando atualmente?

    a. ☐ Sim ☐Não

    b. Se não que é sua ocupação?

    ☐Estudante ☐aposentado ☐Dona de casa ☐desemprego
11. Qual é sua profisão? _____

Renda

12. Somando o seu trabalho principal com outros tipos de renda, quanto você ganhou ao todo no mês passado?

    ☐Até 1 salário mínimo (622 reais)

☐ Mais de 1 a 2 salários mínimos
☐ Mais de 2 a 4 salários mínimos
☐ Mais de 4 salários mínimos
☐ Não teve renda

13. Somando a sua renda das pessoas que moram com você, de quanto foi aproximadamente a renda familiar em sua casa no mês passado?
☐ Até 2 salários mínimos
☐ Mais de 2 a 5 salários mínimos
☐ Mais de 5 a 10 salários mínimos
☐ Mais de 10 a 20 salários mínimos
☐ Não teve renda

14. Alguém em sua família já recebeu a bolsa família?
☐ Sim
☐ Não

References

Affigne, Tony. 2014. *The Latino Voice in Political Analysis, 1970–2014: From Exclusion to Empowerment.* New York: New York University Press.

Aguilar, Rosario, Saul Cunow, Scott Desposato, and Leonardo Barone. 2015. "Ballot Structure, Candidate Race, and Vote Choice in Brazil." *Latin American Research Review* 50(3): 175–202.

Alexander, Michelle. 2012. *The New Jim Crow: Mass Incarceration in the Age of Colorblindness.* New York: The New Press.

Almeida, Alberto Carlos. 2007. *A Cabeça do Brasileiro.* Rio de Janeiro: Editora Record.

Alves, Jaime. 2014. "From Necropolis to Blackpolis: Necropolitical Governance and Black Spatial Praxis in São Paulo, Brazil." *Antipode* 46(2): 323–339.

Anderson, Mark. 2009. *Black and Indigenous: Garifuna Activism and Consumer Culture in Honduras.* Minneapolis: University of Minnesota Press.

Andrews, George Reid. 1991. *Blacks and Whites in Sao Paulo, Brazil, 1888–1988.* Madison: University of Wisconsin Press.

Angel, Ronald J. 2014. "The Rise of Ethnic Politics in Latin America." *Ethnic and Racial Studies* 37(10): 1884–1886.

Arcand, Jean-Louis, and Béatrice D'Hombres. 2004. "Racial Discrimination in the Brazilian Labour Market: Wage, Employment and Segregation Effects." *Journal of International Development* 16(8): 1053–1066.

Arias, Omar, Gustavo Yamada, and Luis Tejerina. 2004. "Education, Family Background and Racial Earnings Inequality in Brazil." *International Journal of Manpower* 25(3/4): 355–374.

Arruda, Roldão. 2014. "População negra é maior beneficiária dos programas sociais." *Estadão,* October 15, http://politica.estadao.com.br/blogs/roldao-arruda/populacao -negra-e-maior-beneficiaria-dos-programas-sociais/ (accessed December 11, 2016).

Azevedo, Thales de. 1996 [1953]. *As Elites de Cor Numa Cidade Brasileira: Um Estudo de Ascensão Social e Classes Sociais e Grupos de Prestígio.* Salvador: Editoria da Universidade Federal da Bahia.

Bailey, Stanley R., and Edward E. Telles. 2006 "Multiracial vs. Collective Black Categories: Census Classification Debates in Brazil." *Ethnicities* 6: 74–101.

Bailey, Stanley, Mara Loveman, and Jeronimo Muniz. 2013. "Measures of 'Race' and the Analysis of Racial Inequality in Brazil." *Social Science Research* 42(1): 106–119.

Bailey, Stanley. 2009a. *Legacies of Race: Identities, Attitudes, and Politics in Brazil.* Palo Alto: Stanford University Press.

Bailey, Stanley. 2009b. "Public Opinion on Nonwhite Underrepresentation and Racial Identity Politics in Brazil." *Latin American Politics and Society* 51(4): 69–99.

Bairros, Luiza. 1991. "Mulher Negra: O Reforço da Subordinação." In *Desigualdade Racial no Brasil Contemporâneo,* ed. Peggy Lovell, 177–193. Belo Horizonte: MGSP Editores, Ltda.

Bancario Rio. 2013. Salvador Tem Maior População e é a Mais Discriminada. Online Bancario. November 2. http://www.bancariosrio.org.br/2013/ultimas-noticias/item /25008-salvador-tem-maior-populacao-negro-do-pais-e-e-a-mais-discriminada (accessed July 8, 2017).

Baran, Michael D. 2007. "'Girl, You Are Not Morena. We Are Negras!': Questioning the Concept of 'Race' in Southern Bahia, Brazil." *Ethos* 35(3): 383–409.

Barreto, Matt. 2007. "Sí se puede! Latino Candidates and the Mobilization of Latino Voters." *American Political Science Review* 101(3): 425–441.

Bastide, Roger, and Florestan Fernandes. 1959. *Relações Raciais Entre Negros e Brancos em São Paulo: Ensaio Sociológico Sôbre as Origensm as Manifestações Atuais e Efeitos do Preconceito de Côr na Sociedade Paulistana.* São Paulo: Companhia Editoria Nacional.

Bianchi, Paula, and Tais Vilela. 2014. "Cresce o número de quem se diz 'preto' e 'pardo'; grupo chega a 53% no país." September 18. http://noticias.uol.com.br/cotidiano /ultimas-noticias/2014/09/18/ibge-n-de-autodeclarados-pretos-e-pardos-sobe-e-neg ros-sao-45-no-pais.htm (accessed July 8, 2017).

Bohn, Simone. 2011. Social Policy and Vote in Brazil: Bolsa Familia and the Shifts in Lula's Electoral Base. *Latin American Research Review* 46(1): 54–79.

Bohn, Simone. 2013. "The Electoral Behavior of the Poor in Brazil: A Research Agenda." *Latin American Research Review* 48(2): 25–31.

Bonilla-Silva, Eduardo and Karen Glover. 2006. "'We Are All Americans': The Latin Americanization of Race Relations in the United States." In *The Changing Terrain of Race and Ethnicity,* eds. Maria Krysan and Amanda E. Lewis. New York: Russell Sage Foundation.

Bonilla-Silva, Eduardo. 2004. "From Bi-Racial to Tri-Racial: Towards a New System of Racial Stratification in the USA." *Ethnic and Racial Studies* 27(6): 931–950.

Bourdieu, Pierre, and Loïc Wacquant. 1999. "On the Cunning of Imperialist Reason." *Theory Culture and Society* 16(1): 41–58.

Branscombe, Nyla R., Michael T. Schmitt, and Richard D. Harvey. 1999. "Perceiving Pervasive Discrimination among African Americans: Implications for Group Identification and Well-Being." *Journal of Personality and Social Psychology* 77(1): 135–149.

Brubaker, Rogers, and Frederick Cooper. 2000. Beyond "Identity." *Theory and Society* 29: 1–47.

Bueno, Natália S. and Thad Dunning. 2017. "Race, Resources, and Representation: Evidence from Brazilian Politicians." *World Politics* 69(2): 327–365.

Buras, Kristen L. 2011. "Race, Charter Schools, and Conscious Capitalism: On the Spatial Politics of Whiteness as Property (and the Unconscionable Assault on Black New Orleans)." *Harvard Educational Review* 81(2): 296–331.

Burdick, John. 1998. "The Lost Constituency of Brazil's Black Movements." *Latin American Perspectives* 25: 136–155.

Burdick, John. 2009. "Collective Identity and Racial Thought in São Paulo's Black Gospel Music Scene." *Music and Arts in Action* 1(2): 16–29.

Butler, Kim. 1998. *Freedoms Given, Freedoms Won: Afro-Brazilians in Post-Abolition São Paulo and Salvador.* New Brunswick: Rutgers University Press.

Caldwell, Kia. 2007. *Negras in Brazil: Re-envisioning Black Women, Citizenship, and the Politics of Identity.* New Brunswick: Rutgers University Press.

Carey, Tony E., Regina P. Branton, and Valerie Martinez-Ebers. 2014. "The Influence of Social Protests on Issue Salience among Latinos." *Political Research Quarterly* 67(3): 615–627.

Carneiro, Sueli. 2003. "Mulheres em Movimento." *Estudos Avançados* (17): 49. http://dx.doi.org/10.1590/S0103–40142003000300008 (accessed July 8, 2017).

Carta Capital. 2016. "Sociedade: Preconceito. 'O fosso entre brancos e negros no mercado de trabalho: Em 13 anos, Renda de Pretos e Pardos Avançou Mais que a dos Brancos, mas Disparidade ainda é Gritante'." http://www.cartacapital.com.br/blogs/parlatorio /o-fosso-entre-brancos-e-negros-no-mercado-de-trabalho (accessed July 8, 2017).

Cassilde, Stéphanie. 2008. On the Endogeneity of Self-Declared Skin Colour in Contemporary Brazil. 11th IZA Summer School, Buch/Ammersee, Germany.

Castro, Mônica. 1993. "Raça e Comportamento Político." *Dados* 36: 469–491.

Cleland, Danielle. 2017. The Power of Race in Cuba: Racial Ideology and Black Consciousness during the Revolution. Cary: Oxford University Press.

Cohen, Cathy. 1999. *The Boundaries of Blackness: AIDS and the Breakdown of Black Politics.* Chicago: University of Chicago Press.

Cohen, Cathy. 2010. *Democracy Remixed: Black Youth and the Future of American Politics.* Cary: Oxford University Press.

Collins, Patricia Hill. 1990. *Black Feminist Thought: Knowledge, Consciousness, and the Politics of Empowerment.* London: Harper Collins.

Costa, Alexandre Emboaba. 2014. *Reimagining Black Difference and Politics in Brazil: From Racial Democracy to Multiculturalism.* New York: Palgrave MacMillan.

Covin, David. 2006. *The Unified Black Movement in Brazil 1978–2002.* Jefferson: McFarland Press.

Crenshaw, Kimberlé. 1991."Mapping the Margins: Intersectionality, Identity Politics, and Violence against Women of Color." *Stanford Law Review* 43(6): 1241–1299.

Crissien, Jean Paul. 2015. "Stand For" and Deliver? Reserved Seats, Ethnic Constituencies, and Minority Representation in Colombia. Doctoral Dissertation. Arizona State University.

Daniel, G. Reginald. 2006. "Race and Multiraciality in Brazil and the United States: Converging Paths? University Park: Pennsylvania State University Press.

Darity Jr., William, Jason Dietrich, and Darrick Hamilton. 2005. "Bleach in the Rainbow: Latin Ethnicity and Preference for Whiteness." *Transforming Anthropology* 13(2): 103–109.

Darity Jr., William. 2003. "Employment Discrimination, Segregation, and Health." *American Journal of Public Health* 93(2): 226–231.

Davenport, Lauren D. 2016. "Beyond Black and White: Biracial Attitudes in Contemporary U.S. Politics." *American Political Science Review* 110(1): 52–67.

Davenport, Lauren. 2016a. "Beyond Black and White: Biracial Attitudes on Contermporary I.S. Politics." *The American Political Science Review* 110(1): 52–67.

Davenport, Lauren. 2016b. "The Role of Gender, Class, and Religion in Biracial Americans Racial Labeling Decisions." *American Sociological Review* 8(1): 57–84.

Davis, Daríen, Tianna Paschel, and Judith Morrison. "Pan Afro-Latin African Americanism Alliances Revisited: Legacies and Lessons for Transnational Alliances in the New Millennium." In *Afro-Descendants, Identity, and the Struggle for Development in the Americas*, eds. Bernd Reiter and Kimberly Simmons, 19–50. East Lansing: Michigan State University Press.

Dawson, Michael. 1994. *Behind the Mule: Race and Class in African American Politics.* Princeton, NJ: Princeton University Press.

Degler, Carl. 1986. *Neither Black nor White: Slavery and Race Relations in Brazil and the United States.* Madison: The University of Wisconsin Press.

Delgado, Richard, and Jean Stefancic. 2012. *Critical Race Theory: An Introduction.* New York: New York University Press.

Dietrich, Erich. 2015. "Ambition with Resistance: Affirmative Action in Brazil's Public Universities." In *Race, Politics, and Education in Brazil Affirmative Action in Higher Education*, eds. Rosana Heringer and Ollie Johnson III, 155–177. New York: Palgrave Macmillan.

Edmonds, Alexander. 2010. *Pretty Modern: Beauty, Sex, and Plastic Surgery in Brazil.* Durham: Duke University Press.

Escobar, Arturo. 2008. *Territories of Difference: Place, Movements, Life, Redes.* Durham: Duke University Press.

Fernandes, Florestan. 1965. *A Integração do Negro na Sociedade de Classes.* São Paulo: Dominus Editora.

Fernandes, Sujatha. 2014. "Malandreo Negro: Gangsta Rap and the Politics of Exclusion in Venezuela." In *Comparative Perspectives on Afro-Latin America*, eds. Kwame Dixon and John Burdick, 72–92. University Press of Florida.

Figo, Anderson. 2017. "Preço de Aluguel Recua 0,12% em Junho. http://exame.abril.com .br/seu-dinheiro/preco-do-aluguel-recua-012-em-junho/ (accessed July 29, 2017).

Figureido, Angela. 2010. "Out of Place: The Experience of the Black Middle Class." In *Brazil's New Racial Politics*, eds. Bernd Reiter and Gladys Mitchell, 51–64. Colorado: Lynne Rienner Press.

Floyd-Alexander, Nikol. 2012. "Disappearing Acts: Reclaiming Intersectionality in the Social Sciences in a Post-Black Feminist Era." *Feminist Formations* (24)2:1–25.

Forde, Kaelyn. 2015. "Where Police Kill 6 Times More People Than in the U.S." *Refinery29.* August 26. https://google.com/amp/www.www.refinery29.com/amp/2015 /08/92326/brazil-black-lives-matter-police-brutality-protest (accessed July 8, 2017).

Fraga, Luis; John Garcia; Rodney Hero; Jones-Correa, Michael; Valerie Martinez-Ebers, and Gary Segura. 2006. "Su Casa Es Nuestra Casa: Latino Politics Research and the Development of American Political Science." *American Political Science Review* (10)4: 515–521.

Francis, Andrew M. and Maria Tannuri-Pianto. 2012. "Using Brazil's Racial Continuum to Examine the Short-Term Effects of Affirmative Action in Higher Education," *Journal of Human Resources* 47(3): 754–784.

Francisco, Flavio. 2010. Fronteiras em Definição: Identidades Negras e Imagens dos Estados Unidos e da África no Jornal O Clarim da Alvorada (1924–1932). MA Thesis. Universidade de São Paulo.

Frank, Reanne, Ilana Redstone Akresh and Bo Lu. 2010. "Latino Immigrants and the U.S. Racial Order: How and Where Do They Fit In?" *American Sociological Review* 20 (10):1–24.

Frasure, Lorrie. 2010. "The Burden of Jekyll and Hyde: Barack Obama, Racial Identity and Black Political Behavior." In *Whose Black Politics: Cases in Post-Racial Black Leadership*, ed. Andra Gillespie, 133–154. New York: Routledge.

French, Jan. 2009. *Legalizing Identities. Becoming Black or Indian in Brazil's Northeast.* University of North Carolina Press: Chapel Hill, NC.

French, Jan. 2013. "Rethinking Police Violence in Brazil: Unmasking the Public Secret of Race." *Latin American Politics and Society* 55(4): 161–181.

Freyre, Gilberto. 1956. *The Masters and the Slaves: (Casa Grande & Senzala) A Study in the Development of Brazilian Civilization.* New York: Knopf.

Fried, Brian. 2012. "Distributive Politics and Conditional Cash Transfers: The Case of Brazil's Bolsa Família." *World Development* 40(5):1042–1053.

Fuente, Alejandro da la. 2001. *A Nation for All: Race, Inequality, and Politics in Twentieth-Century Cuba.* Chapel Hill: University of North Carolina Press.

Galtung, Johan. 1990. "Cultural Violence." *Journal of Peace Research* 27(3): 291–305.

Garcia, Chris, and Gabriel Sanchez. 2008. *Moving (into) the Mainstream?: Latinos in the U.S. Political System?* Saddle River: Pearson and Prentice Hall.

Gay, Claudine. 2002. "Spirals of Trust? The Effect of Descriptive Representation on the Relationship between Citizens and Their Government." *American Journal of Political Science* 46(4): 717–732.

Gillam, Reighan. 2016. "The Help, Unscripted: Constructing the Black Revolutionary Domestic in Afro-Brazilian Media." *Feminist Media Studies.* http://dx.doi.org /10.1080/14680777.2015.1137338 (accessed July 8, 2017).

Gilliam, Angela and Onik'a Gilliam. 1999. "Odyssey: Negotiating the Subjectivity of Mulata Identity in Brazil." *Latin American Perspectives* 26(3): 60–84.

Golash-Boza, Tanya and William Darity Jr. 2008. "Latino Racial Choices: The Effects of Skin Colour and Discrimination on Latinos' and Latinas' Racial Self-Identifications" *Ethnic and Racial Studies* 31(5): 1–36.

Golash-Boza, Tanya. 2011. *Yo Soy Negro: Blackness in Peru.* Gainsville: University Press of Florida.

Goldsmith, Arthur H., Darrick Hamilton and William Darity, Jr. 2007. "From Dark to Light: Skin Color and Wages among African-Americans." *Journal of Human Resources* 42(4): 701–738.

Goldstein, Donna M. 1999. "'Interracial' Sex and Racial Democracy in Brazil: Twin Concepts?" *American Anthropologist* 101(3): 563–578.

González, Lélia. 1988. "For an Afro-Latin Feminism." *Confronting the Crisis in Latin America: Women Organizing for Change.* Isis International & Development Alternatives with Women for a New Era: 95–101.

Gregory, Patricia C., Thomas A. LaVeist, and Crystal Simpson. 2006. "Racial Disparities in Access to Cardiac Rehabilitation" *American Journal of Physical Medicine & Rehabilitation* 85(9): 705–710.

Guimarães, Antonio Sergio. 2001. The Race Issue in Brazilian Politics (The Last Fifteen Years). Fifteen Years of Democracy in Brazil Conference. Paper presented at the Institute of Latin American Studies at the University of London, London, England, February 15–16.

Guimarães, Antonio Sergio. 2002. *Classes, Raças e Democracia*. São Paulo: Editora 34.

Hagopian, Francis. 1996. *Traditional Politics and Regime Change in Brazil*. New York: Cambridge University Press.

Hamilton, Darrick, Arthur Goldsmith and William Darity Jr. 2009. "Shedding "Light" on Marriage: The Influence of Skin Shade on Marriage for Black Females." *Journal of Economic Behavior and Organization* 72(1): 30–50.

Hanchard, Michael. 1994. *Orpheus and Power: The Movimento Negro of Rio de Janeiro and São Paulo, Brazil, 1945–1988*. Princeton: Princeton University Press.

Harris, Marvin. 1970. "Referential Ambiguity in the Calculus of Brazilian Racial Identity." *Southwestern Journal of Anthropology* 26(1): 1–14.

Harrison, Faye. 2008. *Outsider Within*. Champaign: University of Illinois Press.

Hasenbalg, Carlos and Nelson do Valle Silva. 1988. *Estrutura Social, Mobilidade e Raça*. Rio de Janeiro: Instituto Universitário de Pesquisas do Rio de Janeiro.

Hasenbalg, Carlos. 1978. Race Relations in Post-Abolition Brazil: The Smooth Preservation of Racial Inequalities. Ph.D. dissertation, University of California, Berkeley.

Hellwig, David. 1992. *African American Reflections on Brazil's Racial Paradise*. Philadelphia: Temple University Press.

Henriques, Ricardo. 2005. "Apresentação." In *Educação anti-racista: Caminhos abertos pela Lei Federal no 10.639/03*, eds. Ana Flávia Pinto, Andréia Lisboa de Sousa, Dmaris Lúcia de Santana Braga, and Sales Augusto dos Santos, 7–10. Brasilia: SECAD-Secretaria de Educação Continuada, Alfabetização e Diversidade.

Hernandez, Tanya. 1998. "Multiracial Discourse: Racial Classifications in an Era of Color-blind Jurisprudence." *Maryland Law Review* 57: 97–173. Available at http://ir.lawnet.fordham.edu/faculty_scholarship/23 (accessed July 8, 2017).

Hernandez, Tanya. 2011. "The Value of Intersectional Comparative Analysis to the 'Post-Racial' Future of Critical Race Theory: A Brazil – U.S. Comparative Case Study." *Connecticut Law Review* 43(5): 1407–1437.

Hernandez, Tanya. 2013a, "Affirmative Action in the Americas The hemisphere-wide drive to make equality a human right" *Americas Quarterly*, August 1, http://www.americas quarterly.org/affirmative-action-in-the-americas (accessed July 8, 2017).

Hernandez, Tanya. 2013b. Racial Subordination in Latin America: The Role of the State, Customary Law and the New Civil Rights Response. New York: Cambridge University Press.

Hernandez, Tanya. 2016. "Envisioning the United States in the Latin American Myth of 'racial democracy Mestizaje." *Latin American and Caribbean Ethnic Studies* 11(2):1– 17.

Hochschild, Jennifer L. and Vesla Weaver. 2007. "The Skin Color Paradox and the American Racial Order'." *Social Forces* 86(2): 643–670. doi: 10.1093/sf/86.2.643

Hordge-Freeman, Elizabeth. 2015. *The Color of Love: Racial Features, Stigma, and Socialization in Black Brazilian Families*. Austin: University of Texas Press.

Htun, Mala. 2016. *Inclusion without Representation: Gender Quotas and Ethnic Reservations in Latin America*. New York: Cambridge University Press.

Ikawa, Daniela. 2014. "The Construction of Identity and Rights: Race and Gender in Brazil." *International Journal of Law in Context* 10(4): 494–506.

Janusz, Andrew. 2017. "Candidate Race and Electoral Outcomes: Evidence from Brazil." *Politics, Groups, Identities*: 1–23. http://dx.doi.org/10.1080/21565503.2017.1279976

Johnson III, Ollie and Rosana Heringer. 2015. Race, Politics, and Education in Brazil: Affirmative Action in Higher Education. New York: Palgrave MacMillan.

Johnson III, Ollie. 1998. "Racial Representation and Brazilian Politics: Black Members of the National Congress, 1983–1999." *Journal of Interamerican Studies and World Affairs* 40: 97–118.

Johnson III, Ollie. 2006. "Locating Blacks in Brazilian Politics: Afro-Brazilian Activism, New Political Parties, and Pro-Black Public Policies." *International Journal of Africana Studies* 12: 170–193.

Johnson III, Ollie. 2007. "Black Politics in Latin America: An Analysis of National and Transnational Politics." In *African American Politics on Political Science*, ed. Wilbur C. Rich, 55–75. Philadelphia: Temple University Press.

Johnson III, Ollie. 2012. Race, Politics and Afro-Latin Americans." In *Routledge Handbook of Latin American Politics*, eds. Peter Kingstone and Deborah J. Yashar, 302–318. New York: Routledge.

Johnson III, Ollie. 2014. "Black Activism in Ecuador, 1979–2009." In *Comparative Perspectives on Afro-Latin America*, eds. Kwame Dixon and John Burdick, 176–197. University Press of Florida.

Johnson III, Ollie. 2015. "Blacks in National Politics." In *Race, Politics, and Education in Brazil: Affirmative Action in Higher Education*, eds. Ollie Johnson III and Rosana Heringer, 17–58. New York: Palgrave MacMillan.

Joseph, Tiffany. 2015. *Race on the Move: Brazilian Migrants and the Global Reconstruction of Race*. Palo Alto: Stanford University Press.

Kay, Kristen, Gladys Mitchell-Walthour and Ismail White. 2015. "Framing Race and Class in Brazil: Afro-Brazilian Support for Racial versus Class Policy." *Politics, Groups, and Identities* (3)2: 222–238.

Lamont, Michèle, Graziella Moraes Silva, Jessica S. Welburn, Joshua Guetzkow, Nissim Mizrachi, Hanna Herzog, and Elisa Reis. 2016. *Getting Respect: Responding to Stigma and Discrimination in the United States, Brazil, and Israel*. Princeton: Princeton University Press.

Layton, Matthew and Amy Smith. 2017. "Is it Race, Class, or gender? The Sources of Perceived Discrimination in Brazil." *Latin American Politics and Society* 59(1): 52–73.

Leal, David. 1999. "It's Not Just a Job: Military Service and Latino Political Participation." *Political Behavior* 21: 153–174.

Lefebvre, Henri. 1991. *The Production of Space*. Cambridge: Blackwell.

Levitt, Barry. 2015. "Discrimination and the Distrust of Democratic Institutions in Latin America." *Politics, Groups and Identities* 3(3): 417–437.

Lima, Márcia. 2015. "Açoes Afirmativas e Juventude Negra no Brasil." *Cadernos Adenauer* (São Paulo), v. Xvi: 27–43.

Lipman, Pauline. 2011. "Contesting the City: Neoliberal Urbanism and the Cultural Politics of Education Reform in Chicago." *Discourse: Studies in the Cultural Politics of Education* 32(2): 217–234.

Lisboa, Vinícius. 2014. "Renda dos Negros Cresce, mas Não Chegar a 60% da dos Brancos." January 30. EBC Agência Brasil (accessed July 8, 2017).

Lopez Bunyasi, Tehama. 2015. "Brown Ballots in the Buckeye State." In *Latinos and the 2012 Election: The New Face of the American Voter*, ed. Gabriel R. Sanchez. Lansing: Michigan State University Press.

Lovell, Peggy. 2006. "Race, Gender, and Work in São Paulo Brazil 1960–2000." *Latin American Research Review* 41(3): 63–87.

Loveman, Mara, Jeronimo Muniz, and Stanley R. Bailey. 2012. "Brazil in Black and White? Race Categories, the Census, and the Study of Inequality." *Ethnic and Racial Studies* 35(8): 1466–1483.

Madrid, Raul L. 2012. *The Rise of Ethnic Politics in Latin America*. New York: Cambridge University Press.

Marx, Anthony. 1998. *Making Race and Nation: A Comparison of South Africa, the United States, and Brazil*. New York: Cambridge University Press.

McCallum, Cecilia. 2005. Racialized Bodies, Naturalized Classes: Moving through the City of Salvador da Bahia. *American Ethnologist* 32(1): 100–117.

McCallum, Cecilia. 2007. "Women Out of Place? A Micro-Historical Perspective on the Black Feminist Movement in Salvador da Bahia, Brazil." *Journal of Latin American Studies* 39(1): 55–80.

Meade, Teresa. 1997. *Civilizing Rio: Reform and Resistance in a Brazilian City, 1889–1930*. University Park: The Pennsylvania State Press.

Melo, Débora. 2012. Em Dez Anos, População que se Autodeclara Negra Aumenta, e Número de Brancos Cai. Noticias UOL. June 29. http://noticias.uol.com.br/cotidiano /ultimas-noticias/2012/06/29/em-dez-anos-populacao-que-se-autodeclara-negra-sobe -e-numero-de-brancos-cai-diz-ibge.htm (accessed July 8, 2017).

Mendonça, Ricardo. 2014. "Dilma Cresce Onde Há Pouco Bolsa Famlia." Folha de São Paulo. November 2. http://www1.folha.uol.com.br/poder/2014/11/1542052-dilma -cresceu-onde-ha-pouco-bolsa-familia.shtml (accessed on December 11, 2016.)

Ministério da Educação 2015. "Marcha das Mulheres Negras reúne 50 mil Pessoas em Protesto Contra Racismo."November 18. http://portal.mec.gov.br/component/content /222-noticias/537011943/32111-marcha-das-mulheres-negras-reune-50-mil-pessoas -em-protesto-contra-racismo-e-desigualdade-social?Itemid=86 (accessed July 8, 2017).

Minority Rights Group International. 2014 "Afro-Colombians." https://www.justice .gov/sites/default/files/eoir/legacy/2014/02/19/Afro-Colombians.pdf (accessed July 8, 2017).

Mitchell-Walthour, Gladys and William Darity Jr. 2014. "The Endogeneity of Race: Choosing Blackness in Salvador and São Paulo, Brazil." *Latin American and Caribbean Ethnic Studies* (9)3: 318–348.

Mitchell-Walthour, Gladys. 2012. "Afro-Brazilian Black Linked Fate in Salvador and São Paulo, Brazil." *National Political Science Review* 13: 41–62.

Mitchell-Walthour, Gladys. 2012. "Racism in a Racialized Democracy and Support for Affirmative Action Policy in Salvador and São Paulo, Brazil." In *Afro-Descendants, Identity, and the Struggle for Development in the Americas*, eds. Bernd Reiter and Kimberly Simmons, 207–230. East Lansing: Michigan State University Press.

Mitchell-Walthour, Gladys. 2015. "Afro-Brazilian Support for Affirmative Action." In *Race, Politics, and Education in Brazil: Affirmative Action in Higher Education*, eds. Ollie Johnson III and Rosana Heringer, 133–153. New York: Palgrave Macmillan.

Mitchell, Gladys. 2009a. "Campaign Strategies of Afro-Brazilian Politicians: A Preliminary Analysis." *Latin American Politics and Society* 51(3): 111–142.

Mitchell, Gladys. 2009b. "Identidade coletiva negra e escolha eleitoral no Brasil" *Opinião Pública* 15(2): 275–305.

Mitchell, Gladys. 2010. "Politicizing Blackness: Afro-Brazilian Color Identification and Candidate Preference" In *Brazil's New Racial Politics*, eds. Bernd Reiter and Gladys Mitchell. Colorado: Lynn Rienner Publishers.

Mitchell, Michael and Charles Wood. 1998. "The Ironies of Citizenship: Skin Color, Police Brutality and the Challenges to Brazilian Democracy," *Social Forces* 77: 1001–1020.

Mitchell, Michael, K. C. Minion Morrison, and Ollie Johnson III. 2009. "Creating a Transnational Network of Black Representation in the Americas: A Profile of the Legislators at the First Meeting of Black Parliamentarians in Latin America." *National Political Science Review* (12): 227–246.

Mitchell, Michael. 1977. Racial Consciousness and the Political Attitudes and Behavior of Blacks in São Paulo, Brazil. PhD dissertation, Indiana University.

Mitchell, Michael. 1997. "Blacks in Electoral Politics: The Case of Celso Pitta." Paper presented at the Fourth Meeting of the Brazilian Studies Association, Washington, DC, November 12–15.

Mitchell, Michael. 2007. "Race and Democracy in Brazil: The Racial Factor in Public Opinion." Paper presented at the National Conference of Black Political Scientists, San Francisco, CA, March 21–24.

Moldonado, Marta. 2009. "It Is Their Nature to Do Menial': The Racialization of. 'Latino/a Workers' by Agricultural Employers." *Ethnic and Racial Studies* 32(6): 1017–1036.

Morrison, Judith. 2007. "Race and Poverty in Latin America: Addressing the Development Needs of African Descendants." UN Chronicle. XLIV (3) https://unchronicle.un.org /article/race-and-poverty-latin-america-addressing-development-needs-african-descen dants (accessed July 8, 2017).

Morrison, Judith. 2012. "Race and Ethnicity by the Numbers." *AmericasQuarterly.* http://www.americasquarterly.org/morrison (accessed July 8, 2017).

Nascimento, Abdias do. 1989. *Brazil, Mixture or Massacre?: Essays in the Genocide of a Black People.* Dover: Majority Press.

Nascimento, Elisa. 2009. *The Sorcery of Color: Identity, Race, and Gender in Brazil.* Philadelphia: Temple University Press.

Neely, Brooke and Michelle Samura. 2011. "Social Geographies of Race: Connecting Race and Space." *Ethnic and Racial Studies* 34(11): 1933–1952. http://dx.doi.org /10.1080/01419870.2011.5592622011. 34 (11).

Néri, Felipe. 2013. "CCJ da Câmara aprova cota racial para deputados federaise estaduais." Globo.com October 30. http://g1.globo.com/politica/noticia/2013/10 /ccj-da-camara-aprova-cota-racial-para-deputados-federais-e-estaduais.html (accessed on July 20, 2017).

Nobles, Melissa. 2001. *Shades of Citizenship: Race and the Census in Modern Politics.* Stanford: Stanford University Press.

Nogueira, Oracy. 1985 [1954]. *Tanto Preto quanto Branco: Estudos de Relações Raciais.* São Paulo: T. A. Queiroz.

Nogueira, Oracy. 2007. "Preconceito racial de marca e preconceito racial de origem: Sugestão de um quadro de referência para a interpretação do material sobre relações raciais no Brasil." *Tempo Social* 19(1): 287–308.

Oliveira, Cloves Luiz P. 1997. *A Luta por um Lugar: Gênero, Raça, e Classe: Eleições Municipais de Salvador-Bahia, 1992.* Salvador: Serie Toques Programa A Cor da Bahia-UFBA.

Oliveira, Cloves. 2007. *A Inevitável Visibilidade de Cor: Estudo comparativo das cam-panhas de Benedita da Silva e Celso Pitta às prefeituras do Rio de Janeiro e São Paulo, nas eleições de 1992 e 1996*. PhD dissertation, Instituto Universitário de Pesquisa do Rio de Janeiro (Iuperj).

Oliveira, Dennis. 2016. "The Racist Roots of the coup d'état against President Dilma Rousseff." https://blackwomenofbrazil.co/2016/05/16/the-racist-roots-of-the-coup -detat-against-president-dilma-rousseff/ (accessed July 20, 2017).

Oliveira, Mirela. 2014. "O Nosso Lugar é na Periferia: O Racismo Sutil Deixando de Ser Sutil." *Blogueiras Negras*. http://blogueirasnegras.org/2014/07/12/o-nosso-lugar-e -na-periferia-o-racismo-sutil-deixando-de-ser-sutil/ (accessed December 28, 2016).

Osuji, Chinyere. 2013. "Racial 'Boundary-Policing': Perceptions of Black-White Interracial Couples in Los Angeles and Rio de Janeiro." *DuBois Review: Social Science Research on Race* 10(1): 179–203.

Osuji, Chinyere. 2014. "Divergence or Convergence in the U.S. and Brazil: Understanding Race Relations through White Family Reactions to Black-White Interracial Couples. *Qualitative Sociology* 37: 93–115.

Paixão Marcelo and Luiz M. Carvano. 2008. *Relatório Anual das Desigualdades Raciais no Brazil; 2007–2008*. Rio de Janeiro: Editora Garamond Ltda.

Paixão Marcelo, Irene Rossetto, Fabiana Montovanele, and Luiz M. Carvano. 2011. *Relatório Anual das Desigualdades Raciais no Brazil; 2009–2010*. Rio de Janeiro: Editora Garamond Ltda.

Paixão, Marcelo; Carvano, Luiz Marcelo, and Rossetto, Irene. 2010. Desigualdade racial e crise: indicadores de acesso ao mercado de trabalho metropolitano desagregados por cor ou raça em 2009. *Versus: Revista de Ciências Sociais Aplicadas do CCJE/UFRJ (Impresso)*, v. ano II:72–84.

Paixão, Marcelo. 2015. Discriminação de cor ou raça no acesso ao crédito produtivo no Brasil. Latin American Studies Association Conference. San Juan, Puerto Rico.

Pardue, Derek. 2004. "Putting Mano to Music: The Mediation of Race in Brazilian Rap." *Ethnomusicology Forum* 13: 253–286.

Park, Robert E. 1931. "Mentality of Racial Hybrids." *American Journal of Sociology* 36 (4): 534–551.

Paschel, Tianna S. 2016. *Becoming Black Political Subjects: Movements and Ethno-Racial Rights in Colombia and Brazil*. Princeton: Princeton University Press.

Penha-Lopes, Vânia. 2013. *Pioneiros: Cotistas na Universidade Brasileira*. São Paulo: Paco Editorial.

Pereira, Amilcar. 2015. "From the Black Movement's Struggle to the Teaching of African and Afro-Brazilian History." In *Race, Politics, and Education in Brazil Affirmative Action in Higher Education*, eds. Rosana Heringer and Ollie Johnson III, 59–72. New York: Palgrave Macmillan.

Pereira, João Baptista Borges. 1982. "Aspectos do Comportamento Político do Negro em São Paulo." *Ciência e Cultura* 34: 1286–1294.

Pereira, Júnia Sales. 2008."Reconhecendo ou construindo uma polaridade étnico-identitária? Desaios do ensino da história no imediato contexto pós-Lei no 10.639." *Estudos Históricos* 21(41): 21–43.

Perry, Keisha-Khan. 2013. *Black Women against the Land Grab: The Fight for Racial Justice in Brazil*. Minneapolis: University of Minnesota Press.

Petruccelli, José and Ana Lucia Saboia. 2013. *Pesquisa de Características Étnico-Raciais da População*. Instituto Brasileira de Geografia e Estatística. Rio de Janeiro: Rio de Janeiro. http://biblioteca.ibge.gov.br/visualizacao/livros/liv63405.pdf (accessed July 7, 2017).

Pierson, Donald. 1942. *Negroes in Brazil: A Study of Race Contact at Bahia*. Chicago: University of Chicago Press.

Pinho, Patricia de Santana. 2010. *Mama Africa: Reinventing Blackness in Bahia*. Durham: Duke University Press.

Prandi, Reginaldo. 1996. Raça e Voto na Eleição Presidencial de 1994. *Estudos Afro-Asiaticos* 30: 61–78.

Price, Patricia L. 2012. "Race and Ethnicity: Latino/a Immigrants and Emerging Geographies of Race and Place in the USA." *Progress in Human Geography* 36(6): 800–809.

Racusen, Seth. 2010. "Affirmative Action and Identity." In *Brazil's New Racial Politics*, eds Bernd Reiter and Gladys Mitchell, 89–122. Colorado: Lynn Rienner Publishers.

Racusen, Seth. 2012. "The Grammar of Color Identity in Brazil." In *Afro-Descendants, Identity, and the Struggle for Development in the Americas*, eds. Bernd Reiter and Kimberly Simmons, 141–178. East Lansing: Michigan State University Press.

Rahier, Jean Muteba. 2012. "Afro-Ecuadorian Community Organizing and Political Struggle: Influences on and Participation in Constitutional Processes." In *Comparative Perspectives on Afro-Latin America*, eds. Kwame Dixon and John Burdick, 198–218. New York: Routledge.

Rangel, Marcos. 2015. "Is Parental Love Colorblind? Human Capital Accumulation within Mixed Families." *The Review of Black Political Economy* (42): 57–86.

Reis, João. 1995. *Slave Rebellion in Brazil: The Muslim Uprising of 1835 in Bahia*. Baltimore: Johns Hopkins University Press.

Reiter, Bernd and Gladys Mitchell. 2010. *Brazil's New Racial Politics*. Boulder: Lynne Rienner Publishers.

Rezende, Cludia Barcelos and Marcia Lima. 2004. "Linking Gender, Class, and Race." *Social Identities* 10(6): 757–773.

Ribeiro, Luiz César de Queiroz, Juciano Martins Rodrigues, and Felipe Souza Corrêa. 2010. "Segregação Residencial e Emprego nos Grandes Espaços Urbanos Brasileiros." *Caderno Metropolitano* 12(23): 15–41.

Rockquemore, Kerry and Patricia Arend. 2002. "Opting for White: Choice, Fluidity and Racial Identity Construction in Post Civil-Rights America." *Race and Society* 5:49–64.

Rogers, Reuel. 2006. *Afro-Caribbean Immigrants and the Politics of Incorporation: Ethnicity, Exception, or Exit*. New York: Cambridge University Press.

Rossi, Marina. "Mais brasileiros se declaram negros e pardos e reduzem número de brancos Desde 2007 IBGE constata que população branca cai e hoje representa 45,5% do país." *El País*. November 16. http://brasil.elpais.com/brasil/2015/11/13/politica /1447439643_374264.html (accessed July 8, 2017).

Sansone, Livio. 2004. *Negritude sem Etnicidade: O Local e o Global Nas Relações Raciais e na Produção Cultural Negra do Brasil*. Salvador, BA: EDUFBA.

Santana, Emilce. 2013. "Table: Afro-descendant and Indigenous Population in Latin America by Country." PerlaPrinceton.edu https://perla.princeton.edu/table-afro-descen dant-and-indigenous-population-in-latin-america-by-country/ (accessed July 29, 2017).

Santos, Hélio. 2015. "Cotas Racias: O Acinte das Fraudes." Geledes.org.br https://www .geledes.org.br/cotas-raciais-o-acinte-das-fraudes/#gs.PiDeaHw (accessed July 7, 2017).

Santos, Jaqueline. 2014. "Hiphop and the Reconfiguration of Blackness in São Paulo: The Influence of African American Political and Musical Movements in the 20th Century." *Social Identities* 22(2): 160–177.

Santos, Renato E. 2010. "New Social Activism: University Entry Courses for Black and Poor Students." In *Brazil's New Racial Politics*, eds. Bernd Reiter and Gladys Mitchell, 197–225. Boulder: Lynne Rienner Publishers.

Santos, Sales Augusto dos. 2000. *A Ausência de uma Bancada Suprapartidária Afro-Brasileira no Congreso Nacional (Legislatura 1995/1998). Brasília: Centro de Estudos Afro-Asiaticos*, 2 Vols. Brasília: Centro de Estudos Afro-Asiaticos.

Santos, Sales Augusto dos. 2006. "Who Is Black in Brazil? A Timely or a False Question in Brazilian Race Relations in the Era of Affirmative Action?" *Latin American Perspectives* 33: 30–48.

Santos, Sales Augusto dos. 2010. "Black NGOs and "Conscious" Rap: New Agents of the Antiracism Struggle in Brazil." In *Brazil's New Racial Politics*, eds. Bernd Reiter and Gladys Mitchell, 165–177. Colorado: Lynn Rienner Publishers.

Santos, Sales Augusto dos. 2014. *Educação um Pensamento Negro Contemporâneo*. Jundiaí: Paco Editorial.

Santos, Sônia Querino dos Santos e Vera Carbalho Machado. 2008. "Políticas Públicas Educacionais: Antigas Reivindicações, Conquistas (Lei 10.639) e Novos Desafios." *Ensaio: Avaliação e Políticas Públicas em Educação. Rio de Janeiro* 16(58): 95–112.

Saunders, Tanya. 2009. "La Lucha Mujerista: Krudas CUBENSI and Black Feminist Sexual Politics in Cuba." *Caribbean Review of Gender Studies*, Mona, Jamaica: University of the West Indies. http://sta.uwi.edu/crgs/november2009/journals/CRGS%20Las%20Krudas.pdf (accessed July 12, 2017).

Saunders, Tanya. 2012. "Black Thoughts, Black Activism: Cuban Underground Hip-Hop and Afro-Latino Countercultures of Modernity." *Latin American Perspectives* 39(2): 42–60.

Saunders, Tanya. 2015. *Cuban Underground Hip Hop: Black Thoughts, Black Revolution, Black Modernity*. Austin: University of Texas Press.

Sawyer, Mark. 2005. *Racial Politics in Post-Revolutionary Cuba*. New York: Cambridge University Press.

Scott, Joan. 1991. "The Evidence of Experience." *Critical Inquiry* 17(4): 773–797.

Seltzer, Richard and Robert C. Smith. 1991. "Color Differences in the Afro-American Community and the Differences They Make." *Journal of Black Studies* 21(3): 279–286.

Shabazz, Rashad. 2015. *Spatializing Blackness: Architectures of Confinement and Black Masculinity in Chicago*. Urbana: University of Illinois Press.

Sheriff, Robin. 2001. *Dreaming Equality: Color, Race, and Racism in Urban Brazil*. New Brunswick: Rutgers University Press.

Sidanius, Jim, Yesilernis Pena and Mark Sawyer. 2001. "Inclusionary Discrimination: Pigmentocracy and Patriotism in the Dominican Republic." *Political Psychology* 22 (4): 827–851.

Silva, Graziella and Marcelo Paixão. 2014. "Mixed and Unequal: New Perspectives on Brazilian Ethnoracial Relations." In *Pigmentocracies: Ethnicity, Race, and Color in Latin America*, 172–217. Chapel Hill: University of North Carolina Press.

Silva, Graziella and Silva Reis. 2011. "Perceptions of Racial Discrimination among Black Professionals in Rio de Janeiro." *Latin American Research Review* 46(2): 55–78.

Silva, Graziella Moraes D and Elisa P. Reis. 2012. "The Multiple Dimensions of Racial Mixture in Rio de Janeiro, Brazil: From Whitening to Brazilian Negritude." *Ethnic and Racial Studies* 35(3): 382–399.

Silva, Hédio Jr. 1998. *Anti-racismo: Coletânea de Leis Brasileiras (Federais, Estaduais, Municipais)*. São Paulo: Oliveira Mendes.

Silva, Rosana Aparecida da. 2016 "Povo negro se une contra o golpe, na luta pela democracia." *Rede Brasil Atual*. http://www.redebrasilatual.com.br/blogs/blog-na-rede /2016/04/povo-negro-se-une-contra-o-golpe-na-luta-pela-democracia-7361.html (accessed July 7, 2017).

Skidmore, Thomas. 1974. *Black into White: Race and Nationality in Brazilian Thought*. New York: Oxford University Press.

Smith, Candis Watts. 2014. *Black Mosaic: The Politics of Black Pan-Ethnic Diversity*. New York: New York University Press.

Smith, Christen. 2014. "For Cláudia Silva Ferreira: Death and the Collective Black Female Body." *The Feminist Wire*, May 5. http://www.thefeministwire.com/2014/05/for-clau dia-silva-ferreira-death-black-female-body/ (accessed December 1, 2016).

Smith, Christen. 2016. *Afro-Paradise: Blackness, Violence, and Performance in Brazil*. Champaign: University of Illinois Press.

Soares, Glaucio Ary Dillon and Nelson do Valle Silva. 1987. "Urbanization, Race, and Class in Brazilian Politics." *Latin American Research Review* 22: 155–176.

Souza, Amaury de. 1971. "Raça e Política no Brasil urbano." *Revista de Administração de Empresas* 11: 61–70.

Souza, Beatriz. 2004. *As 200 Cidades Mais Populosas do Brasil*. Exame.abril.com.br. http://exame.abril.com.br/brasil/as-200-cidades-mais-populosas-do-brasil/ (accessed July 7, 2017).

Steffensmeier, Darrell and Stephen Demuth. 2000. "Ethnicity and Sentencing Outcomes in U.S. Federal Courts: Who Is Punished More Harshly?" *American Sociological Review* 65(5): 705–729.

Sue, Christina and Tonya Golash-Boza. 2013. "'It Was Only a Joke': How Racial Humour Fuels Colour-Blind Ideologies in Mexico and Peru." *Ethnic and Racial Studies*: 36 (10): 1582–1598.

Sue, Christina. 2013. *Land of the Cosmic Race: Race Mixture, Racism, and Blackness in Mexico*. New York: Oxford University Press.

Sue, Cristina. 2009. "An Assessment of the Latin Americanization Thesis." *Ethnic and Racial Studies* 32(6): 1058–1070.

Sueli, Carneiro. 2010. *Insumias: Racismo, Sexismo, Organizacion Politica y Desarollo de Mujer Afrodescendiente*. Lima: CEDET, Centro de Desarrollo Étnico.

Sugiyama, Natasha Borges and Wendy A. Hunter. 2013. "Whither Clientelism? Good Governance and Brazil's Bolsa Família Program." *Comparative Politics* 46(1): 43–62.

Tajfel, Henry and Turner, John C. 1986. "The Social Identity Theory of Inter-Group Behavior." In *Psychology of Intergroup Relations*, eds. Stephen Worchel and William Austin, 7–24. Chicago: Nelson-Hall.

Tate, Katherine. 2003. *Black Faces in the Mirror: African Americans and Their Representatives in the U.S. Congress*. Princeton: Princeton University Press.

Taylor, Keeanga-Yamahtta. 2016. *From #Blacklivesmatter to Black Liberation*. Chicago: Haymarket Books.

Telles, Eduard and Lim, Nelson. 1998. "Does It Matter Who Answers the Race Question? Racial Classification and Income Inequality in Brazil." *Demography* 35(4): 465–474.

Telles, Edward and Stan Bailey. 2013. "Understanding Latin American Beliefs about Racial Inequality." *American Journal of Sociology* 118(6): 1559–1595.

Telles, Edward. 2004. *Race in Another America: The Significance of Skin Color in Brazil.* Princeton: Princeton University Press.

Telles, Edward. 2014. *Pigmentocracies: Ethnicity, Race, and Color in Latin America.* Chapel Hill: University of North Carolina Press.

Terra 2011. Negros e pardos são maioria em 56,8% das cidades, diz estudo. Terra.com .br http://noticias.terra.com.br/brasil/cidades/negros-e-pardos-sao-maioria-em -568-das-cidades-diz-estudo,475c55e5c56fa310VgnCLD200000bbcceb0aRCRD.html (accessed July 7, 2017).

Terra. 2007. Conhece a Biografía de ACM. http://noticias.terra.com.br/brasil/noticias/0 „OI1700581-EI306,00-Conheca+a+biografia+de+ACM.html (accessed July 7, 2017).

Toledo, José Roberto. 2013. "62% Apoiam Cotas Para Alunos Negros, Pobres e da Escola Pública, diz Ibope." Estadão. http://educacao.estadao.com.br/noticias/geral,62 -apoiam-cotas-para-alunos-negros-pobres-e-da-escola-publica-diz-ibope,997758 (accessed December 16, 2016).

Tukufu, Zuberi, and Eduardo Bonilla-Silva. 2008. *White Logic, White Methods: Racism and Methodology.* New York: Rowman and Littlefield.

Twine, France Winddance and Jonathan Warren. 1999. *Race and Research, Researching Race: Methodological Dilemmas in Critical Race Studies.* New York: New York University Press.

Twine, France Winddance. 1998. *Racism in a Racial Democracy: The Maintenance of White Supremacy in Brazil.* New Jersey: Rutgers University Press.

Tyner, James A. 2012. *Space, Place, and Violence: Violence and the Embodied Geographies of Race, Sex, and Gender.* New York: Routledge.

Tyson, Karolyn, Wiliam Darity Jr. and Domini Castellino. 2005. "It's Not "a Black Thing": Understanding the Burden of Acting White and Other Dilemmas of High Achievement." *American Sociological Review* 70(4): 582–605.

Valente, Ana Lúcia E.F. 1986. *Política e Relações Raciais: Os Negros e às Eleições Paulistas de 1982.* São Paulo: FFLCH-US.

Valente, Rubia R. and Brian J. L. Berry. 2017. "Performance of Students Admitted through Affirmative Action in Brazil." *Latin American Research Review* 52(1): 18–34.

Valentino, Nicholas A., Vincent L. Hutchings and Ismail K. White. 2002. "Cues That Matter: How Political Ads Prime Racial Attitudes during Campaigns." *American Political Science Review*, March: 75–90.

Vargas, João Costa. 2004. "Hyperconsciousness of Race And Its Negation: The Dialectic Of White Supremacy in Brazil." *Identities* 11(4): 443–470.

Vargas, João Costa. 2006. "When a Favela Dared to Become a Gated Condominium: The Politics of Race and Urban Space in Rio de Janeiro." *Latin American Perspectives July* 2006 (33)4: 49–81.

Vasconcelos, Fábio. "Ganho de votos de Dilma no 2º turno não tem relação com Bolsa Família" O Globo. October 29, 2014. http://blogs.oglobo.globo.com/na-base-dos -dados/post/ganho-de-votos-de-dilma-no-2-turno-nao-tem-relacao-com-bolsa-fam ilia-553452.html (accessed on December 11, 2016.)

Wade, Peter. 1993. *Blackness and Race Mixture: The Dynamics of Racial Identity in Colombia.* Baltimore: Johns Hopkins University Press.

Wade, Peter. 1997. *Race and Ethnicity in Latin America.* Chicago: Pluto Press.

Wagley, Charles. 1971. *An Introduction to Brazil.* New York: Columbia University.

Williams, David. 1999. Race, Socioeconomic Status, and Health: The Added Effects of Racism and Discrimination. *Annals of the New York Academy of Sciences* 896: 173–188.

Williams, Erica Lorraine. 2013. *Sex Tourism in Bahia: Ambiguous Entanglements.* Champaign: University of Illinois Press.

Wong, Janelle S., Karthick Ramakrishnan, Taeku Lee, and Jane Junn. 2011. *Asian American Political Participation: Emerging Constituents and Their Political Identities.* Russel Sage Foundation.

Xongani, Ana Paula. 2016. "Foi Golpe" Ana Paula Xongani's YouTube Channel. https://www.youtube.com/watch?v=8eC2CfPUTRI (accessed on July 20, 2017).

Yashar, Deborah. 2015. "Does Race Matter in Latin America?: How Racial and Ethnic Identities Shape the Region's Politics." *Foreign Affairs*, Mar/Apr 94(2): 33–40.

Zepeda-Millán, Chris. 2016. "Weapons of the (Not So) Weak" Immigrant Mass Mobilization in the US South." *Critical Sociology* 42(2): 269–287.

Zucco, Cesar, and Timothy J. Power. 2013. "Bolsa Família and the Shift in Lula's Electoral Base, 2002–2006: A Reply to Bohn." *Latin American Research Review* 48 (2): 3–24.

Index